Focus on Grammar

An **Advanced** Course for Reference and Practice

Jay Maurer

Sharon Hilles, grammar consultant

Longman

Focus on Grammar: An Advanced Course for Reference and Practice

Copyright © 1995 by Addison-Wesley Publishing Company, Inc.
All rights reserved.
No part of this publication may be reproduced,
stored in a retrieval system, or transmitted
in any form or by any means, electronic, mechanical,
photocopying, recording, or otherwise,
without the prior permission of the publisher.

Editorial Director: Joanne Dresner
Senior Development Editor: Joan Saslow
Assistant Editor: Jessica Miller
Production Editorial: Lisa Hutchins
Text Design: Six West Design
Cover Design: A Good Thing, Inc.
Book Production: Circa 86, Inc.
Text Art: Alex Bloch, Circa 86, Meryl Treatner

Library of Congress Cataloging-in-Publication Data
Maurer, Jay
    Focus on grammar. An advanced course for reference and practice
Jay Maurer.
      p.   cm.
    Includes index.
    ISBN 0-201-65693-0
    1. English language—Textbooks for foreign speakers.   2. English
language—Grammar—Problems, exercises, etc.   I. Title.
PE1128.M3547   1995
428.2'4—dc20
                                                     94-39043
                                                      CIP

7 8 9 10 -CRK- 01 00 99 98

For Thain and Zeya

Contents

Focus on Grammar: An Advanced Course for Reference and Practice

Appendices

About the Author

Jay Maurer has taught EFL in colleges, universities, and binational centers in the Somali Republic, Spain, Portugal, and Mexico. He has taught ESL in Washington State and at Columbia University's American Language Program. In addition, he was professor of college composition and literature for seventeen years at Santa Fe Community College and Northern New Mexico Community College. He is the coauthor of the popular and widely used series *Structure Practice in Context.* Currently he writes and teaches in Seattle.

Focus on Grammar: An Advanced Course for Reference and Practice has grown out of the author's experiences as a practicing teacher of both ESL and college writing.

Introduction

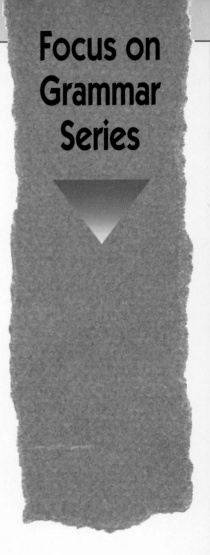

Focus on Grammar: An Advanced Course for Reference and Practice is the fourth text in the four-level *Focus on Grammar* series. Written by practicing ESL professionals, the series focuses on English grammar through lively listening, speaking, reading, and writing activities. Each of the four Student's Books is accompanied by a Workbook, Cassettes, and a Teacher's Manual. Software is also available. Each Student's Book stands alone as a complete text in itself or can be used as part of the *Focus on Grammar* series.

Both Controlled and Communicative Practice

Research in applied linguistics suggests that students expect and need to learn the formal rules of a language. However, students need to practice new structures in a variety of contexts to help them internalize and master these structures. To this end, *Focus on Grammar* provides an abundance of both controlled and communicative exercises so that students can bridge the gap between knowing grammatical structures and using them. The many communicative activities in each unit enable students to personalize what they have learned in order to talk to each other with ease about hundreds of everyday issues.

A Unique Four-Step Approach

The series follows a unique four-step approach. The first step is **contextualization.** New structures are shown in the natural context of passages, articles, and dialogues. This is followed by **presentation** of structures in clear and accessible grammar charts and explanations. The third step is **focused practice** of both form and meaning in numerous and varied controlled exercises. In the fourth step, students engage in **communication practice,** using the new structures freely and creatively in motivating, open-ended activities.

A Complete Classroom Text and Reference Guide

A major goal in the development of *Focus on Grammar* has been to provide a Student's Book that serves not only as a vehicle for classroom instruction but also as a resource for self-study. The combination of grammar charts, grammar notes, and extensive appendices provides a complete and invaluable reference guide for the student at the advanced level. Exercises in the Focused Practice sections of each unit are ideal for individual study, and students can check their work by using the complete Answer Key at the back of the book.

Thorough Recycling

Underpinning the scope and sequence of the series as a whole is the belief that students need to use target structures many times in many contexts at increasing levels of difficulty. For this reason, new grammar is constantly recycled so that students will feel thoroughly comfortable with it.

Comprehensive Testing Program

SelfTests at the end of each of the eight parts of the Student's Book allow for continual assessment of progress. In addition, diagnostic and final tests in the Teacher's Manual provide a ready-made, ongoing evaluation component for each student.

PART AND UNIT FORMAT

Focus on Grammar: An Advanced Course for Reference and Practice is divided into eight parts comprising twenty-one units. Each part contains grammatically related units, with each unit focusing on a specific grammatical structure or related groups of structures.

In this advanced-level text, some structures are grouped together because of their related application to writing. The infinitive of purpose, for example, is taught together with participial phrases because both kinds of structures function adverbially. But, more importantly, they have similar applications to the acquisition of two important concepts: sentence combining and avoiding dangling modifiers.

Each unit has one or more major themes relating the exercises to one another and providing a context that serves as a vehicle for the structure. All units have the same clear, easy-to-follow format:

Introduction

The Introduction presents the grammar focus of the unit in a natural context. The Introduction texts, all of which are recorded on cassette, present language in various formats. These include newspaper and magazine excerpts, stories, transcripts of speeches, news broadcasts, radio shows, and other formats that students encounter in their day-to-day lives. In addition to presenting grammar in context, the Introduction serves to raise student motivation and provides an opportunity for incidental learning and lively classroom discussions. All Introductions are preceded by Questions to Consider, a feature that allows students to explore the topic that follows.

Grammar Charts

Grammar Charts follow each Introduction. These focus on the form and variety of the unit's target structure. As in all the *Focus on Grammar* texts, the charts are clear and easy to understand. These charts provide students with a clear visual reference for each new and reviewed structure.

Grammar Notes

The Grammar Notes that follow the charts focus on the meaning and use of the structure. Each note gives a clear explanation of the grammar point and is always followed by one or more examples. *Be careful!* notes alert students to common ESL/EFL errors. Subtleties of meaning and use are thoroughly explored in this advanced-level text. Cross-references to other related units and the Appendices make the book easy to use.

Focused Practice Exercises

These exercises follow the Grammar Notes. This section provides practice for all uses of the structures presented in the notes. Each Focused Practice section begins with a "for recognition only" exercise called Discover the Grammar. Here, the students are expected to recognize either the form of the structure or its meaning without having to produce any language. This activity raises awareness of the grammar as it builds confidence.

Following the Discover the Grammar activity are exercises that practice the grammar in a controlled, but still contextualized, environment. The exercises proceed from simpler to more complex. There is a large variety of exercise types including fill-in-the-blanks, matching, multiple choice, question and sentence formation, sentence combining, and error analysis through editing. As with the Introduction, students are exposed to many different written formats, including letters, journal entries, broadcast transcripts, essays, and newspaper and magazine articles. Topics are varied, providing rich and interesting contexts for meaningful practice. All Focused Practice exercises are suitable for self-study or homework. A complete Answer Key is provided at the end of this book.

Communication Practice Exercises

These exercises are intended for in-class use. The first exercise in this section is called Practice Listening. Having had exposure to and practice with the grammar in its written form, students now have the opportunity to check their aural comprehension. After listening to the tape (or hearing the teacher read the tapescript, which can be found in the Teacher's Manual), they complete a task that focuses on either the form or the meaning of the structure. It is suggested that students be allowed to hear the text as many times as they wish to complete the task successfully. In some units, an optional dictation follows the comprehension task to pave the way for the writing activity that is to follow later in the unit. In others, an open-ended discussion of the taped text is suggested to enhance the use of the tape.

Practice Listening is followed by a variety of activities that provide students with the opportunity to use the grammar in open-ended, interactive activities. Students work in pairs, small groups, or as a whole class, in discussions, role plays, and debates. Every unit gives students an opportunity to write an essay especially formulated to elicit practice of the unit's structures. Finally, a Picture Discussion in each unit enables students to apply their mastery of structure in a new and unrelated context. Many of the Picture Discussions are generated from reproductions of famous paintings esteemed throughout the world.

Review or SelfTest

At the conclusion of each of the eight parts, there is a review feature that can be used as a self-test. The exercises in this section test the form and use of the grammar content of the units in the part just concluded. Each test contains one exercise formatted in the same way as the Structure and Written Expression section of the TOEFL®.

From Grammar to Writing

This special feature of the advanced-level text in the *Focus on Grammar* series is designed to help students bridge the gap between writing in the ESL/EFL classroom and the less controlled writing that students may need to do outside of class, whether in everyday or academic settings. These optional units occur after the SelfTests and focus on such writing issues as the sentence; subject-verb agreement; parallelism; avoiding fragments, run-on sentences, and comma splices; punctuating adjective clauses; and capitalization and punctuation of direct and indirect speech. Although these writing issues are not solely ESL/EFL related, they are highly important to the ESL/EFL student who wants to write successfully.

In each From Grammar to Writing unit, the topic presented is related to the grammar content of the part just concluded. For example, the second writing unit on parallelism naturally and logically accompanies the gerund and infinitive part, since mixing gerunds and infinitives in a series is a common parallelism error.

Appendices

The twenty-five Appendices provide useful information, such as lists of common irregular verbs, common adjective-plus-preposition combinations, spelling rules, and lists of countries. The Appendices can help students do the unit exercises, act as a springboard for further classroom work, and serve as a reference source.

SUPPLEMENTARY COMPONENTS

The supplementary components of *Focus on Grammar*—the Workbook, the Cassettes, and the Teacher's Manual—are all tightly keyed to the Student's Book, ensuring a wealth of practice and an opportunity to tailor the series to the needs of each individual classroom.

Cassettes

All of the Introduction texts and all of the Practice Listening exercises, as well as other selected exercises, are recorded on cassette. The symbol ▭ appears next to these activities. Listening scripts appear in the Teacher's Manual and may be used as an alternative way of presenting the listening activities.

Workbook

The Workbook accompanying *Focus on Grammar: An Advanced Course for Reference and Practice* provides a broad range of additional exercises appropriate for self-study of the target grammar of each unit in the Student's Book. Most of the exercises are fully contextualized with interesting and useful themes. There are also eight tests, one for each of the eight Student's Book parts. These tests have questions in the format of the Structure and Written Expression section of the TOEFL®. Besides reviewing the material in the Student's Book, these questions provide invaluable practice to those who are interested in taking this widely administered test.

Teacher's Manual

The Teacher's Manual, divided into three parts, contains a variety of suggestions and information to enrich the material in the Student's Book. The first part gives general suggestions for each section of a typical unit. The next part offers practical teaching suggestions and cultural information to accompany specific material in each unit. The Teacher's Manual offers suggestions to enhance students' vocabulary acquisition, both in presenting the meanings of new words and in aiding students to derive meaning from context on their own.

The Teacher's Manual also offers ready-to-use diagnostic and final tests for each of the eight parts of the Student's Book. In addition, a complete script of the cassette tapes is provided, as is an answer key for the diagnostic and final tests.

Software

The *Focus on Grammar* Software provides individualized practice based on each unit of the Student's Book. Fully contextualized and interactive, the activities broaden and extend practice of the grammatical structures in the reading, listening, and writing skill areas. The software includes grammar review, review tests, and all relevant refere/nce material from the Student's Book. It can also be used alongside the *Longman Dictionary of American English* software.

Acknowledgments

Writing this book has been an excellent experience. I should really thank everyone I've ever met for inspiring me in the writing, especially my students over the years. Specifically, though, I want to express my appreciation and gratitude to the following folks:

Lyn McLean, who suggested me as the author for this book.

Joanne Dresner, who oversaw this project and inspired me all along the way. It wouldn't have been possible without her.

Jessica Miller, who provided encouragement and edited with a keen eye.

Allen Ascher, who was a driving force behind this project, kept it on track, and kept me laughing.

Lisa Hutchins, who guided the book through the production process with a good hand and good cheer.

Tom Finnegan, for perceptive and comprehensive copyediting.

Laura McCormick, for timely and helpful support on permissions.

The reviewers Laura T. LeDrean, Douglas Oliver, Ellen Rosenfield, Cynthia Wiseman, and Ramón Valenzuela, who made many valuable suggestions.

Special thanks are due to grammar consultant Sharon Hilles.

West Side, in all ways.

April, Becky, David, Diana, Jack, James, Jean, Jeff, Mackenzie, Marg, Rolleen, Thain, Zeya, and Mom. You were all there, and you're all here.

Above all, Joan Saslow. This is her book too.

Credits

Grateful acknowledgment is given for the following material:

"OUT, OUT—". From *The Poetry of Robert Frost*. Edited by Edward Connery Lathem. Henry Holt and Company.

Grateful acknowledgment is given to the following for providing photographs:

The Verb Phrase: Selected Topics

INTRODUCTION

Mark Williams, an American student, is spending a year studying abroad in a bilingual international student program in Spain. Read and listen to the three letters from Mark to his sister Emily, written at different times: before, during, and after the year in Spain.

Questions to Consider

1. Do events always turn out as expected?
2. Do you hold any stereotypes about certain groups of people?
3. How can stereotypes be harmful?

Saturday, August 20

Dear Emily,

We **leave** for Spain in just three weeks! It**'ll be** a great trip over there because we**'re stopping** in London for five days before we **go on** to Madrid. Classes **begin** on September fifteenth. I**'ll be taking** Spanish language and literature, world history, anthropology, and biology—not a heavy load. It**'s going to be** a fun and easy year in the land of mañana. The classes **will** mostly **be** in Spanish, of course, so my fluency **will have improved** tremendously by the end of the year. When I **get** to Spain, I**'m going to be rooming** with two other guys, one from Brazil named Luis and one from Japan named Isao. I**'ll meet** them in London, so we**'ll have gotten to know** each other a little by the time we **get** to Madrid. Everyone thinks that all year long we**'ll be having** fun—singing and playing guitars and serenading the señoritas on their balconies. And that siesta in the middle of the day **will be** fantastic. So **will** the food!

    Enough for now. Tell Mom and Dad I**'ll write** them as soon as I **get** a spare moment.

Love,
Mark

December 15

Dear Emily,

Well, my first term at the University of Madrid **is** just about over, and things **are going** OK. I**'m** right in the middle of exams. As a matter of fact, I**'ve been studying** all afternoon, and I'm going to keep studying until midnight. I **need** a break, though, so I**'m writing** you. It**'s been** a challenging experience getting used to living in a foreign country, but well worth it. Madrid **is** actually a lot like any big city anywhere. Take the famous siesta, for example. I **haven't had** time for one single siesta yet! It **seems** like I'm always either **studying** or **going shopping** for food or **cooking** because Luis, Isao, and I **love** to eat, and we**'ve** all **discovered** the joy of cooking! Hardly anyone else **takes** a siesta, either. A lot of people **work** far away from where they **live,** and traffic **is** so bad that it **takes** forever to get anyplace—just like back in Dallas! So people just **take** long lunches. School **is** pretty difficult, too. Spanish students **study** very hard, and we**'ve** only **had** one party. I **have had** time to study the guitar, though, and my conversational Spanish **is getting** better and better. And everyone **is** really friendly and natural. But there**'s** not too much singing in the streets or serenading the girls. No one **has** time. The food **is** truly great, however, and I **love** it!

Enough for the moment. I**'ve bought** presents for everyone, but I'm going to send them after the New Year because I **don't have** time to get to the post office. Enjoy the holidays!

Love,

Mark

(continued on next page)

June 15

Dear Emily,

The school year **ended** two weeks ago, and I **got** my marks. I **did** much better than I **thought** I **would**—two 4s and two 3s, but I **had to knock** myself **out** to do it. I **was** sure I **was going to fail** anthropology because I**'d failed** the first exam. It **was** a gigantic class, and you never **got** a chance to talk to the professor, who **lectured** with a microphone. But a few weeks into the term, Luis and I **set up** a study group with some other students. We **would get together** three afternoons a week and **quiz** each other about the important points, which really **helped** us pull through. I never **thought** it **would be** so difficult.

I **left** Madrid last week, and on the plane I **was thinking** about how different Spain **turned out** to be from what I **had expected.** I **used to think** the Spanish people **were** all carefree and happy-go-lucky. Well, the Spanish people I **met were** friendly and outgoing and **liked** having a good time, just like I**'d heard,** but they **were** also businesslike and dedicated. I **was** surprised to learn that Spanish students **studied** really hard, too. Boy, **did** they **set** me a good example! I **studied** more in Madrid than I ever **had** back at home. Spain definitely **turned out** not to be the land of mañana…. but the food **was** wonderful.

Love,

Mark

TENSE AND TIME

PRESENT TIME: NOW

SIMPLE PRESENT
Spanish students **study** hard.

PRESENT PROGRESSIVE			
SUBJECT	*AM/IS/ARE*	**BASE FORM + -ING**	
Mark	**is**	**studying**	at the University of Madrid.

PRESENT TIME: BEFORE NOW

PRESENT PERFECT			
SUBJECT	*HAS/HAVE*	**PAST PARTICIPLE**	
He	**has** not	**had**	much spare time.

PRESENT PERFECT PROGRESSIVE			
SUBJECT	*HAS/HAVE BEEN*	**BASE FORM + -ING**	
Mark	**has been**	**studying**	all day.

*   *   *

PAST TIME: A TIME IN THE PAST (GENERAL OR SPECIFIC)

SIMPLE PAST
Mark and Luis **set up** a study group.

PAST PROGRESSIVE			
SUBJECT	*WAS/WERE*	**BASE FORM + -ING**	
They	**were**	**worrying**	about their marks.

USED TO + BASE FORM
Mark **used to think** the Spanish people were all happy-go-lucky.

general

WOULD + BASE FORM
Mark and Luis **would meet** with their study group three afternoons a week.

specific

PAST TIME: BEFORE THAT TIME IN THE PAST

PAST PERFECT			
SUBJECT	*HAD*	**PAST PARTICIPLE**	
Mark and Luis	**had**	**failed**	the first exam.

PAST PERFECT PROGRESSIVE			
SUBJECT	*HAD BEEN*	**BASE FORM + -ING**	
They	**had** not **been**	**studying**	enough.

(continued on next page)

PAST TIME: AFTER THAT TIME IN THE PAST (BUT BEFORE NOW)

FUTURE IN THE PAST

	WAS/WERE GOING TO	*BASE FORM*	
Mark thought he	**was going to**	**fail**	anthropology.

	WOULD	*BASE FORM*	
He knew he	**would**	**find**	time to study.

	WOULD BE	*BASE FORM + -ING*	
Mark	**would be**	**doing**	a lot more studying.

* * *

FUTURE TIME: A TIME IN THE FUTURE (GENERAL OR SPECIFIC)

	WILL	*BASE FORM*	
Mark	**will**	**enjoy**	taking a siesta every afternoon.

general

	BE GOING TO	*BASE FORM*	
His classes	**are going to**	**be**	easy.

specific

FUTURE PROGRESSIVE			
	WILL BE	*BASE FORM + -ING*	
He	**will be**	**taking**	four classes.

SIMPLE PRESENT
Classes **begin** on September 15.

PRESENT PROGRESSIVE			
	AM/IS/ARE	*BASE FORM + -ING*	
The group	**is**	**stopping**	in London on the way to Madrid.

FUTURE TIME: BEFORE THAT TIME IN THE FUTURE (BUT AFTER NOW)

FUTURE PERFECT			
	WILL HAVE	*PAST PARTICIPLE*	
They	**will have**	**improved**	their Spanish by then.

FUTURE PERFECT PROGRESSIVE			
	WILL HAVE BEEN	*BASE FORM + -ING*	
They	**will have been**	**waiting**	for two hours by the time we get there.

Grammar Notes

Verb tenses convey a sense of relationships in time that link states, events, and actions.

1. Present time: We can describe present states, events, or actions in existence or happening now by using simple present tense or present progressive. We use present perfect or present perfect progressive to describe those events which began or occurred before now and either continue now or have continued <u>until</u> now.

> NOW:
> Mark **lives** with two other students.
> His Spanish **is getting** better and better.
>
> BEGAN OR OCCURRED BEFORE NOW:
> He **hasn't had** a chance to take one single siesta.
> He **has been studying** very hard.

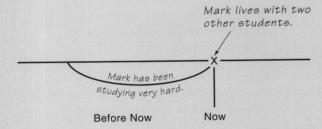

Mark lives with two other students.

Mark has been studying very hard.

Before Now   Now

2. Past time: We can express past states, events, or actions in terms of a <u>specific time</u> in the past with simple past tense.

> simple past
> Yesterday Mark **wrote** Emily a letter.
> Emily **read** it while she was eating lunch.

We use past progressive, *used to* + verb, or *would* + verb to describe states, events, or actions that occurred <u>during a period of time in the past</u>.

> past progressive
> Isao **was cooking** dinner when the phone rang.
>
> used to + verb
> Mark **used to study** French, but now he studies Spanish.
>
> would + verb
> He **would close** his books every night before ten.

To express those states, actions, or events that occurred <u>before then</u>, we use past perfect or past perfect progressive.

> past perfect
> She **hadn't seen** him in many years.
> past perfect progressive
> Mark **had been studying** all evening, and he was very tired.

To express those states, actions, or events that occurred <u>after then but before now</u>, we use future in the past.

> Mark thought Gina **was going to come** to the party.
> He thought he **would fail.**

Study the following sentences. The verb tenses convey the order of events in past time.

> Mark and Luis **had heard** about their anthropology teacher's demanding reputation before they **began** the course.
> Isao **had been having** difficulty in his math course before Mark **helped** him.
> He **thought** he **was going to fail** the course.
> Mark **used to think** that the weather in Spain **was** always hot because he **had seen** so many pictures of people at the beach.

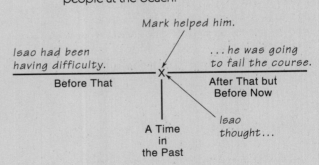

Mark helped him.

Isao had been having difficulty.

Before That

. . . he was going to fail the course.

After That but Before Now

A Time in the Past

Isao thought . . .

Future in the past and habitual past: Future in the past is expressed with *was/were going to* or *would* + base form of verb. It is often used to refer to events that were supposed to take place but did not.

> Isao and Elena **were going to attend** a concert after dinner. (They had planned to attend but didn't.)

(continued on next page)

Would + verb often has a slightly different meaning. It implies a possibility or expectation, but no specific plan.

> Mark thought he **would be serenading** girls on balconies when he got to Spain. (He expected this but had no plan.)

Be careful! Habitual past is expressed with *used to* and *would*. Both forms describe actions that were repeated in the past.

> Mark **used to study** every evening when he was in Spain.
> Mark **would study** every evening when he was in Spain.

In the examples above, *used to* and *would* are interchangeable, since the sentences describe past <u>actions</u>. Although both *used to* and *would* can be used to describe repeated or continuing past actions that no longer exist, only *used to* can be used to describe past <u>location</u>, <u>state</u>, or <u>possession</u>.

> Mark **used to live** in Dallas. (location) NOT ~~He would live in Dallas.~~
> He **used to be** overweight. (state) NOT ~~He would be overweight.~~
> He **used to have** a dog. (possession) NOT ~~He would have a dog.~~

3. **Future time:** *Will, be going to* + base form of verb, simple present tense, present progressive, or future progressive can be used to describe states, events, and actions that will occur at some time in the future.

> A TIME IN THE FUTURE:
> *will + verb*
> Mark **will go** back to Dallas in July.
> *be going to + verb*
> Luis and Isao **are going to stay** another
> *simple present*
> year after Mark **leaves.**

Future perfect or future perfect progressive describe those states, events, and actions that will occur before that time in the future but after now.

BEFORE THAT TIME BUT AFTER NOW
> *future perfect*
> Mark's Spanish **will have improved** greatly by next July.

> *Mark will go to Dallas.*
> Mark's Spanish will have improved greatly.
> Luis and Isao are going to stay another year.

Now — Before That ← A Time in the Future → After That

Be careful! Many sentences describing states, events, or actions in the future are made up of two clauses, one with *if, after,* or similar words and a verb in the simple present tense and the other clause with a future form.

> Mark **will write** his parents as soon as he **gets** a spare moment.
> As soon as he **gets** a spare moment, Mark **will write** his parents.

Remember that in these sentences, the simple present tense is always used to describe the action that occurs first in time, and the future form is used to describe the action that occurs second. It doesn't matter which clause comes first in the sentence.

Be careful! Do not use *will* or *be going to* in both clauses. The following sentence is incorrect: ~~After he will get his bachelor's degree, Mark will return to Spain for advanced study.~~

4. Both simple and progressive verb forms indicate the time when something occurs. Remember, however, that a progressive form suggests a state, event, or action that is in progress, incomplete, or temporary in relation to the moment of speech.

> Mark **is cooking** dinner. (in progress at the moment of speech)
> He **has been studying** Spanish for eight years. (incomplete at the moment of speech)
> Isao **was speaking** Japanese yesterday. (temporary)

5. In past, present, and future sentences, stative verbs—verbs that express senses, feelings, possession, or thoughts—do not

usually occur in the progressive or perfect progressive forms. Remember that when stative verbs do occur in the progressive, they take on special active meanings. See Appendix 3 on page A9 for a list of stative verbs.

> Mark **has** a Spanish dictionary. (stative: "possesses")
> Mark and his roommates **are having** dinner. (active: "eating")

Usage note: Some native speakers use stative verbs in the progressive in informal conversational speech.

> **Will** you **be needing** a ride to the airport?
> **I'm** really **wanting** a cup of coffee right now.

6. Remember that verb tenses often follow a certain sequence that indicates relationships in time. This feature is called <u>sequence of tenses</u>. In general, past forms go with other past forms, and present forms go with other present forms or with future forms.

> present   present
> Mark **thinks** the Spanish people **are** carefree.

> past   past
> Mark **thought** the Spanish people **were** carefree.
> present
> Mark **expects** that his fluency in Spanish
> future perfect
> **will have improved** greatly by the end of the year.
> present perfect
> The boys **have rented** an apartment and
> present progressive
> **are moving** in next weekend.

Remember, though, that there are many occasions where meaning makes mixing of tense forms necessary.

> She **says** she **used to have** long hair.

Remember also the formal sequence of tenses that is observed in the following types of sentences.

> She **said** she **didn't know.** (indirect speech)
> If Mark **spoke** Japanese, he **would take** a trip to Japan. (conditional sentence)
> When Isao **gets** to class, he **will take** a test. (time clauses)
> Mark **wishes** he **were** in Spain right now. (after **wish**)

FOCUSED PRACTICE

1. Discover the Grammar

Look again at some of the sentences from Mark's letters to Emily. On the lines provided, write the events in the order in which they happened or will happen.

1. I've been studying all afternoon, and I'm going to keep studying until midnight. I need to take a break, though, so I'm writing you.

First: _____ I've been studying all afternoon. _____

Second: _____ I need to take a break. I'm writing you. _____

Third: _____ I'm going to keep studying until midnight. _____

(continued on next page)

2. I've bought presents for everyone, but I'm going to send them after the New Year because I don't have time to go to the post office.

First: _____

Second: _____

Third: _____

3. I was sure I was going to fail anthropology because I'd failed the first exam.

First: _____

Second: _____

Third: _____

4. When I get to Spain, I'm going to be rooming with two other guys. We'll have gotten to know each other really well by then.

First: _____

Second: _____

Third: _____

2. Homesickness

Mark is inviting his friend Alicia to a party. Fill in the blanks in their conversation, choosing between the verb forms given. If a stative verb has an active meaning, remember to use the progressive.

See page 19 at back of book

Mark: Hi, Alicia. This is Mark. _____ We're having _____ a party tonight. Can you come?
1. (We have / We're having)

Alicia: Sure, I'd love to. Do you need anything? _____ some gazpacho
2. (I make / I'm making)

right now. What if _____ that? And what time
3. (I bring / I'm bringing)

_____ there?
4. (does everybody get / is everybody getting)

Mark: About 8:00, but maybe you could come earlier. Yes, bring the gazpacho, please.

_____ it. _____ to invite Gina?
5. (I love / I'm loving)   6. (Do you want / Are you wanting)

Alicia: I don't know. Something's wrong. _____ really distant these days,
7. (She was / She's being)

and she hasn't _____ out of her room all morning.
8. (come / been coming)

I _____ on her door an hour ago and she
9. (knocked / was knocking)

_____ at me to go away because she
10. (yelled / was yelling)

_____ on her term paper and didn't want to be bothered. I don't
11. (worked / was working)

think that's it, though. There was a faint sound of sobbing coming from her room, and at first

I thought I _____ things because Gina never
12. (heard / was hearing)

_____. You know how much she
13. (cries / is crying)

_____ her emotions in control.
14. (keeps / is keeping)

Mark: What do you think it is, then?

Alicia: Well, for one thing, she and Jaime _____ each other, but they
15. (saw / were seeing)

_____ it off. The other thing is that
16. (broke / were breaking)

→ dating is an idiomatic expression

_____ ~~adjective~~ homesick for Italy. She just hasn't
  17. (she's / she's being)

_____ used to Spain.
  18. (gotten / been getting)

Mark: That's too bad. A party is just what Gina _____.
                                                         19. (needs / is needing)

_____. That should cheer her up. Try to get her to come. She
  20. (We dance and sing / We're going to be dancing and singing)

should be with others.

Alicia: OK, I will. I'll be there as soon as _____ some errands.
                                                    21. (I run / I'm running)

3. Perceptions

_Jihan and Luis are having a conversation about Spain. Fill in the blanks in their
conversation with simple and perfect forms of the indicated verbs. Use contracted
forms with pronouns._

Jihan: Why are you in Spain, Luis?

Luis: Well, my school awarded a scholarship to study abroad to the person who

_____had studied_____ Spanish the longest. I _____
        1. (study)   2. (study)

Spanish since elementary school, and I jumped at the chance to be in this program when I won

the award.

Jihan: What _____ of Spain?
                   3. (think)

Luis: Well, I really like it, but a lot of my perceptions _____ since
                                                                 4. (change)

I _____ here. In Brazil I thought most Spaniards
    5. (be)

_____ Portuguese, but since then I
  6. (speak)

_____ that's not the case. I also thought everybody
  7. (discover)

_____ a siesta every afternoon. Actually, hardly anybody
  8. (take)

_____. What about you? Do you like Spain?
  9. (do)

Jihan: I love it. My expectations _____ too, though. A Spanish-speaking
                                         10. (change)

family, the Sotos, lived next door to us in Alexandria when I was a girl. They

_____ a daughter my age named Pilar and we
  11. (have)

_____ good friends. Our family got to know her family really well.
  12. (become)

Since then I _____ close to the Spanish people. I'll tell you one
               13. (always feel)

thing, though: I expected Spanish women to be like Mrs. Soto. She

_____ sweet and submissive, always deferring to her husband.
  14. (be)

The Spanish women I _____ since I got here
                       15. (meet)

_____ that way at all!
  16. (not be)

Luis: Yeah, Spanish women can be very assertive. How's your Spanish coming?

(continued on next page)

Jihan: Pretty well. By the time the program _____ in June, I

17. (end)

_____ fluent, I think. What about yours?

18. (become)

Luis: I guess I'm fluent, but I'd better be; by next January I _____ on it

19. (working)

for ten years. I still make plenty of mistakes, though!

4. Country and City

Isao and Elena are talking about life in the country and the city. Fill in the blanks in their
*conversation with correct forms of **used to** or **would**. Use **would** if it is possible to do so.*

→ location, state, possession   see page 8

Isao: Have you always lived in Madrid, Elena?

Elena: No. In fact, I've only been here for a year. I _____used to live_____ in San Acasio; it's a small

1. (live)

town north of here. And when I was a little girl, from 1980 to 1984, my father was a visiting

professor at the University of Salamanca. We _____ there every summer

2. (go)

during those four years, and we _____ a farmhouse outside the city. My father

3. (rent)

_____ his classes in the mornings and _____ us on outings

4. (teach)   5. (take)

in the afternoons. How about you? I know you live in Tokyo now, but _____ in

6. (you, not live)

Sapporo?

Isao: Yes, we did when I was young. We also _____ a summer house in a small

7. (have)

village near there. We don't have it anymore, though. It's too bad, because I have some fond

memories of the place. We _____ a month there in the early summer and

8. (spend)

another month in the winter. It was great for us children because we _____

9. (not have to)

think about school or homework for a whole month. I really miss that simple life in the country.

Elena: Me too. I'd like to go back to it.

university bulletin board in Barcelona

5. Plans and Expectations

A year ago, when Mark was on the plane to Madrid, he wrote down some of his expectations for the coming year; some of them came true, and some didn't. Now Mark is back in the United States and is telling his friends about his experiences. Write Mark's sentences. Use the indicated future-in-the-past constructions: **was/were going to** + *verb or* **would** + *verb. Be sure to respect the sequence of tenses.*

1. I imagine that I'll fall in love with a Spanish girl, (would)

   I imagined that I'd fall in love with a Spanish girl ,

   but I didn't.

2. I think I'll make a lot of new friends, (would)

   _____ ,

   and I did.

3. I'm sure I won't have to study very much, (would)

   _____ ,

   but I had to study a whole lot.

4. I'm sure I'm not going to have any difficulty with my courses, (was/were going to)

   _____ ,

   but I had tremendous difficulty for quite a while.

5. I think I'm going to be doing a lot of serenading of señoritas on their balconies, (was/were going to)

   _____ ,

   but I only did that once, and that was sort of a joke.

6. I expect that I'll love Spanish food and will learn to prepare it, (would)

   _____ ,

   and I did. You're all invited to dinner.

7. I'm sure that the Spanish people will turn out to be fun-loving and carefree, (would)

   _____ ,

   but that was an oversimplification. They're fun-loving and serious.

8. I hope that I'm going to write in my diary every day, (was/were going to)

   _____ ,

   but I rarely had time. I did write in it occasionally.

6. Misconceptions

At the beginning of the year, all the students in the International Program had some misconceptions about people from other countries—some silly and some that could be hurtful. Using the following prompts and the indications of time in parentheses, write sentences describing their misconceptions and their discoveries. Make sure to follow the sequence of tenses.

1. Mark/be/under the impression that/Spain/be/the land of mañana. (past time)

   Mark was under the impression that Spain was the land of mañana.

2. Isao/think/people in Spain/wear/large Mexican sombreros. (past time)

3. He/discover,/however,/that/large sombreros/be/relatively uncommon in Spain. (present time)

4. Luis/assume that/everyone in Spain/can/speak/Portuguese. (past time)

5. Until she/meet Mark,/Alicia/believe/a lot of Americans/be/arrogant. (past time)

6. She/learn/that/this/be not/necessarily true. (present time)

7. Mark and Alicia/think/all Italians/express their emotions/freely. (past time)

8. They/find out that/not all Italians/be/outwardly emotional. (present time)

9. Elena/think/Japanese and American people/always have/plenty of money until she/meet Isao and Mark. (past time)

10. Now she/expect that/she/have to/lend them money. (present time)

11. When Luis/tell/Isao/he/go/introduce him to a young woman from Egypt, Isao/expect that/the woman/will/be wearing a veil. (past time)

12. He/learn from Jihan that/many Muslim women/not wear/veils. (past or present time)

7. Editing

Find and correct the twenty mistakes in verb tense usage in the following composition.

> "I am writing these words in English because I am ~~needing~~ _need_ the practice. At this moment I have been on an airplane over the Pacific Ocean, en route to a year of study at New York University in the United States. I am looking forward to being there, but I am also a little afraid. What will I find when I will get to America? Will the Americans be arrogant and violent? Would I make friends? Am I happy?"
>
> These had been the words I had written in my diary on the airplane last month. When I arrived at John F. Kennedy Airport, I used to be timid and nervous. I have heard a lot about crime before I left Japan, so I am very scared when I arrived. People in Japan had also told me that Americans will be rude, unfriendly, and unhelpful. For this reason, I was very surprised when the taxi driver from the airport would carry my luggage and spoke kindly and slowly to me. He even asked if there was anything else he can do. And when I had been arriving at the college, everyone seemed concerned about me. I found that the majority of people here are friendly and are going out of their way to help you if you need it.
>
> On television, the news programs speak a lot about bad events like accidents, murders, diseases, and fights. But I don't see as much violence in my life as I do on television. I had not been mugged, and I don't worry all the time about my safety.
>
> Two of the ideas I would have about the United States, however, seem to be true. One is that Americans don't seem to pay much attention to rules. One of my best American friends says, in fact, "Rules are made to be broken." The other idea I had that seems to be true is about the American family. In Japan the family is very important, but some Japanese people are thinking that the family is meaning nothing in the United States. Anyway, I am going to have a chance to see a real American family. I will have been going with my roommate, Susan, to spend Thanksgiving break with her family in Pennsylvania. When I see her family, I will have understood more!

COMMUNICATION PRACTICE

8. Practice Listening

🔲 *It is the end of the year in Spain. Mark is leaving tomorrow to return to the United States, and he, Luis, and Isao are talking about this past year and the year to come. Listen to their conversation on the tape. Then listen again and circle true (T) or false (F) in response to the questions.*

___T___ 1. Luis and Isao will stay another year in Spain.

_____ 2. Mark will return to Spain before getting his bachelor's degree.

_____ 3. Mark left Dallas. Then he and Jane agreed not to see each other anymore.

_____ 4. Mark still misses Jane.

_____ 5. Mark was writing Jane regularly before she sent him a letter.

_____ 6. Mark will telephone the Hills for train directions to Brighton before he leaves Madrid.

_____ 7. Isao will get a tan before he returns to Madrid.

_____ 8. First Luis will get his visa. Then he'll take a boat to Alexandria.

_____ 9. Luis will tutor for a month. Then he'll go to Alexandria.

_____ 10. Isao and Luis will earn money. Then they'll go to Dallas.

9. Small Group Discussion

Reread the composition on page 15. In small groups, write down all the things this student believed about Americans before she arrived and what she believes now. Discuss with your classmates your own beliefs that have changed similarly as a result of travel, living in a foreign country, or meeting people from a group you had never known before. Some ideas to consider: Where did the stereotype come from? What makes a stereotype change? How can stereotypes be harmful?

10. Essay

Write a short essay (one or two paragraphs) on a misconception or stereotype that you have experienced—either a misconception that you held which you later changed, or someone else's misconception of you. Choose one of the following openers:

Topic 1. I used to have the misconception that . . . , but my ideas have changed.

Topic 2. People used to believe that I . . . , but they have had to change their views.

Topic 3. I have learned a great deal about the dangers of stereotyping.

11. Picture Discussion

Look at this picture of the sinking of the Titanic *in 1912. Divide into three groups. Each group will describe the situation from a different point of view: a passenger at the beginning of the voyage, an officer at the moment of sinking, and a survivor a week after the sinking.*

Example:
Officer at the moment of the sinking: We **are sinking,** and we . . .

Henry Reuterdalh: The Mansell Collection

2

Certainty and Necessity (Modals)

INTRODUCTION

Read and listen to the following letter to an advice columnist and the columnist's response to the letter.

Questions to Consider

1. Should people having difficulty in a marriage try to work out their problems and stay together?
2. What are ways of keeping a marriage, or any relationship, in good shape?

Pamela's corner

DEAR PAMELA: I'm at my wits' end about how to save my marriage. When my husband, Bruce, and I got married three years ago, everything was wonderful. But recently I've begun to think he **must not love** me anymore because he works all day and then goes out in the evenings to be with his friends. He never even eats dinner with us any longer, and when I try to talk to him about it, he shuts down and only says I **ought to go** to school to learn housekeeping because the place looks like a pigsty.

A few weeks ago things all came to a head when I told the kids they **could get** a puppy. Bruce already had a dog, but she was old, sick, and incontinent. He **was supposed to have** her put to sleep but kept refusing to do it. So one day I took her to the vet and had her euthanized. When Bruce found out about it and then saw the new dog, he lost his temper. I thought he **might make** a scene in front of the kids, so I took them and spent the night at my mother's.

Another thing is that he's very stingy. He told me I **should get** a "real" job if I want more money. My mother says I **should file** for divorce because Bruce **can't** possibly **love** me, the way he's been acting. In fact, she says I never **should have married** him in the first place. Pamela, I still love Bruce and want this marriage to work, but he's acting like a jerk. What **should I do?**

Clueless in Cleveland

DEAR CLUELESS: Honey, I sympathize with your problems, but it takes two to tango. Bruce **may** well **be** in the wrong, but you **have to take** some of the responsibility for this mess. The first thing you**'ve got to do** is stop relying on your mother. It sounds like she's been poking her nose into places it doesn't belong. Regarding the dog problem, you really blew it! You **couldn't have been thinking** very rationally or sensitively if you had his dog put to sleep without his knowledge, and you never **should have allowed** the children to get a new dog so soon.

As for your housekeeping, Bruce **may have** a point. There's no doubt the work of housewives (or house-husbands, for that matter) is undervalued, but you **may not be** holding up your end of the bargain. That's something you **can fix.**

As for the money situation, Bruce **could be** right again. You **might look** for a part-time job—not because you don't already have a "real" job but so that you **can establish** some financial independence. Maybe you **could find** something to do at home, like writing or telephone sales.

Above all, you **must take** control of your life. You and Bruce obviously **have got to find** a way to talk about your problems. If Bruce **won't talk,** you **ought to find** a counselor or some neutral party (not your mother!) to act as referee, and then you need to keep talking. I don't think you **should file** for divorce, at least not until you've tried to work things out. Good luck, and hang in there!

Pamela

CERTAINTY AND NECESSITY (MODALS)

DEGREE OF CERTAINTY: AFFIRMATIVE (PRESENT AND PAST)

SPEAKER IS ALMOST CERTAIN.			
SUBJECT	**MODAL OR MODAL-LIKE EXPRESSION**	**BASE FORM (OR PAST PARTICIPLE)**	
He	**must**	**be**	angry.
He	**has to**	**be**	angry.
He	**'s got to**	**be**	angry.
He	**must have**	**been**	angry.

SPEAKER IS LESS CERTAIN.			
SUBJECT	**MODAL OR MODAL-LIKE EXPRESSION**	**BASE FORM (OR PAST PARTICIPLE)**	
He	**may**	**be**	angry.
He	**might**	**be**	angry.
He	**could**	**be**	angry.
He	**may have**	**been**	angry.
He	**might have**	**been**	angry.
He	**could have**	**been**	angry.

(continued on next page)

DEGREE OF CERTAINTY: NEGATIVE (PRESENT AND PAST)

SPEAKER IS VERY SURE; ALMOST CERTAIN.			
She	**couldn't**	**be**	happy.
She	**couldn't have**	**been**	happy.
She	**can't**	**be**	happy.
She	**can't have**	**been**	happy.

SPEAKER IS A LITTLE LESS SURE BUT STILL THINKS SITUATION PROBABLE.			
She	**must** not	**be**	happy.
She	**must** not **have**	**been**	happy.

SPEAKER IS EVEN LESS SURE BUT STILL THINKS SITUATION POSSIBLE.			
She	**may** not	**be**	happy.
She	**may** not **have**	**been**	happy.
She	**might** not	**be**	happy.
She	**might** not **have**	**been**	happy.

DEGREE OF CERTAINTY: FUTURE

SPEAKER IS QUITE SURE.			
She	**should**	**be**	here by twelve o'clock.
She	**ought to**	**be**	here by twelve o'clock.

SPEAKER IS LESS SURE BUT CONSIDERS SITUATION POSSIBLE.			
She	**may**	**be**	here by twelve o'clock.
She	**might**	**be**	here by twelve o'clock.
She	**could**	**be**	here by twelve o'clock.

DEGREE OF NECESSITY

ABSOLUTELY NECESSARY; OBLIGATORY			
You	**must**	**have**	a blood test to get married.
You	**have to**	**take**	the test before you can get your license.

STRONGLY EXPECTED			
You	**'re to**	**be**	at the doctor's office at eight o'clock.

STRONGLY ADVISED			
You	**'d better**	**take**	some action soon.
You	**'ve got to**	**go**	into therapy right away.
You	**have to**	**communicate**	better if you want your marriage to survive.

ADVISED			
She	**should**	**stop**	relying on her mother.
They	**ought to**	**seek**	counseling.

SUGGESTED			
Alice	**could**	**go away**	for a while.
You	**might**	**look for**	a part-time job.

CLASSIFICATION OF MODALS AND MODAL-LIKE EXPRESSIONS

	Certainty	Necessity
must	X	X
have to	X	X
have got to	X	X
could	X	X
might	X	X
should	X	X
ought to	X	X
may	X	
can't	X	
couldn't	X	
had better		X
be to		X
be supposed to		X

Grammar Notes

We express greater or lesser degrees of certainty or necessity in different ways. In this unit, we look at the modals and modal-like expressions we use in making statements of certainty or necessity.

1. **Certainty:** *must, have to, have got to, may, might, can't, couldn't, should,* and *ought to* These modals express varying degrees of certainty. They are used when the speaker is concluding something based on logic and the facts as understood by the speaker. (Remember that when we want to state a fact we are absolutely—100 percent—sure of, we don't use modals.)

> (Speaker is 100 percent sure.)
> Alice **knows** what's wrong.
>
> (Speaker is very sure.)
> Alice **must know** what's wrong.
> Alice **has to know** what's wrong.
> Alice **has got to know** what's wrong.
>
> (Speaker is less sure.)
> Alice **may know** what's wrong.
> Alice **might know** what's wrong.
> Alice **could know** what's wrong.

Varying degrees of certainty are expressed in different ways in affirmative and negative statements and in statements about the future. Refer to the Degree of Certainty grammar boxes on pages 19 and 20 for examples of some different ways to express these degrees.

The following grammar notes describe some interesting features of these modals and modal-like expressions.

a. *May* and *might*
Some speakers feel that *may* shows more optimism than *might*.

> They **may be able** to save their marriage. (more optimistic)
> They **might be able** to save their marriage. (less optimistic)

With these and many other modals and modal-like expressions, however, emphasis and tone of voice, point of view, context, and other factors may color a modal slightly, changing its intensity.

b. *Might have* and *may have*
Might have is occasionally used in questions, but *may have* never is. In negative questions, *might* normally contracts with *not*.

> **Mightn't** he **have** gone out with his friends?

c. *Can't, can't have, couldn't,* and *couldn't have* These are used when a speaker feels that it would be impossible to believe or conclude otherwise.

> She **can't** possibly **love** me. She's so mean to me all the time.
> You **couldn't have meant** what you just said. You must have been very angry.

Can't and *couldn't* can also express feelings of denial, as when something awful has occurred.

> John died? Oh, that **can't be!** He was so young!

Be careful! *Can't* can be used to express certainty, but *can* is only used to express ability.

d. *Should, ought to, may, might,* and *could* These can be used to express future probability. *Should* and *ought to* express a greater degree of certainty, and *may, might,* and *could* express a lesser degree.

> I heard there's no traffic. They **should arrive** on time. (Speaker thinks this is likely.)
> They had some car trouble. But they **may arrive** on time anyway. (Speaker thinks this is possible.)
> It's been raining. They **could arrive** on time, but traffic always gets so backed up in bad weather. (Speaker thinks this is possible though not likely.)

e. *Could have*
In statements about the past, *could have* can express either a lack of certainty or a missed opportunity. Compare these two sentences.

Alice **could have told** him how mad she was at him, but I'm not sure what she told him. (uncertain guess about the past)

Alice **could have discussed** the situation with Bruce. It's unfortunate that she didn't. (missed opportunity)

2. **Necessity:** *must, be to, have to, have got to, had better, should, ought to, could,* and *might*
These modals and modal-like expressions are used to express varying degrees of necessity. See the grammar boxes on pages 20 and 21 for examples of these degrees.

The following grammar notes describe some interesting features of these modals and modal-like expressions.

a. *Must, have to,* and *have got to*
These modals and modal-like expressions are used when something is required or prohibited by law or formal rules. Statements such as these are obligating; they do not allow for choice in following them. Although *must* is more formal than *have to* and *have got to*, the three forms are equally obligating in this context.

You **must have** a blood test to get married.
You **have to carry** your driver's license with you whenever you drive.
You**'ve got to show** proper identification to enter this room.
Students **must not smoke** in the building.

b. *Have to* and *have got to*
These can also be used in conversation to make extremely strong suggestions that the speaker wants to insist on, but they are not actually obligating. Suggestions, however strong, do not have to be followed.

You look awful. You really **have to see** a doctor.

Be careful! *Have to* in the negative is used to show a lack of necessity.

He **doesn't have to pay** for the first counseling session.

c. *Must*
Be careful! *Must* and *must not* are generally not used to make extremely strong suggestions because their use suggests that the speaker has more authority or power than the listener. This would be impolite in many situations.

d. *Need not (needn't), needn't have*
In formal speech and writing, you will hear or see the form *need not* or *needn't* in place of *don't/doesn't have to*. Its past form is *needn't have* + past participle.

You **needn't be** there before the others arrive.
You **needn't have brought** a present.

e. *Be to* and *be supposed to*
These are used to express strong expectation.

You **were to appear** in court in October 1. Why weren't you there?
Noncustodial parents **are supposed to pay** child support.

Be to carries more power, intensity, and authority than *be supposed to* and for this reason would be rude in conversation. *Be to* also carries a threat that there will be consequences if the expectation is not met.

f. *Had better*
Had better is used to offer strong advice. Since advice, however strong, doesn't have to be followed, it is not obligating. When a speaker uses *had better,* though, there is a suggestion of a consequence for not following the advice.

You**'d better pay** that bill right away.

Be careful! *Had better* is almost never used in affirmative questions.

g. *Had better have*
Had better used in the past (*had better have* + past participle) suggests present or past consequences for past actions.

She**'d better not have invited** her mother! She's in trouble if she did! (present consequences)
He**'d better have gotten** there on time! Everyone else did. (past consequences)

(continued on next page)

h. *Should* and *ought to*

These are used to make suggestions and give advice. The speaker wants to convince the listener to do something. *Ought to* is used less than *should* in questions, the negative, or the past.

You **should go** into marital counseling.
You **ought to try** to communicate better with each other.

i. *Might* and *could*

These are used to make suggestions when the speaker is not trying to influence the listener too strongly.

You **might try** working as a teacher's aide. You would be good at it. Or you **could try** writing.

Be careful! *Migh*t occurs in the negative, but it doesn't generally contract with *not*.

j. *Shall*

Shall is often used in questions to ask about a course of action. It is only used with *I* or *we*.

Shall I open the window?
Yes, please do. It's really stuffy in here.

When *shall* is used with *we*, it is often followed by a sentence with *let's*.

A: Shall we go to a movie tonight?
B: No, **let's** just **stay** home and **rent** a video. I'm too tired to go out.

k. *Must have, might have, may have, could have,* and *ought to have*

These combine with *had to* to make conclusions and guesses about past obligation.

Bruce **must have had to** go to court.

Ms. Adams **must not have had to** pay child support.
Alice **might have had to** leave early.

l. *Must, might, may, could, should,* and *ought to*

These combine with *be able to* to make guesses about future ability.

They **may be able to** work out their differences.

3. Modals don't add *-s* in the third-person singular form.

She may get married next year. NOT ~~She mays get married next year~~.

Modals are followed by the base form of a verb without *to*.

I can get a divorce. NOT ~~I can to get a divorce~~.

Two modals cannot be used together in the same verb phrase.

We may be able to settle our argument. NOT ~~We may can settle our argument~~.

4. Remember that modals and modal-like expressions occur in four patterns.

modal + base form:
Bruce and Alice **might go** into therapy.

modal + **have** + past participle:
Alice **should have told** Bruce she was getting a new dog.

modal + **be** + present participle:
Bruce and Alice **might be thinking** about divorce.

modal + **have been** + present participle:
They **might have been arguing** last night.

FOCUSED PRACTICE

1. Discover the Grammar

Read the two letters to Pamela and Pamela's responses. Choose one of the descriptions from the box to explain the function of each of the numbered modals and modal-like expressions.

advice ✓	near certainty ✓	obligation
possibility ✓	strong advice ✓	

Dear Pamela:

My wife's mother means well, but she's always asking questions about our personal finances. Somehow she found out that we were denied credit on a loan, how I don't know. What *suggestion* <u>should I do</u>?
1.

Puzzled in Punxsutawney

Dear Puzzled:

Your wife <u>must have told</u> her about the
2.
obl. near cert.
denial of credit. Tell your mother-in-law
s. adv
<u>she'd better mind</u> her own business. Then
3.
have a talk with your wife. Tell her this is the kind of information that <u>shouldn't go</u>
4.
outside your household.

Pamela

Dear Pamela:

When our son Gerardo turned sixteen, my husband and I gave him a car with the condition that he <u>had to pay</u> the insurance
5.
obl.

on it. He has been staying out till all hours of the night with his friends and has missed the first insurance payment. When we tried to talk to him about it, he was sullen and told us to mind our own business. Any suggestions? The car is in our name.

Mortified in Monterey

Dear Mortified:

<u>Could your son be</u> just a little bit
6.
pos
spoiled? He <u>may not have thought</u> your
7.
pos
were serious about his paying the car insurance. Sit down and have a no-nonsense talk with him. Tell him you're taking his car keys away until he comes up with the insurance money. Be firm. Make sure he understands <u>he's got to act</u>
8.
obl. / strong advice can be either
responsibly.

Pamela

2. Children and Discipline

Mr. and Mrs. Mendoza are talking to a family counselor about problems with their children. Choose from the modals and modal-like expressions in the box and write them in the appropriate blanks.

must	shall	should	ought to
should have	shouldn't have	needn't	had better
had to	don't have to	has to	didn't have to

Mr. Mendoza: _____Should_____ children help around the house? I _____ do a
1.   2.
lot of chores when I was a child. I _____ get up at the crack of dawn
                                                                        3.
and slave away all day long, but my parents made me do my share. Today it seems like a

lot of children _____ do anything.
                                4.

Counselor: Absolutely. Children _____ feel that they're making a valuable
                                                                5.
contribution to the household. Chores are crucial.

Mrs. Mendoza: What about paying them for work they do?

Counselor: You can give them an allowance if you want to, but it _____ be tied to
                                                                                                                6.
the completion of tasks. My son gets an allowance every week, but it's simply his share of

the family money. He knows he still _____ clean his room, wash the
                                                                        7.
dishes, and do other things.

Mr. Mendoza: What about spanking? My son Tony deliberately broke a window last week. I was so angry

that I spanked him, but I didn't feel good about it afterwards. I know I probably

_____ resorted to spanking, but I'm not sure what would have been an
                        8.
appropriate punishment.

Counselor: Spanking rarely solves anything. I think you _____ made him pay for
                                                                                        9.
the window.

Mrs. Mendoza: Just one more question. We've found out that Sara, our oldest daughter, has been

skipping school. We talked to her about it, and now she's refusing to go to school at all.

She seems depressed.

Counselor: Well, the law says that children _____ attend school at least until they
                                                                        10.
are sixteen. I think you _____ bring her in for a talk with me. It sounds
                                        11.
like something pretty serious is going on. _____ we go ahead and
                                                                        12.
make an appointment for her to see me? How about next Thursday at four?

Mrs. Mendoza: Yes, let's do that.

3. Family Values

Write sentences using the prompts given. Use contracted modals for the negative forms.

1. Children/attend school/until the age of eighteen. (must)

   Children must attend school until the age of eighteen.

2. Parents/allow/their children to drink alcohol. (should not)

   _____

3. Physical abuse in families/be tolerated. (must not)

   _____

4. Parents/help their children/with their homework. (ought to)

   _____

5. Spouses/consider divorce/except as a last resort. (should not)

   _____

6. Parents/give their children/an allowance. (should)

   _____

7. Parents/pay their children/for doing household chores. (need not)

   _____

8. When they are wrong, /parents/apologize/to their children. (should)

   _____

9. Spouses/take separate vacations. (should not)

   _____

10. Parents/use corporal punishment/on their children. (must not)

    _____

11. Spouses/work at a marriage/to make it succeed. (must)

    _____

12. Families/hold regular family councils/to air problems. (ought to)

    _____

4. Trepidation

Bruce and Alice have agreed to talk with a family therapist to iron out their communication problems. Bruce hasn't shown up for the appointment. Write Alice's and the therapist's statements, placing the given expressions in the correct tenses.

a family counseling session

Therapist: Well, we _____ were supposed to _____ start this session at ten o'clock and it's 10:30.
1. (be supposed to)
Do you have any idea where Bruce is?

Alice: No, not really. He _____ car problems. His car has been in the
2. (could / have)
shop, but it was supposed to be ready by eight this morning. They

_____ working on it.
3. (might not / finish)

Therapist: Did you talk this morning?

Alice: No, he'd left the house by the time I got up. I did leave him a note about it last night, though. But he

got home very late, so he _____ the note.
4. (may not / see)

Therapist: Are you sure he knows that today's the day we _____?
5. (be supposed to / meet)

Alice: Well, actually we haven't talked about it since at least a week ago. He

_____.
6. (must / forget)

Therapist: I wonder. You _____ some wishful thinking. Based on what I know
7. (may / doing)
of Bruce, I'd say he _____ some trepidation . . . either that or he
8. (must / feeling)
_____ this thing seriously. We'll reschedule the meeting for next
9. (may not / taking)
Wednesday at 4:30. Tell him he _____ another session. I'm
10. (be not to / miss)
charging you for my time.

5. Anxiety

Mr. and Mrs. Mendoza have left their children with a babysitter and have gone to a play. It's intermission, and they are calling home to check on things. Choose from the list of modals and modal-like expressions in the box and write them in the appropriate blanks.

must have	must be	can't be	is
must not have	must not be	could have	can't have

Mr. Mendoza: (telephone rings) There's no answer. Jessica said she was going to take them out for ice

cream. They _____ must not be _____ back yet.

1.

Mrs. Mendoza: Albert, it's ten o'clock. It _____ taken them this long. Something

2.

_____ happened. Lord only knows; they _____ had

3.   4.

an accident. Jessica just got her license, you know.

Mr. Mendoza: Now, Cecilia, don't jump to conclusions. Jessica is very responsible. She

_____ a good driver.

5.

Mrs. Mendoza: Try again.

Mr. Mendoza: (dials) Still no answer!

Mrs. Mendoza: This _____ happening! We leave them for two hours, and . . .

6.

Mr. Mendoza: Hello? Oh, hello, Jessica. Is everything all right? I've called two times in the last five minutes.

Jessica: All right? Well yes, of course. We were out in the back yard watching the fireworks from the

stadium. I _____ heard the telephone.

7.

6. Communication

Bruce and Alice have succeeded in getting together with their therapist to work on their problem in communication. The therapist is making some suggestions about how they can improve things. Complete her sentences, choosing from the cues provided.

Since I've been observing the way you two communicate, or don't communicate, I've noticed a number of things. I have several suggestions.

1. You talk about each other, not to each other. Start using the word "you." That

_____ ought to _____ help you for starters.

(must / ought to)

2. You don't look at each other when you talk. Try looking the other person in the eye, at least briefly. That also

_____ improve the general climate. Bruce, you're especially prone to

(ought to / must)

looking away from Alice when you're talking to her.

3. I'm not sure but I think it _____ help if you jot down a list of points you

(had better / might)

want to make when you are discussing a problem. Sometimes people forget about the issues and just start

shouting at each other because they get rattled and can't remember what they wanted to say.

(continued on next page)

4. Truly consider the other person. Alice, you _____ thinking much about
(couldn't have been / didn't have to be)

Bruce's feelings when you had his dog put to sleep.

5. Focus on dialogue rather than battle. If you start exploring issues instead of trying to win, you

_____ be able to resolve your differences. I'm cautiously optimistic on this
(may / must)

point. Learn to ask the other person "What do you think about this?"

6. Stop bottling up your feelings. Express them. You _____ be headed toward
(had better / could)

disaster if you don't do something to change your pattern.

7. Editing

Read the following journal entry. Find and correct the fifteen errors in modals and modal-like expressions.

April 18—Things couldn't ^be worse between Pat and me. I don't know
how things could ^have gotten so bad so fast. I really get irritated, though,
when I come home after working hard all day long, and the house is a
mess and dinner isn't ready. I don't know what Pat does all day long,
but she must be spend a lot of time with her friends or something
because the housework is never done.

Today I came home about six and looked for my blue suit because I was
supposed to wear it to my club meeting tonight. I said, "Pat, where's my
suit? I had to wear it to my club meeting later this evening." Pat giggled
and said, "Oh, I must have forgetting to pick it up at the cleaner's. Wear
your blue jeans instead. You haven't to dress up to go to a club
meeting." I was furious, and I guess I may had raised my voice a little.
Pat started crying and said, "Stop yelling at me. I didn't have time to
pick it up because I must have gone to Mother's to give her a ride to her
bridge club meeting." I was even more furious. Why can Pat take care
of her own household responsibilities before she spends time chauffeur-
ing her mother around? I was so mad that I left the house and didn't
come back until late. I didn't go to my meeting.

I've been thinking, though; maybe we ought go to family counseling.
Maybe we should have going to counseling all along. It can hurt to try
it out, I suppose. I think we might growing apart, and I guess we hadn't
better do something.

COMMUNICATION PRACTICE

8. Practice Listening

*Sara and Tony, two of the Mendozas' children, are having a conversation.
Listen to their conversation on the tape. Then listen again and circle the letter
of each sentence that correctly describes the situation.*

1. a. Tony is very sure his parents won't notice the broken window.
   b. Tony thinks it's possible his parents won't notice the broken window.

2. a. Sara is giving Tony strong advice to tell their parents.
   b. Sara is giving Tony weak advice to tell their parents.

3. a. In the Mendoza family, telling the truth is a requirement.
   b. In the Mendoza family, telling the truth is a nice thing to do.

4. a. Tony is almost sure that his dad tells about the broken window.
   b. Tony thinks it is possible that Dad notices if he tells about the broken window.

5. a. Tony thinks it's possible that the ball hit the window.
   b. Tony is almost sure that the ball hit the window.

6. a. Tony thinks it is possible that someone else broke the window.
   b. Tony is almost sure that someone else broke the window.

7. a. Sara thinks it's possible that Tony broke the window.
   b. Sara is almost sure that Tony broke the window.

8. a. Sara thinks it was a bad idea for Tony to be playing ball in the front yard.
   b. Sara thinks it didn't matter that Tony was playing ball in the front yard.

9. a. In the Mendoza family, the children are required to play ball in the back yard.
   b. In the Mendoza family, the children are expected to play ball in the back yard.

10. a. Tony and Sam felt it was necessary to play ball in the front yard.
    b. Tony and Sam felt it would be fun to play ball in the front yard.

11. a. Sara thinks it's possible that Dad is in a good mood.
    b. Sara is almost sure that Dad is in a good mood.

12. a. Sara thinks that Dad will probably be satisfied if Tony tells him about the broken window.
    b. Sara thinks it's possible that Dad will be satisfied if Tony tells him about the broken window.

13. a. It is possible that Tony will tell Dad later.
    b. It is almost certain that Tony will tell Dad later.

9. Pair or Small Group Discussion

*In pairs or small groups, choose one item from exercise 3 and discuss whether you
agree, disagree, or are undecided. Explain your reasons to the members of the group.*

10. Role Play in Pairs

Working with a partner, choose one of the following situations and role-play it. When you have done the role play once, reverse the roles and play it again. Use appropriate modals or modal-like expressions in your role play.

Example:
A (parent): Billy, I think we **might have** a problem, and I wonder what we **should do** about it.
B (child): What's that, Dad (or Mom)?
A (parent): Well, your mother and I found these cigarettes in the garage, and neither of us smoke. Have you been smoking?

1. A parent and a fourteen-year-old child are discussing evidence that the child has been smoking.
2. A parent and teenaged child are discussing the child's possible failure in algebra at school.
3. A parent feels that his or her child has been unjustly accused of cheating on an exam. The parent and the instructor are discussing the issue.
4. A parent and teenaged child have had a shouting match. They are talking about it afterwards.
5. A teenager was grounded and can't attend the rock concert. The teenager and the parents are discussing the punishment.
6. One spouse feels the other spouse has been very uncommunicative lately. He or she is raising the issue with the uncommunicative spouse.
7. A parent has heard a rumor that there are drugs at school. He or she is discussing the situation with the school principal.
8. Lately one neighbor has been bothered a great deal by a neighbor's dogs, which bark at all hours of the day and night. The two neighbors are discussing the problem.
9. A former spouse has been cited by the court for nonpayment of child support. His or her spouse has telephoned to discuss the nonpayment.

11. Essay

Write a short essay (three or four paragraphs) about a less-than-satisfactory relationship you have had—with a parent, friend, boyfriend, girlfriend, spouse, or any other kind of partner. Briefly describe the situation and how it was unsatisfactory. Speculate on why you and the other person acted as you did. Give yourself some advice as to how you might avoid such a relationship in the future.

12. Picture Discussion

Look at the picture. In small groups speculate about who Christina is. Could she be the woman in the picture? Or could Christina be someone else? Why is this woman in the field? What might she be doing?

Andrew Wyeth: *Christina's World*. (1948)
Tempera on gessoed panel, 32 ¼ x 47 ¾".
The Museum of Modern Art, New York.
Purchase.
Photograph © 1995
The Museum of Modern Art, New York.

INTRODUCTION

Read and listen to a segment of a radio call-in show with psychologist Mariana Maguire.

Questions to Consider

1. What is your definition of *conscience?*
2. Where do notions of right and wrong come from?

Maguire: Good evening. I'm psychologist Mariana Maguire with tonight's edition of "How Can I Help You?" The toll-free number is 1-800-555-9999. Sally from Toronto, you're on the air.

Sally: Hi, Mariana. First let me tell you how much I enjoy your show. I don't like most of the stuff on radio, but I **do** listen to you.

Maguire: Thanks, Sally. What's on your mind tonight?

Sally: Well, I've been dating a man named Bob for a long time. We're engaged to be married, but I just don't feel I can go through with it.

Maguire: Why? Don't you love him?

Sally: I **did** love him at first—or at least I thought I did—and I **do** think a lot of him as a person. But the wedding is in three weeks. I've been thinking of just running away and never coming back.

Maguire: Why haven't you done something before this?

Sally: I **did** try to tell him a couple of weeks ago, but he just dismissed it as typical prewedding jitters.

Maguire: Well, Sally, I guess my main question is whether you're sure of your feelings.

Sally: No. . . I **am** sure. I'm just worried about hurting him.

Maguire: You don't have to hurt Bob, but you **do** have to level with him and tell him the truth. Honesty is always the best policy. I wish you good luck. Hello, Jerry from Tulsa.

Jerry: Evening, Mariana. Thank you for taking my call. I wanted to ask you about a problem with my children.

Maguire: OK, go ahead. What's the problem?

Jerry: They only call me when they want something, and all they really seem to care about is getting their inheritance. I'm not a rich man, but I **am** pretty well off, and I **have** got some money put away for them. The trouble is that they never come to see me. We **do** live in different parts of the country, so I guess that part is understandable. They've both written me recently, asking if they could have their inheritance early. My son wants to buy a house. He doesn't have the cash for a down payment, but he **does** earn enough to make the monthly payments. And my daughter and her husband want to buy a boat.

Maguire: How old are they?

Jerry: They're both in their late twenties.

Maguire: OK. What's your question, then?

Jerry: I agreed to send the money. Can I withdraw my offer? I mean, would it be ethical? Or fair?

Maguire: Well, your children **do** sound pretty selfish. If you feel it'd be wrong to give them this money now, I'd suggest you just tell them you've changed your mind. That **may** start them thinking a bit and might even make them a little more concerned about you in the long run. Good luck. Now, caller number 3, Helen from Kingston, New York, talk to me. . . .

CONTRAST AND EMPHASIS (AUXILIARIES)

WITH *BE*

I'm not a tax expert.	I **am** an accountant, though.

WITH *BE* AND OTHER VERBS AS AUXILIARIES

Zeya doesn't eat meat.	She **does** eat fish.
You don't know how to use a computer?	Who **does** know how to use a computer?
I can't recommend Mr. Isaacs for the top position in the company.	I **can**, however, recommend him for a management position.
I know where Chichicastenango is.	I **have** been to Guatemala, you know

Grammar Notes

1. When speakers want to place special emphasis on a verb (or any other word), they pronounce it with stress. Speakers stress words for insistence or for contrast with a prior statement.

   You can ask me about the multiplication tables. I **HAVE** been to fourth grade, you know. (Stressing **have** indicates insistence.)
   I'm not a miracle worker. I **AM** a doctor, though, and I'll try my best to save her. (Stressing **am** expresses contrast with prior statement.)

   Note, however, that if the verb is not *be* and it is in the simple present or simple past tense, the auxiliary *do, does,* or *did* can appear before the verb to express emphasis or contrast.

   I don't love Scott. I **DO** like him a lot, though.

   A: You didn't do your homework.
   B: I **DID** do my homework! I turned it in yesterday.

   You didn't bake the cookies? Who **DID** bake them, then?

   A: I think I recognize that man.
   B: Yes, you **DO** recognize him. He's your long-lost brother.

2. If a writer makes a contrast with a preceding statement, the reader can pronounce with stress the verb, auxiliary verb, or modal in the contrasting statement.

   While what she did wasn't illegal, it **WAS** unethical.
   Anne doesn't speak Spanish, but she **DOES** speak German.

3. Be careful! We do not contract the subject and verb in statements of contrast or emphasis.

   I haven't spoken to the doctor, but I **HAVE** spoken to the nurse, NOT ~~I haven't spoken to the doctor, but **I've** spoken to the nurse.~~

FOCUSED PRACTICE

1. Discover the Grammar

▣▣ *Brent Washburn is having a conversation with his thirteen-year-old son, Jeremy, about Jeremy's behavior. Listen to their conversation on the tape. Then listen again. Circle the ten verbs that show emphasis and/or make a contrast with a preceding statement.*

Brent: Jeremy, come on into the living room. There are some things we need to talk about.

Jeremy: Dad, if it's about the broken window in the bathroom, I can explain. I *did* break it, but I didn't mean to. It was an accident, really.

Brent: It wasn't the window I wanted to talk about, though I am a little bit angry about that.

Jeremy: It's not the window? What do you want to talk about, then?

Brent: Well, for one thing, I got a letter in the mail from your teacher. She says that you haven't been studying and that you might fail. You do want to pass the seventh grade, don't you?

Jeremy: Of course. And I have been studying, Dad. I just keep forgetting to turn in my homework.

Brent: She also says that you don't pay attention in class and that you're always staring out the window.

Jeremy: Aw, she's just got it in for me. I do pay attention, Dad. Just because I'm not looking at her doesn't mean I'm not paying attention. Mrs. Hammond just doesn't like me. She's a boring teacher, too.

Brent: Jeremy, I've known Mrs. Hammond for a long time. Her classes may not be all fun and games, but she does know how to teach. From now on, I want you to study every evening from seven till nine, and I'm going to call Mrs. Hammond every week to see if you're turning in your homework. And I will call every week. Don't think I won't.

Jeremy: Do I still get to watch TV or play video games?

Brent: Not till your grades improve. You're to study for two hours every evening. You can't have any friends over in the evening, either. You can read a library book if you've got your homework done. OK. Now let's talk about the window. What happened?

Jeremy: Well, you know how the lock on the bathroom door hasn't been working? I couldn't get the door open, so I had to go out the window, and it's so small that it broke while I was squeezing out of it.

Brent: Jeremy, tell me the truth. What really happened?

Jeremy: That is the truth, Dad. I swear it.

Brent: All right. You know how I feel about telling the truth. I hope I don't find out later that this was just a story.

Jeremy: You won't, Dad. I promise.

2. A Letter Home

Priscilla Hammond, Jeremy Washburn's seventh-grade teacher, has written a second letter to Brent and Anne, Jeremy's parents. It has been a month since the Washburns received the first letter, and Mrs. Hammond is reporting on Jeremy's progress. In the blanks in the letter, write the correct forms of the verbs provided, using emphatic forms.

February 22

Dear Mr. and Mrs. Washburn,

I'm writing to give you a progress report on Jeremy. In general I'd say he's not out of trouble yet, though he ___is___ doing better than before. He still has a tendency to daydream a little too much, but he ___does seem___ to be paying better attention in class. His weakest subject is math, which he's still not passing. He ___did score___ high in math on the national achievement tests a month ago, however. He ___did not have___ a chance to pass that subject. He's also not passing science, but he ___is___ doing very well in English, history, and art.

The main problem I'm having with Jeremy is getting him to turn in his work. He ___did submit___ three assignments last week, but he's still missing four others. There are just so many distractions for children these days. I ___do appreciate___ your efforts to monitor his study time in the evenings. You're definitely doing the right thing, even though it may not make you very popular with Jeremy for a while. I only wish other parents were as concerned as you are.

Jeremy could still fail the seventh grade, but he ___does have___ a chance to make it, so please keep up the supervised work at home.

Sincerely,

Priscilla Hammond

Priscilla Hammond

3. Did They Do the Right Thing?

Examine the following statements about famous world figures. Fill in the blanks in the statements with regular or emphatic forms of the verbs provided, placing emphatic forms in the parts of sentences that make a contrast.

On August 9, 1974, Richard M. Nixon _____resigned_____ the presidency of the United States, disgraced by
1. (resign)

his involvement in the Watergate scandal. Many _____predicted_____ he would always be hated, but he
2. (predict)

persevered and _____did manage_____ to rehabilitate himself politically by the time of his death in 1994.
3. (manage)

On September 8, 1974, President Gerald R. Ford _____pardoned_____ Richard M. Nixon for any federal
4. (pardon)

crimes he might have committed while he was president. This action probably _____cost_____ Ford
5. (cost)

the 1976 presidential election, but it _____did help_____ the United States to recover from Watergate.
6. (help)

On March 26, 1979, Egyptian president Anwar el-Sadat _____signed_____ the Camp David Accords with
7. (sign)

Prime Minister Menachem Begin of Israel. This action probably _____caused_____ Sadat's assassination
8. (cause)

in 1981, but it _____did promote_____ peace between Egypt and Israel.
9. (promote)

On February 11, 1990, South African president F. W. de Klerk _____freed_____ black nationalist leader
10. (free)

Nelson Mandela from imprisonment, initiating the process of dismantling apartheid and creating a multiracial

society. While South Africa's road ahead may be fraught with peril, the country _____did have_____ a
11. (have)

good chance to become a racially harmonious society.

In the late 1800s, Elizabeth Cady Stanton and Susan B. Anthony _____founded_____ the National Woman
12. (found)

Suffrage Association. Their actions _____led_____ to the eventual granting of the vote to women in
13. (lead)

the United States and _____influenced_____ the achievement of women's rights elsewhere in the world.
14. (influence)

While women today may not yet enjoy complete equality with men, they _____do have_____ vastly
15. (have)

increased political power.

Susan B. Anthony

COMMUNICATION PRACTICE

4. Practice Listening

A police chief is interrogating a man who has been arrested. This man is insisting on his innocence. Listen to their conversation on the tape. Auxiliaries, pronoun subjects, and some main verbs have been deleted from the text in your book. Listen again and fill in the blanks in their conversation. Pay close attention to emphatic and nonemphatic auxiliaries. Distinguish carefully between contractions and full forms.

Police Chief: All right, Mr. Grinker, where _____were you_____ on the morning of June 14 at
1.
5:30 A.M., and what ___Were you___ doing? ___You weren't___ at home;
2.   3.
___That's___ for sure.
4.

Man: ___I was___ at home, sleeping. Some people ___do sleep___, you
5.   6.
know. And what makes you think ___I wasn't___ at home? Why
7.
___haven't you___ checked this out?
8.

Police Chief: ___We have___ checked it out. We called your landlady, and she said
9.
___you ___ told her ___you were going to be___ gone from your apartment
10.   11.
from the twelfth to the fourteenth of June on a business trip to Portland.
___I'd___ advise you to tell the truth, Mr. Grinker.
12.

Man: ___I am___ telling the truth. ___I did go___ to Portland, but I got
13.   14.
back late on the night of the thirteenth. I went right to sleep because I had to be at work by
eight the next morning.

Police Chief: Your car ___was seen___ seen in the East Valley. We have reason to believe
15.
___It was___ the getaway car used in the robbery of the Circle Q in
16.
Auburn at 5:15.

Man: ___That is___ nonsense. ___I don't___ live anywhere near Auburn.
17.   18.
Why ___do you___ think I had anything to do with this?
19.

Police Chief: Well, ___you do have___ a police record, and ___you did do___ some time in
20.   21.
jail. ___I wouldn't___ exactly describe you as a law-abiding citizen.
22.

Man: ___I am___ a law-abiding citizen. ___that was___ ten years ago.
23.   24.
___I was___ just a teenager. ___I did___ commit a crime, but I
25.   26.
served my time, and I learned my lesson.

(continued on next page)

Police Chief: You have a blue 1992 Ford Escort, _____don't you_____? A bystander witnessed the
27.
robbery and saw your car. She called the police.

Man: _____I do have_____ a blue Ford, but it's a Taurus, not an Escort, and
28.
_____It's a_____ a 1991, not a 1992. Those models _____do look_____ alike,
29.   30.
you know. But _____I still don't_____ understand why you think _____It was_____
31.   32.
my car. Without a license number, how . . .

Police Chief: _____She did get_____ a license number, Mr. Grinker—DCN494.
33.

Man: _____That is_____ my license number, but _____It is_____ easy to make a
34.   35.
mistake. _____She could have_____ confused one of the numbers. And a D
36.
_____does look_____ an awful lot like a B, you know, especially when
37.
_____It's not_____ completely light yet.
38.

Police Chief: You say that you have a blue '91 Taurus and not a '92 Escort?

Man: _____That's_____ right.
39.

Police Chief: All right, Mr. Grinker. _____I am not_____ completely convinced
40.
_____You are giving_____ me a straight story, but _____I am going to give_____ you the benefit of
41.   42.
the doubt. _____Can you_____ prove _____you were_____ at work at 8 A.M. on the
43.   44.
morning of the fourteenth?

Man: Sure _____I can_____.
45.

Police Chief: OK, Mr. Grinker. _____You can go_____ on home. _____We will be_____ in touch.
46.   47.
_____It may take_____ a while, but _____we will get_____ to the bottom of this.
48.   49.

Tape Discussion

*How difficult is a police officer's job? What should a person do if he or she is
unjustly accused of a crime?*

6. Role Play in Pairs

Work with a partner. Choose one of the following situations and role-play it. Then switch the roles and play it again.

1. A parent and son or daughter are having a discussion. The son or daughter got home two hours after curfew.

   Example:
   Parent: Jim, it was two o'clock when you got home last night.
   Son: Sorry, Mom (or Dad). I had a flat tire on the way back from the concert. It took a long time to get it fixed. I didn't have a spare tire with me.
   Parent: Why didn't you call? We were ready to call the police.
   Son: I **did** call. I called about 12:30, but there was no answer.

2. A parent believes his or her child took some money from the parent's pocket or purse. They are talking about it.

3. A boss has written a job evaluation which an employee doesn't agree with. They are discussing the evaluation.

4. Two friends are discussing capital punishment. They are on opposite sides of the issue.

5. One friend wants to borrow some money from another friend who is reluctant to lend it because the last time the friend borrowed he or she didn't pay the money back.

6. A neighbor accuses another neighbor's child of committing some vandalism on his or her property. The parent of the child is convinced that the child did not commit the vandalism.

7. Group Discussion

Listen to Helen Giuliani talk about herself. When you have finished, talk in groups about Helen's strengths and weaknesses. What kind of person is she? Do you think she is overly critical of herself?

8. Writing

*Choose one of the topics in the role play in exercise 6 and write a conversation about it. Use **do, does,** and **did** in affirmative sentences and noncontracted forms where they are appropriate.*

9. Picture Discussion

With a partner, talk about the picture. Then create a conversation between the young man and the woman from Matchmakers, Inc.

Example:
> **A:** Tell me a little bit about the woman of your dreams.
> **B:** Well, she doesn't have to have much formal education, but she **does** have to have a lot of interests.

I. *Complete the following conversation with correct forms of* **be going to** **(was/were going to** *or* **is/are going to)** *and* **would** *or* **will.** *Use* **will** *or* **would** *if* **be going to** *is not specified.*

Elena: I wonder where Isao and Mark are. Isao said _____they'd be_____ here by 12:30. It's already 12:45.
1. (they / be)

Jihan: Well, when I talked to Mark this morning, he told me he _____ stop at the post office to mail a
2. (be going to)
package. That's the only thing I can think of.

Elena: These men! They can never be anywhere on time. We _____ the train if they don't come soon.
3. (be going to miss)

Jihan: What about lunch? Did Isao say _____ bring
4. (he / be going to)
sandwiches?

Elena: No, he says _____ at a restaurant near the
5. (we / eat)
museum. . . . Oh, there they come. . . . At last. Where have you
guys been? _____ a new leaf and not be late
6. (you / be going to / turn over)
anymore? That's what you said.

Mark: Well, we promised that _____ not to get
7. (we / try)
places late! We're working on it. Oh, by the way, Luis is coming
after all. He says _____ a later train and meet
8. (he / take)
us at three o'clock. OK, ladies, time's a-wasting. Let's get on the
train!

II. *Complete the conversations with* **used to** *or* **would.** *Use* **would** *if possible.*

1. **A:** _____Didn't you use to smoke_____?
a. (not / you / smoke)

   B: Yeah, I _____, but I quit six months ago.
b.

   A: Good. I _____ smoke, too. It was terrible. When I was a serious
c.
smoker, I _____ smoke two packs a day. I'm glad I stopped.
d.

2. **A:** When I was child, my family spent every summer at a lake in the mountains. The kids
_____ a hike every morning. In the afternoon, we
e. (take)
_____ swimming.
f. (go)

   B: Yeah, our summers were like that, too. My parents _____ a
g. (own)
cabin on the beach. They sold it after we grew up, but when I was ten and eleven, we
_____ every July there. Ah, those were the good old days! Life
h. (spend)
_____ carefree. Now it's just hectic.
i. (be)

42

III. *Complete the letter to a columnist and the columnist's response, choosing between the modals and modal-like expressions given.*

Dear Pamela:

Three years ago I married Jean, a wonderful woman. My relationship with Jean is great, but I

_____can't get along_____ with her three children. Jack is twenty-three and Dave nineteen.
1. (needn't get along / can't get along)

We're living in Jean's house, and they _____ a year and a half ago, but they
2. (must have moved out / were supposed to move out)

haven't, and at the rate things are going, they _____ on their own until the
3. (may not get out / must not get out)

year 2010.

I told Jack he _____ applying for a job at a grocery store nearby because
4. (was to consider / might consider)

I know the manager and could put in a good word for him, but he told me I

_____ to help him—he'll get his own job when he's good and ready.
5. (should try / needn't try)

Dave is in trouble with the government because he _____ with the
6. (was to register / must have registered)

selective service by his nineteenth birthday and didn't. I asked Jean about this and she was unconcerned.

She said, "Oh, he _____; he'll take care of it."
7. (must have forgotten / should have forgotten)

Amy, Jean's seventeen-year-old daughter, is the hardest of the three children to relate to. She sulks most

of the time and refuses to help with chores. If I say anything to her, she tells me

_____ and mind my own business.
8. (I'd better shut up / I may shut up)

Pamela, I'm at the end of my rope, and I don't know what to do. _____
9. (Shall I have it out / Am I to have it out)

with the children and let the chips fall where they may?

Desperate in Denver

Dear Desperate:

Being a stepparent _____ one of the most difficult jobs around; I don't
10. (should be / must be)

envy your position. No, I don't think you _____ with the children. Instead,
11. (may have it out / should have it out)

sit down with Jean and have a private conversation.

The fact that you're still living in Jean's house _____ the cause of the
12. (may be / should be)

problem; after all, it's the children's territory. I think you _____ to Jean that
13. (ought to suggest / are to suggest)

you two find a house of your own as soon as possible. That way, you _____
14. (can get / might get)

a fresh start. Make it clear to the children that, while they are welcome there, the house belongs to you

and Jean. They _____ the message. Also tell Jean that the children's
15. (should get / are supposed to get)

obnoxious treatment of you is unacceptable and that they _____ to be civil.
16. (are supposed to learn / had better learn)

I wish you good luck.

Pamela

IV. *Complete the conversations with sentences containing the indicated modals and modal-like expressions. Be sure to include necessary pronoun subjects or objects.*

1. **A:** Mr. Figueroa, Jason isn't doing very well in math. __Might something be bothering him__ ?

a. (might / something / bothering)

   B: Well, I don't know. _____ rejected. On the phone the other night

b. (could / feeling)
   I heard him asking his friend Amy to go to the prom with him.

   _____. That would depress me if I were seventeen.

c. (may / have / turn down)

   A: I understand. He hasn't been doing his assignments, though. He

   _____ any more assignments or classes. If he does,

d. (not / must / miss)

   _____.

e. (not / may / pass)

   B: He _____ the course, will he?

f. (not / will / have to / repeat)

   A: _____ if he doesn't start turning in his work.

g. (might / have to)

2. **A:** Why do you think Todd left so suddenly? _____?

h. (could / have / be / angry)

   B: No, I don't think so. _____. He's had the flu lately.

i. (may / have / feeling / sick)

   A: Well, _____ that sick. I saw him jogging this morning.

j. (not / can / have / feeling)

   B: Then _____ to an appointment. I don't think anything's wrong.

k. (must / have / have to / go)

V. *Complete the following conversations between a job interviewer and various applicants. Use contracted verbs for nonemphatic statements and full forms for emphatic (contrasting) statements.*

1. **A:** What languages do you know, Ms. Suzuki? Do you speak Mandarin?

   B: No, I __don't speak__ Mandarin. I __do speak__ Japanese and Spanish,

a. (not / speak)   b. (speak)
   though.

   A: Are you fluent in those languages?

   B: I _____ fluent in Japanese. I _____ fluent in Spanish, but I

c. (be)   d. (not / be)
   _____ conversant in it.

e. (be)

2. **A:** Mr. Quinn, your resume says that you attended college. Did you earn a bachelor's degree?

   B: No, I _____ my B.A. I _____ an associate degree, though.

f. (not / earn)   g. (earn)

3. **A:** Ms. Liu, this job requires overseas experience. Have you lived abroad?

   B: I _____ abroad, but I _____ extensively in Europe and

h. (not / live)   i. (travel)
   the Far East.

4. **A:** Mr. Travolta, this _____ a full-time position. It _____ a three-
   j. (not / be)   k. (be)

   quarter-time job, though, and it _____ an excellent benefits package. Are you
                                    l. (offer)

   interested?

   B: The job sounds interesting. I _____ some time to think it over, however. Could I
                                      m. (would like)

   let you know in a few days?

VI. *Each of the following sentences contains four underlined words or phrases, marked A, B, C, or D. Circle the letter of the one word or phrase that is not correct.*

1. Just before the telephone <u>rang</u>, I <u>was hoping</u> someone   **A**   **B**   Ⓒ   **D**
                        A   B

   <u>called</u> <u>to suggest</u> going somewhere.
     C   D

2. Luis <u>doesn't go</u> with us to Toledo today; <u>he's</u> <u>staying</u> home   **A**   **B**   **C**   **D**
          A   B   C

   because he <u>has to</u> finish a term paper.
             D

3. By the time <u>you'll get</u> to Alexandria, <u>I'll</u> <u>have acquired</u> a fantastic tan.   **A**   **B**   **C**   **D**
              A   B   C   D

4. After I <u>got up</u> this morning, I <u>went</u> out, <u>was doing</u> the shopping,   **A**   **B**   **C**   **D**
            A   B   C

   and <u>cleaned up</u> the apartment.
        D

5. I <u>didn't even think</u> there <u>would be</u> a party. Isao and Elena <u>have done</u>   **A**   **B**   **C**   **D**
        A   B   C

   a great job of <u>organizing</u> last night's get-together.
              D

6. <u>We're having</u> a party this afternoon, and <u>we're hoping</u> you   **A**   **B**   **C**   **D**
      A   B

   <u>were able</u> <u>to come</u>.
      C   D

7. The plane <u>has</u> just <u>taken off</u> when I <u>realized</u> that   **A**   **B**   **C**   **D**
             A   B   C

   I <u>had given</u> my parents the wrong arrival date.
      D

8. Mark <u>was</u> surprised when he <u>received</u> an A on the exam   **A**   **B**   **C**   **D**
        A   B

   because he <u>thought</u> he <u>will fail</u> it.
             C   D

9. When the professor <u>asked</u> me where my homework <u>was</u>,   **A**   **B**   **C**   **D**
                  A   B

   I <u>told</u> him <u>I already turned</u> it in.
      C   D

10. We <u>haven't</u> <u>been visiting</u> Toledo for more than a year,   **A**   **B**   **C**   **D**
          A   B

    so I <u>think</u> we <u>ought to go</u> there.
         C   D

From Grammar to Writing

The Sentence

In English a sentence must have at least one <u>independent</u>, or <u>main</u>, clause. A main clause must have a subject and its verb—a verb that shows person, number, and time. Only one type of main clause has no subject: an imperative sentence. In imperative sentences, the subject *you*, is understood. (Note that *Let's dance* is a kind of imperative sentence. *You* is understood.)

A main clause does not depend on another clause to be fully understood.

Other clauses are said to be <u>dependent</u>. Dependent clauses have a subject and a verb, but they are dependent on another clause to be fully understood.

Look at the following sentences. The complete subjects are underlined once and the complete verbs twice.

<u>Mark and his friends</u> <u>are</u> students.

<u>They</u> <u>are spending</u> a year in Spain.

<u>All students in the program</u> <u>will have arrived</u> by September.

<u>Most of them</u> <u>will stay</u> for a year.

<u>Emily</u> <u>has received</u> three letters from Mark.

<u>The letters</u> <u>were written</u> over the course of the year.

<u>Call</u> me.

<u>Are</u> <u>dogs</u> good pets?

The following word groups are not sentences:

Mark sitting and writing a letter. (no verb)
Were taking the train to Barcelona. (no subject)
Such an exciting year. (no verb)
Because he was afraid of heights. (dependent clause)
Which was a beautiful building. (dependent clause)

A. *In the line below each of the following word groups, write **sentence** if the group is an independent clause. If the word group is not a sentence, write **not a sentence** and explain why by writing "no subject," "no verb," or "dependent clause."*

1. Isao at the studio doing his TV program.

   _____ not a sentence: no verb _____

2. All afternoon.

   _____

3. Mark and Luis were at home.

   _____

4. Has been an exciting year.

_____

5. A worthwhile experience meeting students from many nations.

_____

6. They would do it again.

_____

7. Which they had always wanted to do.

_____

8. Think about this question.

_____

B. *Read the following paragraph. You will find eight sentences and nine groups of words that are not sentences. On the lines provided, write the eight sentences.*

In late December, on their way to the French Riviera. Mark, Luis, and Isao took a one-day trip to Barcelona. Not knowing anyone there. They stayed in a youth hostel for a very reasonable price. On their one day in the city. They visited the Sagrada Familia, Gaudí's famous cathedral. Which was unfinished when Gaudí died and is still unfinished. All three boys were impressed by the cathedral's beauty. And decided to climb it to the top instead of taking the elevator. Nearing the top, Isao began to feel vertigo and had to start down again. Mark and Luis continued climbing. Even Mark, who had done a great deal of mountain climbing in the United States. Felt nervous and unprotected at the summit. Both he and Luis agreed that the view was magnificent. And the climb worth it. The three decided to return to Barcelona. As soon as they could.

1. _____Mark, Luis, and Isao took a one-day trip to Barcelona._____

2. _____

3. _____

4. _____

5. _____

6. _____

7. _____

8. _____

2.

The first word of a sentence begins with a capital letter. A sentence ends with some punctuation, most commonly a period, a question mark, or an exclamation point. Sometimes a sentence ends with a semicolon or a colon. When one sentence ends with a semicolon or colon, the first word of the next sentence does not need to be capitalized.

> **W**ho knows the answer**?**
> French food is very delicious**;** **i**t is known all over the world.

C. *Read and study the following paragraph. It contains ten sentences. Find the ten sentences and insert initial capitalization and end punctuation in the appropriate places. Do not add or eliminate any commas.*

A
a year ago Bruce and Alice Corwyn were on the verge of divorce. If they hadn't decided to give counseling a try, they might not have stayed together fortunately, however, they did participate in counseling the process was difficult for both Bruce and Alice at first because each of them had to change the challenge for Alice was to realize that she was married to Bruce and not to her mother for Bruce the difficulty was in learning to express his feelings outwardly, something that he had never really done though there were times when both wanted to throw up their hands in despair, both realized that they would have to stick at the task of rebuilding their marriage if it was going to have any chance of succeeding often feeling that they were progressing at a snail's pace, they somehow managed to renew their commitment to each other in the process they came to understand that no relationship is perfect and that one should never take a relationship for granted in the past year Bruce and Alice have rediscovered their love for each other, and their prospects look bright

The Noun Phrase: Selected Topics

INTRODUCTION

Read and listen to an article by noted futurist Betty Heiser that appeared in a recent issue of Techtime magazine.

Questions to Consider

1. What is your definition of progress?
2. Are you in favor of progress?

Where Are We Going?

Betty Heiser

In the near future, there will be advances in almost every area. Consider **transportation. Pollution** from the **combustion** of **gasoline** will have become so bad all over the world that future cars will run on **electricity.** Long-distance **transportation** will be handled by new high-speed maglev, or magnetic **levitation,** trains. These trains will "levitate," or float, over fixed tracks called guideways. Since they will not touch the guideways, there will be no **friction** or **vibration** to restrict their **speed.** The force of **magnetism** will be used in powering them.

Another area in which we'll see great changes is **genetics.** So much **progress** has been made in genetic **research** that scientists will soon master the **isolation** and **elimination** of certain "negative" genes which cause such phenomena

as **susceptibility** to debilitating diseases, mental **retardation,** mental illnesses such as **schizophrenia,** and physical **deformity.** And simple genetic tests will show whether a person is susceptible to diseases such as **cancer** or **arthritis.**

We will also make great **progress** in **agriculture**

and food **development.** Genetic **engineering** will provide new varieties of drought- and pest-resistant **wheat, corn,** and soybeans, allowing much greater quantities of these crops to be raised, especially in dry **terrain.** Great strides will be made in food **synthesis;** we'll be able to make **food** that tastes exactly like **steak** or **pasta** out of materials such as soybeans and other food bases that will be developed.

Probably the greatest advance of all, however, will take place in the **dissemination** of **information.** We live today in what is called the **Information** Age, and the **centrality** and **availability** of **information** will accelerate. We will have offices without **paper.** Through **membership** in computer networks, most citizens will have **access** to much of the world's **knowledge** through their own home computers. Newspapers will no longer be delivered; instead, people will call up the daily **news** on their TV screens and even study **history, astronomy, biology**—you name it —in the **convenience** of their own homes.

What this all means is that we'll have developed the *how.* What we need to think about is the *why* and the *if.* For this reason, there will come a corresponding interest in **metaphysics** and **mysticism;** there seems to be a natural human tendency to want some things to remain unex-

plained. Do we really want to know everything and be able to control everything? How many of these advances are desirable or even necessary? Will we be able to use them ethically? Will they lead us to greater **happiness?** Only **time** will tell.

NON-COUNT NOUNS

NON-COUNT NOUNS IN "COUNTABLE" FORM

Non-Count Noun	"Countable" Form
I'll have **tea.**	I'll have **a cup of tea.**
You need **advice.**	Let me give you **a piece of advice.**
We saw **lightning.**	We saw **two flashes of lightning.**
We heard **thunder.**	We heard **a clap of thunder.**
Let's play **tennis.**	Let's play **a game of tennis.**

USE OF NON-COUNT NOUNS

Non-Count Nouns in "Mass Use"	Non-Count Nouns In "Count Use"
Work is fundamental.	*Future Shock* is **a literary work.**
I want some **coffee.**	Bring us **two coffees.**
Wine is produced in France.	Chablis is **a white wine.**
This food needs some **spice.**	Turmeric and cardamom are **two spices** that originated in India.
The sun provides **light.**	She saw **two lights** shining in the sky.

Grammar Notes

1. Nouns are names of persons, places, and things. There are two main types of nouns: proper nouns and common nouns. Proper nouns are names of particular persons, places, or things: Leonardo da Vinci, Caracas, The Golden Gate Bridge. They are usually unique. Common nouns refer to people, places, or things, but they are not the names of particular individuals. *Book, courage, heart, rhinoceros, vegetable, and water* are examples of common nouns.

2. There are two types of common nouns: <u>count nouns</u> and <u>non-count nouns</u>. Count nouns name things that can be counted: one woman, nine planets. Non-count nouns (or mass nouns) generally name things that cannot be counted because they exist in a "mass" form. Non-count nouns in their normal meaning are not preceded by *a* or *an*, though they are often preceded by *some* or *the*.

> I bought **rice.** NOT I~~ bought a rice.~~
> Let me give you **some advice.** NOT ~~Let me give you an advice.~~
> **Silver** is mined there. NOT ~~Silvers are mined there.~~

A non-count noun is followed by a singular verb.

> **Information is** essential.
> **Rice feeds** millions.
> **Physics seems** complicated.

3. Notice the following categories of non-count nouns and examples of them:

Abstractions	advice, behavior, chance (luck), energy, evil, fun, good, happiness, honesty, love, responsibility, spontaneity
Activities	bowling, dancing, football, hiking, soccer, tennis
Ailments	AIDS, cancer, malaria, measles
Elements	gold, magnesium, plutonium, silver, titanium, uranium
Foods	barley, beef, broccoli, candy, chicken, meat, rice, wheat
Gases	air, carbon dioxide, oxygen, smoke
Liquids	coffee, gasoline, soda, water, wine
Natural phenomena	aurora borealis, cold, electricity, ice, light, lightning, rain, snow, thunder
Occupations	construction, engineering, nursing, teaching
Particles	dust, pepper, salt, sand, sugar
Subjects	astronomy, business, English, history, Japanese, physics, science, Spanish
Categories	clothing, equipment, fruit, furniture

See Appendix 6 on page A13 for a more complete list of non-count nouns.

4. We frequently make non-count nouns "countable" by adding a phrase which gives them a form, a limit, or a container.

Non-Count Noun	**"Countable State"**
furniture	an article (piece) of furniture
lightning	a flash (bolt) of lightning
meat	a piece of meat
rice	five grains of rice
sand	a grain of sand
tennis	a game of tennis
thunder`	a clap of thunder
water`	a cup of water

See Appendix 7 on page A14 for a more complete list of phrases for counting non-count nouns.

5. Some non-count nouns can be used in a countable sense. When they are, they can be preceded by *a/an* and can occur in the plural. Compare the following non-count nouns in mass use and count use.

Mass Use	Count Use
I ate **meat** for dinner.	There are several **meats** available at most supermarkets. (different types of meat)
We need to take **water** along on the camping trip.	There are carbonated and uncarbonated mineral **waters.**
TV is both good and bad.	Yesterday we bought **a TV.** (informal for "television set")
Too much **salt** in the diet can be unhealthful.	The mixture contains a dissolved **salt.** (a type of chemical compound)
I drink **coffee** every morning.	Please bring us **three coffees.** (cups of coffee)
France produces **wine.**	Cabernet Sauvignon is **a wine** produced in France.
Hard **work** is rewarding.	The *Moonlight Sonata* is **a** musical **work** by Beethoven.
Light is essential for the growth of crops.	We installed **a light** over our front door.
Many events seem governed by **chance.**	I had **a chance** to talk with Sarah. (an opportunity)
I have no **money.**	The state will use tax **monies (moneys)** to fund the project. (amounts of money from different tax sources)
Matter cannot be destroyed.	It's only **a matter** of time before we run out of resources.

6. Be careful! When non-count nouns occur alone or are preceded by *some*, they denote things that don't have any particular boundaries.

> I drank **some soda.** (no particular amount)
> **Work** can be exhausting. (work in general)

When non-count nouns are preceded by *a* or *an*, they acquire a boundary and are limited in some sense. A discrete amount or limit is suggested.

> I drank **a soda.** (a discrete amount—probably a can or a glass)
> *Don Quixote* is **a literary work.** (a single literary work, contained in a book)

7. Study the following non-count nouns ending in -*s* and irregular plural count nouns that occur with great frequency in science.

mathematics, economics, physics	(non-count nouns ending in -*s*)
criterion, phenomenon, nucleus	(singular count nouns)
criteria, phenomena, nuclei	(irregular plural forms)

(continued on next page)

Usage note: *Data* originally was a plural of *datum,* meaning "a fact" or "a piece of information." Today many native speakers use *data* as a non-count noun.

> These **data are** important. (original use of **data** as plural)
> This **data is** important. (common current nonacademic or informal usage)

See Appendix 5 on pages A11 and A12 for a list of irregular plurals.

8. Be careful! In its normal usage, the word *people* is a plural, denoting more than one person. In this meaning, it does not have a singular form.

> **People are** funny and unpredictable.   (people in general—no specific group)

The word *people,* meaning a particular group of humans or particular groups of humans, can have a singular and a plural form.

> The Navajos are **a** native American **people.**
> The different **peoples** of the region live together in harmony.

FOCUSED PRACTICE

1. Discover the Grammar

Listen to the text of the television newscast on the tape. Then listen again as you look at the script. You will find fourteen non-count nouns and thirty count nouns. In the columns at the end of the exercise, classify the non-count and count nouns as they are used in the newscast. Do not include proper nouns.

Good evening. Here are the latest headlines.

☐ A major earthquake has hit near St. Louis. The quake registered 6.6 on the Richter scale, but damage is minor because of the location of the quake.

☐ Scientists at an observatory in Greenland have detected certain unexplained new atmospheric phenomena over the skies of the Arctic Circle. One researcher jokingly described them as resembling "a cross between a UFO and the aurora borealis."

☐ Officials at the United Nations reported in New York today that a final accord has been reached on nuclear nonproliferation, to be signed by all world nations.

☐ Geneticists report new progress in mapping the structure of cellular DNA. This could lead to the capability to boost the intelligence of unborn children.

☐ The new 500-inch reflecting telescope built in the Australian desert goes on-line tomorrow. Astronomers predict that it will vastly expand the frontiers of astronomy, increasing the amount of receivable visual data tenfold.

☐ Physicists at the Jet Propulsion Lab in Pasadena, California, announced the discovery of a new chemical element, to be called pasadenium.

☐ Meanwhile, engineers have found oil in Antarctica, raising the usual issues of environmental protection.

☐ That's news to the hour. Stay tuned for further developments.

Non-Count Nouns

1. aurora borealis
2. nonproliferation
3. progress
4. structure
5. DNA
6. capability
7. intelligence

8. astronomy
9. data
10. pasadenium
11. oil
12. protection
13. news
14.

Count Nouns

1. earthquake
2. quake
3. scale
4. location
5. quake
6. scientists
7. observatory
8. phenomena
9. skies
10. researcher
11. cross
12. UFO
13. officials
14. accord
15. nations
16. geneticists
17. children
18. telescope
19. desert

20. astronomers
21. frontiers
22. amount
23. physicists
24. discovery
25. element
26. engineers
27. issues
28. hour
29. developments
30.
31.
32.
33.
34.
35.
36.
37.
38.

2. Ready for the Future?

Are you prepared for the world of tomorrow? The following concepts are likely to figure significantly in future life. See how many terms you know. Choose from the list of non-count nouns and fill in the blanks to complete the definitions. Use simple present tense forms of the verbs in parentheses.

DNA	intelligence	heredity	genetics
RNA	artificial intelligence	cloning	metaphysics

1. _____RNA_____, or ribonucleic acid, _____is_____ a nucleic acid found in cell
   (be)
   nuclei that _____controls_____ chemical activities in cells.
   (control)

2. _____ _____ the passing on of characteristics from ancestors to their descendants
   (be)
   through the means of genes.

3. _____ _____ a branch of philosophy that _____ the nature of
   (be)   (investigate)
   reality.

4. _____, or deoxyribonucleic acid, _____ an acid found in cell nuclei that
   (be)
   _____ heredity in many organisms.
   (control)

5. _____ _____ the capacity of the mind to understand, learn, and respond to new
   (be)
   and potentially challenging situations.

6. _____ _____ a branch of biology that _____ the study of
   (be)   (involve)
   genes and differences among organisms.

7. _____ _____ the nonsexual reproduction of identical duplicate organisms.
   (be)

8. _____ _____ the capacity of a machine to mirror human intelligence and
   (be)
   perform intelligent acts.

3. Education

It is the year 2000, and much instruction uses interactive television and computer technology. Sam Calderwood is working on a lesson involving word definitions. Choose from the phrases and the list of non-count nouns to help him complete his learning task. Some phrases will be used more than once.

Phrases			Non-Count Nouns		
a speck of	a piece of	a flash of	advice	astronomy	cattle
a branch of	a grain of	an article of	dust	electricity	furniture
a clap of	a game of	a current of	jewelry	lightning	rice
	a herd of		sand	soccer	thunder

1. _____*A piece of*_____ _____*advice*_____ is a statement of recommended behavior.

2. _____ _____ is a single discharge of electrical current between clouds or between clouds and the earth.

3. A collection of bovine mammals is called _____ _____ .

4. A decorative object worn on the body or the clothes is called _____ _____ .

5. _____ _____ is an instance of loud sound usually accompanying lightning.

6. A continuing flow of electrons or protons is termed _____ _____ .

7. A single movable structure on which one sits or sleeps is called _____ _____ .

8. An individual particle of a cereal grown in warm and wet areas is called _____ _____ .

9. A small piece of a very fine, sometimes powdery material is termed _____ _____ .

10. A subcategory of that science which deals with the study of planets, stars, and galaxies is called _____ _____ .

11. A particular staging of an athletic competition played on an outdoor field and using a round ball is called _____ _____ .

12. An individual particle of a material produced by the disintegration of stone and rocks is called _____ _____ .

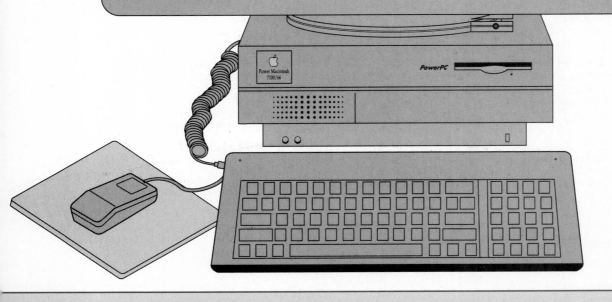

4. Community Bulletin Board

The new interactive bulletin-board channel tells TV viewers about local cultural events, entertainment, and weather. Fill in the blanks in the bulletin-board message, choosing between the forms given. Refer to Appendix 6 on page A13 for help in completing this exercise if necessary.

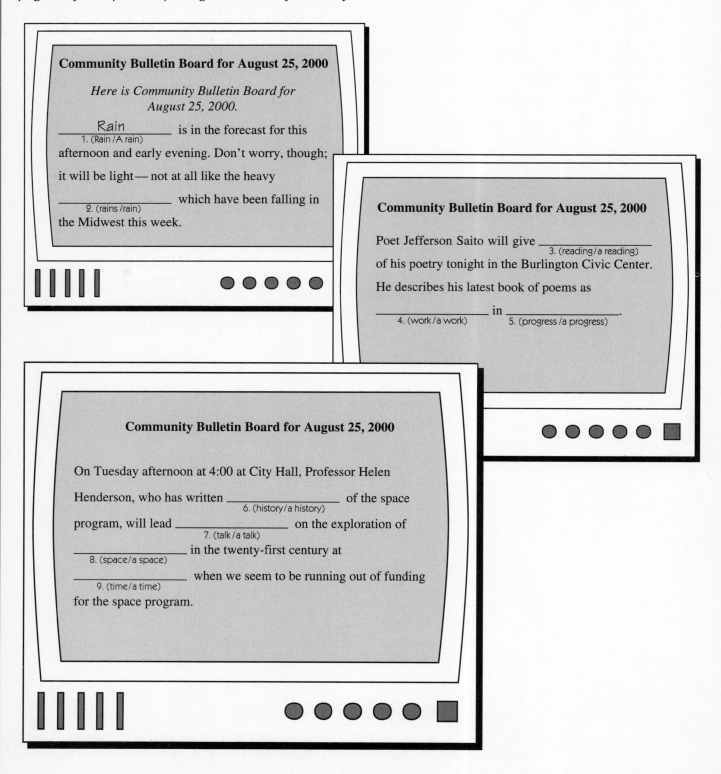

Community Bulletin Board for August 25, 2000

Here is Community Bulletin Board for August 25, 2000.

_____Rain_____ is in the forecast for this
1. (Rain / A rain)

afternoon and early evening. Don't worry, though;

it will be light— not at all like the heavy

_____ which have been falling in
2. (rains / rain)

the Midwest this week.

Community Bulletin Board for August 25, 2000

Poet Jefferson Saito will give _____
3. (reading / a reading)

of his poetry tonight in the Burlington Civic Center.

He describes his latest book of poems as

_____ in _____.
4. (work / a work)   5. (progress / a progress)

Community Bulletin Board for August 25, 2000

On Tuesday afternoon at 4:00 at City Hall, Professor Helen

Henderson, who has written _____ of the space
6. (history / a history)

program, will lead _____ on the exploration of
7. (talk / a talk)

_____ in the twenty-first century at
8. (space / a space)

_____ when we seem to be running out of funding
9. (time / a time)

for the space program.

Community Bulletin Board for August 25, 2000

If you haven't made reservations for the annual Labor Day picnic,

_____ is running short. _____ on the
　　10. (a time / time)　　　　　　　　　11. (Work / A work)

remodeling of Patton Pavilion, where the picnic will be held, is almost

complete. All residents of Burlington are of course invited, but you must

have a ticket, which will cover the price of dinner. The menu will include

fish, meat, and pasta as possible main courses. _____
　　　　　　　　　　　　　　　　　　　　　12. (Soda / A soda)

and _____ are complimentary. Adult
　　13. (a milk / milk)

participants may purchase _____, including
　　　　　　　　　　　14. (wine / a wine)

Columbia Merlot, _____ produced in the eastern part
　　　　　　　　15. (a red wine / red wine)

of the state.

Community Bulletin Board for August 25, 2000

On Friday evening at 8:00 P.M. in the Civic Auditorium, Professor

Mary Alice Waters will present a program on the Xhosa,

_____ of Southern
　　16. (indigenous people / an indigenous people)

Africa. Professor Waters will show _____
　　　　　　　　　　　　　　　　17. (a film / film)

about marriage customs of the Xhosa and other _____
　　　　　　　　　　　　　　　　　　　　　18. (people / peoples)

of the southern third of the African continent.

5. Editing

Read the following composition about genetic engineering. Find and correct the thirteen errors in the use of non-count and count nouns. Some of the errors are made more than once.

Genetic Engineering

People say we will soon be able to perform ✗ genetic engineering. I am against this for several reasons. First, it is dangerous to tamper with the nature because we don't know what will happen. We could upset the balance of the nature. For example, people are against the mosquito because it carries a malaria. Suppose we change the DNA of the mosquito so that it will die off. That will end a malaria, but it will upset the balance of the nature because certain other species eat mosquitoes and won't be able to survive.

Second, genetic engineering will take away a people's control over their own lives. Suppose scientists develop the capability to end violent behavior by eliminating a particular gene from future generations. This may stop a violence, but this type of genetic engineering will make people behave as someone else has determined, not as they themselves have determined, and it will reduce a responsibility.

Third, a genetic engineering will remove a chance from our lives. Part of what makes life interesting is the unpredictability. As far as I am concerned, we should leave a genetic engineering to the Creator.

COMMUNICATION PRACTICE

6. Practice Listening

Futurist Betty Heiser is giving a talk to high school students about her predictions for the future. Listen to their conversation on the tape.

Preparation

Now listen again, filling in the blanks in the conversation in order to prepare yourself for the comprehension section on page 62.

Student 1: Will we continue to explore _____space_____?
1.

Heiser: Yes, absolutely. We'll start with Mars because it's the planet most like Earth. Domed cities will be built. Enormous solar collectors will provide heat and _____light_____ to sustain
2.

_____life_____ inside the domes. Outside the domes, scientists will work on a project to
3.

create _____an atmosphere_____ for the planet. They theorize that oxygen is contained in the Martian soil
4.

and needs to be released.

Student 2: What will _____life_____ be like inside the domes? Will it be tedious and boring since
5.

_____people_____ won't be able to go outside?
6.

Heiser: Not at all. The domed cities will be exciting environments full of _____spirit_____ and
7.

_____atmosphere_____. There will be music and art and many discussions. They will be places of
8.

_____culture_____. Colonists will be carefully selected from a pool of applicants. They'll represent
9.

many different _____peoples_____ from Earth so that there will be a cross-section of all major
10.

_____cultures_____. Anyone emigrating from Earth to Mars will be leading _____an interesting life_____.
11.   12.

Student 3: What about _____food_____? How will the colonists get it?
13.

Heiser: A lot of vegetables will be grown in hydroponic tanks. Animals will be raised in designated dome locations. Other _____foods_____ will be synthesized.
14.

Student 4: When will this happen?

Heiser: There's _____talk_____ in scientific circles of starting the Mars project by 2020, but the exact
15.

date isn't certain yet.

(continued on next page)

Comprehension

Now look at your answers while you listen to the tape again. Circle the letter of the meaning intended by the speaker in each case.

1. (a.) the region beyond the earth's atmosphere

   b. an enclosed area

2. a. an illumination device such as a lamp

   b. light in general

3. a. living beings

   b. a particular life span

4. a. ambience; a feeling or mood

   b. a layer of air surrounding a planet

5. a. a particular life span

   b. existence

6. a. people in general

   b. a specific group of people

7. a. liveliness; animation

   b. a disembodied being; a ghost

8. a. ambience; a feeling or mood

   b. a layer of air surrounding a planet

9. a. the folkways of a particular people

   b. refinement in activities

10. a. people in general

    b. specific groups of people

11. a. specific civilizations

    b. civilization in general

12. a. a particular life span

    b. existence in general

13. a. a specific kind of nourishment

    b. nourishment in general

14. a. specific kinds of nourishment

    b. nourishment in general

15. a. a specific discussion

    b. general conversation

7. Small Group Discussion

Divide into small groups. Discuss the ethics, desirability, and utility of some of the following issues. Take notes about what people in your group think and then report your findings to the other groups.

cloning
test-tube birth
boosting children's intelligence
the 500-channel household

the redesign of species/genetic engineering
lengthening the human life span
space exploration

8. Essay

Choose one of the topics in the preceding exercise and write an essay of two or three paragraphs on it. You may take a position for or against it.

Example:
I am in favor of (*or* I am against) space exploration. . . .

9. Picture Discussion

Working with a partner, look carefully at this painting for a few minutes. Talk to your partner about all the details you see. Then close your books and together see how many details you can remember. Compare your findings with those of other groups.

Example:
There is **snow** on the ground. . . .

Pieter Brueghel: *Return of the Hunters.* (1565)
Oil on oakwood. Kunsthistorisches Museum, Vienna, Austria. Art Resource.

INTRODUCTION

▭▭ *Read and listen to the story and think about the environmental issues raised.*

Questions to Consider

1. What do you consider an environmental problem?
2. Do you think people exaggerate the seriousness of hazards to the environment?
3. How can serious environmental problems be remedied?

ONCE UPON A TIME...

Once upon **a time** there was **a** green and beautiful **planet.** It was **the** third **planet** out from **a** yellowish **sun** in **a** stellar **system** in **a** relatively remote **part** of **the galaxy.** Members of **the** Galactic **Council** knew that **the planet** was between four and five billion years old, but no one was sure exactly how long life had existed there.

The Galactic **Council** had been watching Green, as they called it, for millennia. It was **a job** of **the council** to observe and monitor all planets that harbored life in **an effort** to predict which ones might destroy themselves. Thus **the council** could intervene if it had to. Each planet had its own watcher, and Planet Green's was Gorkon. His job was to visit Green and investigate thoroughly. On this occasion, Gorkon was making his report to **the president** of **the** Galactic **Council.**

The president said, "Well, Gorkon, you're late getting back. There must have been something serious happening to keep you on Green for so long."

Gorkon responded, "Yes, sir, I had to stay longer to be absolutely sure of my calculations. Affairs are not going well there; I'm afraid that if Green doesn't change its ways immediately, life won't be able to endure. Green is now on **a** destructive **path.** There used to be clean air and water, but now there's pollution everywhere. In some large cities, you can hardly see **the sky,** and **the land** is full of garbage and toxic waste dumps. They're cutting down beautiful rain forests in **the** southern **hemisphere.** They've been releasing some very dangerous chemicals—fluorocarbons we would call them—into **the atmosphere,** and **a hole** in **the** ozone **layer** has developed over **the** southern polar **cap.** If something isn't done, **the amount** of ultraviolet radiation in **the atmosphere** will be very dangerous and even lethal within twenty or thirty years. It could happen even sooner."

The president looked sad and asked, "Is that **the** only serious **problem?**"

Gorkon responded, "Unfortunately not. Several individual nations on Green have developed **the bomb.** So far they've avoided using **the weapons** against each other, and right now there's **a sort** of uneasy peace, but there's no guarantee it's going to last. **The** saddest **thing** that's happening on Green, though, is **the extinction** of species. Some have already died off entirely, and many more are endangered. You know what happens to **a planet** when its species start to die off."

"Yes, of course," said **the president.** "We've got to stop that. Well, shall I call **the council** into executive session?"

"Yes, Mr. President," said Gorkon. "Right away. I'm afraid we're going to have to intervene. If we don't, Green may not survive much longer. We wouldn't want to see them suffer **the** same **fate** as Earth did."

ARTICLES

THE: DEFINITE ARTICLE

FOR COUNT NOUNS
We bought a car last week. **The car** was stolen today.
You can see how much of **the forest** has been destroyed by clear-cutting.

FOR NON-COUNT NOUNS
The ozone layer has been damaged.
The rain that fell last night caused some flooding.
The Red Sea is in **the Middle East.**

A/AN: INDEFINITE ARTICLE

FOR SINGULAR COUNT NOUNS
A rain forest has **a delicate ecosystem.**
We bought **a car** last week. The car was stolen today.
She is **an environmentalist.**

ZERO ARTICLE

FOR PLURAL COUNT NOUNS
Environmentalists are against development.
Pollution is destroying air quality in many **places.**

FOR NON-COUNT NOUNS
Environmentalists are against **development.**
Pollution is destroying air **quality** in many places.

FOR PROPER NOUNS
Gorkon traveled to **Green.**
Ms. Trezona negotiated with **Tom Taylor.**

Grammar Notes

1. A noun or noun phrase is <u>specific</u> (or <u>definite</u>) when the speaker and listener both know which specific person, place, or thing is being talked about. Use the definite article, *the,* with singular and plural count and non-count nouns that are specific for you and your listener.

> **The milk** you spilled is all over **the rug** in **the living room.**
> Sean went to **the dentist.**
> The land developers set an enormous fire. **The fire** burned out of control.

2. A noun is also specific when it represents something that is unique—there is only one.

> They say that there is a hole in **the ozone layer.**
> **The president** needs to do something.

3. Certain adjectives can make a noun represent something unique. Some examples of such adjectives are *right, wrong, first, only,* and the superlative forms of adjectives.

> **The best solution** is to talk.
> Sometimes it's **the only solution.**

4. A noun or noun phrase can be made specific by context.

> A: Who are you?
> B: I'm **the doctor.**
> (A is a patient in a hospital. She has just awakened after surgery.)

5. The definite article, *the,* is used with the names of some countries, for example those that are plural or include a "political" word such as *republic, kingdom, union,* or *empire.*

> There is a great interest in the environment in **the United Kingdom.**

See Appendix 8 on page A15 for a list of these countries.

6. The names of some regions are preceded by *the.*

> Camels are native to **the Middle East.**

See Appendix 9 on page A16 for a list of these regions.

7. Many geographical features have the definite article, *the,* as part of their name. This is a kind of specifying.

> **The Pacific (Ocean)** is the world's largest body of water.
> **The Rocky Mountains** run through the United States and Canada.

See Appendix 9 on page A16 for a list of geographical features that have the definite article, *the.*

8. The names of specific airplanes, ships, and hotels often use *the*: the Concorde, the Titanic, the Plaza.

9. The indefinite article, *a/an,* can only be used with singular count nouns.

> **a cat** BUT NOT ~~a rice~~

10. A noun is often <u>indefinite</u> the first time a speaker mentions it. It is usually definite after the first mention.

> Should a petroleum company be allowed to drill for oil on **an unspoiled beach? The beach** might be ruined.

11. Use the indefinite article, *a/an,* with indefinite singular count nouns.

> It is cruel and unfair to harm or displace **a species.**

12. Use no article (zero article) with plural nonspecific count nouns and nonspecific non-count nouns.

> **Environmentalists** are against **development. Siberian tigers** are becoming endangered.

13. Use zero article before the names of people or the designations *Miss, Ms., Mrs.,* or *Mr.* or with professional titles such as *Dr.* or *Professor.*

> **Sally Trezona** negotiated with **Tom Taylor. Ms. Magenheim** called at ten o'clock.

14. A noun is used generically when it represents all members of a class of persons, places, or things. Use *the, a/an,* or zero article with generic nouns to generalize, classify, or define. Generic nouns can be singular or plural count nouns or non-count nouns.

Look at these examples of generalization, classification, and definition with generic nouns.

> **Teachers** are devoted to their profession. (generalization)
> **A monkey** is a primate. (classification)
> **A car** is a four-wheeled vehicle. (definition)

Note that *the* is used with some singular generic count nouns. Singular generic count nouns using *the* fall into three main categories: inventions, musical instruments, and animal species.

> **The wheel** is one of humankind's most important inventions.
> Marjorie plays **the violin.**
> **The Siberian tiger** is endangered.

15. Note the four ways of classifying or defining with generic count nouns.

> indefinite article + singular count noun
> **An orangutan** is a primate.

> zero article + plural count noun
> **Orangutans** are primates.

> definite article + singular count noun
> **The orangutan** is a primate.

> definite article + plural count noun
> **The orangutans** are primates.

These four patterns are approximately the same in meaning when used <u>to classify or define</u> something.

Be careful! In statements where you are <u>not</u> classifying or defining with a generic noun, you may not use *a/an* in front of the noun. Study the following examples.

> They worked to protect **the elephant.**
> They worked to protect **the elephants.**
> They worked to protect **elephants.** NOT ~~They worked to protect an elephant.~~

Remember that no article is used with generic non-count nouns.

> **Carbon** is an element.

FOCUSED PRACTICE

1. Discover the Grammar

Look again at some of the sentences from "Once Upon a Time" on pages 64 and 65. Circle the letter of the sentence that describes the meaning of each sentence from the text.

1. It was the third planet out from a yellowish sun.

   a. We know how many suns there are.

   (b.) We don't know how many suns there are.

2. Members of the Galactic Council knew that the planet was between four and five billion **years old.**

   a. There was one Galactic Council.

   b. There was more than one Galactic Council.

(continued on next page)

3. It was a job of the council to observe and monitor all planets that harbored life.

    a. The council had one job.

    b. The council had many jobs.

4. They're cutting down beautiful rain forests in the southern hemisphere.

    a. They're cutting down some of the rain forests in the southern hemisphere.

    b. They're cutting down all of the rain forests in the southern hemisphere.

5. A hole in the ozone layer has developed over the southern polar cap.

    a. There is one ozone layer.

    b. There are several ozone layers.

6. A hole in the ozone layer has developed over the southern polar cap.

    a. There is one southern polar cap.

    b. There is more than one southern polar cap.

7. Several individual nations on Green have developed the bomb.

    a. They have developed one particular nuclear bomb.

    b. They have developed nuclear bombs in general.

8. You know what happens to a planet when its species start to die off.

    a. This sort of thing can happen to all planets.

    b. This sort of thing can happen to only one planet.

2. Owls or Jobs?

Read this first part of an article that appeared in a recent issue of Impact *magazine.*
Write the correct article and noun choice for each numbered item.

IMPACT

OWLS OR JOBS? YOU DECIDE
by Frank Espinosa

By now you must have heard about

___the controversy___ raging in the Pacific
1. (the controversy / controversy)
Northwest of the United States about

_____ .
   2. (a northern spotted owl / the northern spotted owl)
Environmentalists are pitted against people in the

lumber industry in a battle that could decide the fate

of both _____ and of entire
   3. (the spotted owl / a spotted owl)
families and even towns. Environmentalists say that

this owl,_____ ,
   4. (the endangered species / an endangered species)
must continue to have an old-growth forest habitat if

it is going to survive. Those connected with

_____ say they need to be able
5. (the timber industry / a timber industry)
to log old-growth forests to avert economic disaster.

_____ , obviously feeling it has to
6. (Administration / The administration)
satisfy both camps, is square in _____ .
                       7. (the middle / middle)

    Who is right? The issue is not nearly as black and

white as it might seem at first glance.

3. Disasters

Here are some notable disasters that have occurred in this century. Insert **a/an** *or* **the** *where necessary or leave a blank where no article is required.*

Disaster at Sea
Many Lives Lost

(April 16, 1912) __The__ *Titanic*, a British
     1.
steamer, sank in _____ North Atlantic last
            2.
night after hitting _____ iceberg,
            3.
disproving its builders' claims that it couldn't
be sunk.

Chernobyl Damage Wider than Previously Reported
Details Finally Emerging

On April 26, 1986, _____ fires and explosions following
          14.
_____ unauthorized experiment caused _____ worst
  15.   16.
accident in _____ history of nuclear power at the nuclear
         17.
power plant in Chernobyl, Ukraine. At least thirty-one
people were killed in _____ disaster itself, and _____
          18.   19.
radioactive material was released into the atmosphere.
Approximately 135,000 people were evacuated from
_____ vicinity. Scientists warned of _____ possible
  20.   21.
future cancer deaths and birth defects. _____ accident
                       22.
could have been prevented.

Partial Meltdown at Three Mile Island

(March 29, 1979) _____ worst
         4.
nuclear accident ever to occur in
_____ United States took place at
  5.
the Three Mile Island nuclear
reactor in Pennsylvania yesterday.
_____ causes were _____
  6.   7.
equipment failure and human error,
leading to a loss of coolant in _____
             8.
reactor and a partial meltdown of
_____ reactor's nuclear core. _____
  9.   10.
meltdown of _____ nuclear core
         11.
could have been total. If _____
             12.
coolant hadn't been lost, _____
             13.
accident might not have happened.

MASSIVE OIL SPILL IN ALASKA

(March 24, 1989) _____ oil tanker *Exxon Valdez* struck Bligh Reef in
         23.
Prince William Sound, Alaska tonight, causing _____ worst oil spill in
                         24.
_____ U.S. history. More than ten million barrels of _____ oil were
  25.   26.
spilled, eventually killing _____ many animals and resulting in
               27.
_____ great environmental damage. _____ captain of _____
  28.   29.   30.
Valdez was said to have been drinking in his cabin at _____ time of
                        31.
_____ accident, with _____ ship being piloted by _____ first mate,
  32.   33.   34.
who was inexperienced. Exxon agreed to pay for _____ cost of
                   35.
cleaning up _____ spill. It was determined that _____ captain, rather
        36.   37.
than _____ first mate, should have been piloting _____ vessel.
    38.   39.

4. What's Your EQ?

How much do you know about the environment and the world of nature? Find your Environmental Quotient by matching the two parts of each definition. Circle the choice that uses the correct article or zero article. Then check your answers below.

1. ((The environment)/Environment) is _____
2. A primate is _____
3. A cetacean is _____
4. A marsupial is _____
5. (The ozone layer/An ozone layer) is _____
6. Fluorocarbons are _____
7. (A stratosphere/The stratosphere) is _____
8. Ozone is _____
9. A koala is _____
10. A mammal is _____

a. a form of oxygen with (the distinctive odor/a distinctive odor).
b. the upper portion of the atmosphere, above eleven kilometers.
c. compounds of (fluorine and carbon/the fluorine and carbon) used industrially to lubricate and refrigerate.
d. (a member/the member) of an order of animals that bear their young alive.
e. a member of a group of lower mammals having (a pouch/the pouch) on the abdomen.
f. the collection of physical, biological, and climatological surroundings in which Earth organisms live.
g. a tailless Australian marsupial living in and feeding on (a eucalyptus tree/the eucalyptus tree).
h. (the member/a member) of an order of mammals including dolphins, porpoises, and whales.
i. the part of the atmosphere that normally has high ozone content and that blocks ultraviolet radiation from entering the lower atmosphere.
j. (a member/the member) of a higher order of mammals which includes apes and humans.

Answers: 1. f 2. j 3. h 4. e 5. i 6. c 7. b 8. a 9. g 10. d
Your EQ: 1–3 right: dinosaur   4–6 right: wolf   7–10 right: panda

5. Editing

Each of the following sentences has one error in the use of articles. Correct each sentence.

1. One of the best things we can do to help the environment is to encourage the recycling.
   _____One of the best things we can do to help the environment is to encourage recycling._____

2. Bats are mammals, not the birds.
   _____

3. An orangutan is anthropoid ape dwelling in the jungles of Borneo and Sumatra.
   _____

4. The Mesozoic Era was third of the four major eras of geologic time.

_____

5. Jurassic Period was the period of the Mesozoic Era when dinosaurs were present and birds first appeared.

_____

6. The Milky Way galaxy is galaxy to which the sun and the solar system belong.

_____

7. The meltdown is an inadvertent melting of a nuclear reactor's core.

_____

8. The movie *The China Syndrome* dramatizes a theoretical disaster hypothesizing the meltdown of nuclear reactor so total that the earth would be penetrated.

_____

9. Rain forests in South America are being cleared to make fields for raising the cows.

_____

10. The acid rain is rain with higher-than-normal acidity caused by pollution.

_____

COMMUNICATION PRACTICE

6. Practice Listening

Environmentalist Sally Trezona and lumberman Tom Taylor are having a public debate about the spotted owl. Listen to part of their debate.
{ transcript is on top of next page

Comprehension

Now listen again to certain of Sally's and Tom's sentences. Circle the letter of the sentence that describes the meaning of each sentence.

1. a. Sally thinks Tom is against some spotted owls.
   (b.) Sally thinks Tom is against all spotted owls.

2. a. All owls have to have old-growth forest.
   b. Some owls have to have old-growth forest. *Spotted owls*

3. a. Sally thinks Tom's group wants to cut some of the old-growth forests.
   b. Sally thinks Tom's group wants to cut all of the old-growth forests.

4. a. There is one Endangered Species List.
   b. There is more than one Endangered Species List.

(continued on next page)

5. a. One particular owl can live in different kinds of forests.

   b. Owls in general can live in different types of forests.

6. a. We should consider some humans.

   b. We should consider humans in general.

Optional Dictation

*Now listen once more, filling in the blanks in the following statements with **a/an**, **the**, or no article.*

Trezona: Tom, tell me why you're against ___the___ spotted owls.
1.

Taylor: I'm not against them. I just think there's room for both _____ owls and _____ people.
2. 3.

Trezona: ___the___ owls have to have ___0___ old-growth forest to survive. Your group wants to clear-cut
4. 5.
___the___ old forests.
6.

Taylor: Wrong on both counts. First, we support _____ selective cutting, not _____ clear-cutting. We
7. 8.
also replant everything we cut. ___the___ forest will grow back. Second, ___0___ owls can live in
9. 10.
other places—they don't have to have _____ old-growth forest.
11.

Trezona: What about ___the___ fact that ___the___ spotted owl is on ___the___ Endangered Species List?
12. 13. 14.

Taylor: That's ___a___ good point, but I still think there's ___0___ room for accommodation. ___the___ owl
15. 16. 17.
can live in several different kinds of forests. We need to protect ___the___ owl, but not to ___the___
18. 19.
exclusion of _____ humans.
20.

Trezona: Well, I guess we'll have to agree to disagree.

7. Small Group Discussion

In small groups, discuss the following environmental needs. Come to some kind of consensus in your group about the order of their importance, ranging from the most pressing to the least pressing. Give reasons for your opinions. Report back to the class.

save/whale
stop/destruction/rain forest
prevent/damage/ozone layer
ensure/supply/clean water

stop/destruction/wetland
develop/comprehensive
  system/dispose of/garbage

improve/quality/air
get rid of/nuclear weapon
encourage/recycling

Example:
The most pressing need is to ensure **the** supply of clean water everywhere.
This is because life cannot exist without water.

8. Essay

Choose one of the environmental issues in the preceding exercise and write an essay of three or four paragraphs about it.

9. Debate

Reread the first part of Espinosa's article in exercise 2 on page 68. Then read the rest of the article. Form two groups of students: the environmentalists and the loggers. Prepare your arguments as a group and then have a town meeting to debate the issue.

 OWLS OR JOBS? YOU DECIDE
(continuation)
by Frank Espinosa

Here are the arguments given by the environmentalists in support of their view that the owl should get first consideration:

First, they say, it's the law that an animal on the Endangered Species List must not be harmed and that no development that would impact its habitat may be undertaken. The spotted owl is on the List.

Second, we shouldn't harm or displace a species because it is cruel and unfair to do so.

Most importantly, they say, we must realize that all species are interconnected and that anything harming a single species in the ecosystem will affect all species in the long run.

Says Sally Trezona, spokesperson for a Northwest environmental group: "What we need is a dialogue between the two sides so that people can look at this issue cooperatively instead of competitively. Take the Exxon oil spill in Valdez Bay in Alaska as an example. The spill hurt everyone, not just seals and birds and fish. We might have been able to clean the spill up faster if people had understood that we're all part of the environment and need to work together."

People in the lumber industry take a different view. Tom Taylor, a manager at a lumber company in Oregon, comments: "Sure, I sympathize with some of the points of the environmentalists, but they've gone overboard.

"Remember the Clinch River nuclear plant in Tennessee back in the seventies? It was supposed to be completed in a relatively short time. Its construction was held up for a long time because environmentalists convinced the government that the snail darter, that little fish, would be destroyed because its only habitat was in the river where the reactor was going to be built. Well, it was found out later that the snail darter lives in several other rivers in the area. We could have saved billions of dollars in lost time and resources.

"The same thing is true of the spotted owl. It can live elsewhere. But the best example of the environmentalists' shortsightedness is that they won't admit that people have rights, too, including the ones whose livelihood depends on lumbering. If we can't log these old-growth forests, whole towns are going to be decimated. A lot of people will be out of work. Many of them won't be able to find other jobs because all they know is the timber industry. And here's a word to the wise: The president needs to realize that owls don't vote. He'd better do something if he wants people around here to vote for him."

So there we have it. As you can see, the issue is not simple; it's not a hero-and-villain type of controversy, and it isn't limited to the United States. Should we be cutting down rain forests in Brazil so that farmers can raise cattle that will be slaughtered to make hamburgers for the fast-food industry, which employs millions of people? Should petroleum companies be allowed to drill for oil on beautiful, pristine beaches in Africa? The beaches might be ruined, but jobs will be provided. Which is worth more: jobs or a healthy environment? You be the judge.

10. Picture Discussion

Examine the chart of geologic time. With a partner, choose one period of time that interests you and together prepare a short academic lecture to present to the rest of the class.

Example:
The Jurassic period lasted fifty millon years. . . .

Outline of the earth's history

This geological time scale outlines the development of the earth and of life on the earth. The earth's earliest history appears at the bottom of the chart, and its most recent history is at the top.

Period or epoch and its length		Beginning (years ago)	Development of life on the earth	
Cenozoic Era	Quaternary Period — Holocene Epoch 10 thousand years	10 thousand	Human beings hunted and tamed animals; developed agriculture; learned to use metals, coal, oil, gas, and other resources; and put the power of wind and rivers to work.	Cultivated Plants
	Pleistocene Epoch 2 million years	2 million	Modern human beings developed, Mammoths, woolly rhinos, and other animals flourished but died out near the end of the epoch.	Human beings
	Tertiary Period — Pliocene Epoch 3 million years	5 million	Sea life became much like today's. Birds and many mammals became like modern kinds and spread around the world. Humanlike creatures appeared.	Horses
	Miocene Epoch 19 million years	24 million	Apes appeared in Asia and Africa. Other animals included bats, monkeys, and whales, and primitive bears and raccoons. Flowering plants and trees resembled modern kinds.	Apes
	Oligocene Epoch 14 million years	38 million	Primitive apes appeared. Camels, cats, dogs, elephants, horses, rhinos, and rodents developed. Huge rhinoceroslike animals disappeared near the end of the epoch.	Early horses
	Eocene Epoch 17 million years	55 million	Birds, amphibians, small reptiles, and fish were plentiful, Primitive bats, camels, cats, horses, monkeys, rhinoceroses, and whales appeared.	Grasses
	Paleocene Epoch 8 million years	63 million	Flowering plants became plentiful. Invertebrates, fish, amphibians, reptiles, and mammals were common.	Small mammals
Mesozoic Era	Cretaceous Period 75 million years	138 million	Flowering plants appeared. Invertebrates, fish, and amphibians were plentiful. Dinosaurs with horns and armor became common. Dinosaurs died out at the end of the period.	Flowering plants
	Jurassic Period 67 million years	205 million	Cone-bearing trees were plentiful. Sea life included shelled squid. Dinosaurs reached their largest size. The first birds appeared. Mammals were small and primitive.	Birds
	Triassic Period 35 million years	240 million	Cone-bearing trees were plentiful. Many fish resembled modern kinds. Insects were plentiful. The first turtles, crocodiles, and dinosaurs appeared, as did the first mammals.	Dinosaurs
Paleozoic Era	Permian Period 50 million years	290 million	The first seed plants—cone-bearing trees—appeared. Fish, amphibians, and reptiles were plentiful.	Seed plants
	Carboniferous Period — Pennsylvanian Period 40 million years	330 million	Scale trees, ferns, and giant scouring rushes were abundant. Fish and amphibians were plentiful. The first reptiles appeared. Giant insects lived in forests where coal later formed.	Reptiles
	Mississippian Period 30 million years	360 million	Trilobites had nearly died out. Crustaceans, fish, and amphibians were plentiful. Many coral reefs were formed.	Amphibians
	Devonian Period 50 million years	410 million	The first forests grew in swamps. Many kinds of fish, including sharks, armored fish, and lungfish, swam in the sea and in fresh waters. The first amphibians and insects appeared.	Fish
	Silurian Period 25 million years	435 million	Spore-bearing land plants appeared. Trilobites and mollusks were common. Coral reefs formed.	Corals
	Ordovician Period 65 million years	500 million	Trilobites, corals, and mollusks were common. Tiny animals called graptolites lived in branching *colonies* (groups).	Graptolites
	Cambrian Period 70 million years (?)	570 million (?)	Fossils were plentiful for the first time. Shelled animals called trilobites, and some mollusks, were common in the sea. Jawless fish appeared.	Trilobites
Precambrian Time Almost 4 billion years (?)		4½ billion (?)	Coral, jellyfish, and worms lived in the sea about 1,100 million years ago. Bacteria lived as long as 3½ billion years. Before that, no living things are known.	Bacteria

From *The World Book Encyclopedia.* ©1994 World Book, Inc. By permission of the publisher.

Modification of Nouns

INTRODUCTION

◉◉ *Read and listen to Jessica Taylor's recent article about expectations, from Pocket Digest.*

Questions to Consider

1. What is the difference between hoping for something to happen and expecting it to happen?
2. Does what you expect to happen usually happen?
3. How can expectations be a negative force? How can they be a positive force?

I Hope For It, But I Don't Expect It

by Jessica Taylor

Picture the scene: It's **the seventeenth Winter** Olympics in Lillehammer, Norway. Dan Jansen, **a famous American speed** skater, is about to compete in **the 500-meter** race. This is **the fourth** Olympics he has participated in; in **the first three,** he missed winning **any** medals, but this will be **his last Olympic** competition, so the pressure is on. About halfway through the 500, one of **Dan's** skates catches **a rough** spot on the ice, slowing him down. He wins **no** medal at all. **Three** days later, Dan competes in **the 1,000-meter** race. Everyone knows this is **his last** chance for a medal. **Some** observers have already written him off. Dan starts off well. As he is coming around a turn, though, his skate again hits **a rough** spot on the ice, and he almost falls. But this time he says to himself that he's just going to keep skating and let what happens happen. In effect, he "casts his fate to the winds." The result? Dan sets **a world** record and wins **the gold** medal.

Picture **another** situation: **Your two best film-buff** friends have seen **the reissued** *Citizen Kane.* They rave about **its superb black-and-white** photography and applaud **its profound, sensitive, serious** treatment of **the lonely** life of **an anxiety-ridden busi-ness** tycoon. They say it's **the best American** movie of the century. When you go to see it, though, you feel disappointed.

These situations illustrate what we might call "**the expecta-tion** syndrome." Children often do not meet **their parents' career** expectations of them. Athletes do not always win what people expect them to win. **Great** literature doesn't always seem as good as it should. I asked neurophysiologist Robert Stevens whether there is **an actual scientific** basis for the negativity of expectations or whether this is merely **a philo-sophical** question, **an unpleasant, frustrating** irony of **the human** condition.

Stevens: Well, what we're really talking about here, I think, is **the immense** power of the mind. For example, there is **a documented medical** phenomenon called **focal** dystonia, which is **an abnormal muscle** function caused by **extreme** concentration. Somehow, when athletes are concentrating too hard, they "short circuit" **certain brain** functions and miss the basket, don't hit the ball, or lose the race. So there's **a physiological** counterpart to what the mind manifests.

Pocket Digest: Have you ever had any experience with this phenome-non in your **personal, everyday** life?

Stevens: Yes, I think I have. We're learning more about **the human** brain all the time. It seems that the mind has **immense** power for both **positive** and **negative** things. Let me give you an example from skiing. There are days when, as **a cautious, high-intermediate** skier, I stand at the top of **a steep, icy** slope, plotting **my every** move down the course, fearing that I'll fall. Sure enough, I do fall. **Other** days I feel different. My expecta-tions are miles away. I ski well and don't fall. When we focus exces-sively on goals, our expectations tend to take over, and our mind places us outside the process. On **the other** hand, when we concen-trate on the process instead of the goal, we're often much more successful. Have you heard the phrase "trying too hard"?

Pocket Digest: Very interesting. What would be your recommenda-tion about expectations, then?

Stevens: Well, all I've been able to come up with so far is that it's better to hope for things than to expect them.

speed skater Dan Jansen

MODIFICATION OF NOUNS

NOUN MODIFIERS

	MODIFIER(S)	HEAD NOUN
Dan Jansen is	a famous American **speed**	skater.
He won . . . in . . . in	a **gold*** the 1,000-**meter** the seventeenth **Winter**	medal . . . race . . . Olympics.

ADJECTIVE MODIFIERS

	MODIFIER(S)	HEAD NOUN
Dan Jansen is	a **famous American** speed	skater.
He won . . . in . . . in	a **gold*** the **1,000**-meter the **seventeenth** Winter	medal . . . race . . . Olympics.

NOUN AND ADJECTIVE MODIFIERS OF THE SAME HEAD NOUN

	MODIFIER(S)	HEAD NOUN
Your . . . recommend *Citizen Kane.*	**two best film-buff**	friends
The film has . . . and demonstrates . . . of . . . of	**superb black-and-white** a **profound, sensitive, serious** the **lonely** an **anxiety-ridden business**	photography . . . treatment . . . life . . . tycoon.

*The word *gold* can be considered a noun or an adjective, depending on whether it refers
 to the material or the color.

Grammar Notes

1. Nouns can be modified both by adjectives and by other nouns. The most common pattern is for adjective and noun modifiers to come before the noun they modify. The noun that is modified is called the <u>head noun</u>.

adjective modifier
Dan Jansen is considered an **excellent** skater.

noun modifier
He is a **speed** skater.

2. When there is more than one modifier, the modifiers generally occur in a fixed order. The following list shows the order that modifiers most often follow.* Note that this order is not invariable and can be affected or changed by the emphasis a speaker wishes to give to a particular modifier. Also note that it is unusual for head nouns to have more than three modifiers.

Position	Type of Modifier	Example
1	determiners	a, an, the, this, that, these, those, my, your, Allison's
2	possessive amplifier	own
3	sequence words	first, second, tenth, next, last
4	quantifiers	one, two, few, little, much, many, some
5	opinions or qualities	ugly, beautiful, dull, interesting, intelligent, wonderful, disgusted, interested
6	size, height, or length	big, tall, long, short
7	age or temperature	old, young, hot, cold
8	shapes	square, round, oval
9	colors	red, blue, pink, purple
10	nationalities, social classes, or origins	American, Japanese, Spanish, eastern, upper-class, lower-middle-class, scientific, historic, mythical
11	materials	wood, cotton, denim, silk, glass, stone

*Although many authors have developed lists explaining the order of modifiers, the author wishes to acknowledge particularly Thomas Lee Crowell, *Index to Modern English* (New York: McGraw-Hill, 1964).

The following examples illustrate modifier order as listed above.

determiner	sequence word	quantifier		head noun
the	**first**	**three**		competitions

determiner	opinion or quality	age		
that	**interesting**	**old**		lady

determiner	size	shape	color	
a	**big**	**round**	**red**	ball

determiner	opinion or quality	age	origin	
that	**beautiful**	**old**	**Russian**	vase

determiner	opinion or quality	age	material	
those	**fragile**	**old**	**porcelain**	vases

When a noun has two or more modifiers from the same category, their order is difficult to prescribe.

3. Noun modifiers (also called noun adjuncts) always come before the nouns they modify.

> modifier
> A **house guest** is a guest who is visiting and staying in one's house.
>
> modifier
> A **guest house** is a small house for guests to stay in.

When there are both adjective and noun modifiers, the noun modifiers come closest to the head noun.

> Jansen is a **famous American speed** skater.

4. Compound modifiers are constructed of more than one word. Two types of compound modifiers follow.

> It's a **five-hour** trip (It's a trip lasting five hours.)
> She has a **ten-year-old** daughter. (She has a daughter who is ten years old.)
> He ran at a **record-breaking** speed. (His speed broke records.)
> It's a **crime-related** problem. (It's a problem related to crime.)

These two types of compound modifiers are derived from the phrases in parentheses. In the first type, a number is combined with a noun. In the second type, a noun is combined with a present or a past participle. When compound modifiers precede a noun, they are normally hyphenated.

Be careful! Note how the plural word in the following phrase becomes singular in the compound modifier.

> It's a race of 500 meters.
> It's a 500-meter race. NOT ~~It's a 500-meters race.~~

5. When a noun has two or more adjective modifiers, commas separate only those which are of equal importance. If you are not sure if the modifiers are equally important, it is helpful to see whether the word *and* could be used naturally between them.

> The film has **superb black-and-white** photography and demonstrates a **profound, sensitive, serious** treatment of the lonely life of an anxiety-ridden business tycoon.

In the first group of modifiers, *superb* and *black-and-white* could not naturally have an *and* between them. In the second group, *profound, sensitive,* and *serious* could.

> The film has superb black-and-white photography and demonstrates a **profound and sensitive and serious** treatment of the lonely life of an anxiety-ridden business tycoon.

For this reason, the modifiers are separated by commas.

Speakers usually pause slightly between adjectives of equal importance.

6. Be careful! In written English, it is generally recommended to have no more than two nouns together. Using too many together can be confusing. For example:

> Jerry Jones won the **student portrait painter award.**

Is Jerry a student who won an award for painting portraits? Is Jerry a painter who won an award for painting students? Is the award given by the students? To avoid sentences like this, break up the string of nouns with prepositional phrases or rearrange the modifiers in some other way.

> Jerry Jones won the award for painting portraits of students.
> OR
> Student Jerry Jones won the award for painting portraits.

There is no similar confusion with adjective modifiers.

> The clever little brown-and-white Canadian fox terrier impressed us all. (It is clear that all of the adjectives modify **fox terrier.**)

FOCUSED PRACTICE

1. Discover the Grammar

Examine the following sentences taken from or related to the article that opens this unit. Circle all head nouns which are accompanied by noun or adjective modifiers. Underline adjective modifiers once and noun modifiers twice. Underline only those modifiers that come before the noun. Do not underline determiners in this exercise (**a, an, the, this, that, my, your,** *etc.*).

1. It's the seventeenth Winter Olympics in Lillehammer, Norway.

2. Your two best film-buff friends have seen the reissued *Citizen Kane*.

3. They rave about its superb black-and-white photography and applaud its profound, sensitive, serious treatment of the lonely life of an anxiety-ridden business tycoon.

4. Children often do not meet their parents' career expectations of them.

5. I asked Robert Stevens whether there is an actual scientific basis for the negativity of expectations.

6. There is a documented medical phenomenon called focal dystonia, which is an abnormal muscle function caused by extreme concentration.

7. Can we generalize this phenomenon beyond the sports arena into common, everyday occurrences?

8. I stand at the top of a steep, icy slope, plotting my every move down the course.

9. This skiing example illustrates the basic problem of expectations.

10. Right now we're really in the elementary stages of biological and psychiatric brain research.

2. Reading Aloud

Pam and Alan Murray have taken their son Joshua to Charles Tanaka, a reading specialist, because he cannot read aloud in class. Fill in the blanks in their conversation with compound modifiers, using the phrase in parentheses to create a hyphenated phrase.

Dr. Tanaka: Joshua, tell me about your problems with reading.

Joshua: Well, I get frustrated in my reading class. It's only _____a fifty-minute period_____, but
                  1. (a period that lasts fifty minutes)
to me it seems like a year. Our teacher gives us oral reading assignments every day. When

she calls on me to read aloud, I freeze up, even if it's only

_____. I hate the class.
    2. (an assignment that is one paragraph long)

Dr. Tanaka: But you don't have any problem with silent reading?

Joshua: Nope. I can read _____ in a day or two. I like to read to

3. (a book that is 300 pages long)

myself.

Dr. Tanaka: Uh-huh. Pam and Alan, how long has this been going on?

Alan: Since Josh started the first grade—he's twelve now—so it's been

_____ for him and for us.

4. (an ordeal that has lasted six years)

Dr. Tanaka: Any idea how this started?

Pam: Well, I definitely think it's _____. Joshua lisped when he

5. (a problem related to stress)

started school. He pronounced all his "s" sounds as "th" sounds. That might have had

something to do with it.

Joshua: Yeah! I could read fine silently, but the other kids would laugh at me when I tried to read

aloud and get the "s" sounds right. It just got worse and worse until I couldn't read anything

out loud.

Dr. Tanaka: Uh-huh. But there's another possibility. Maybe this is just

_____. You might need glasses. Let's test your vision. Look

6. (a problem related to eyesight)

at that eye chart on the wall and say the letters on the fifth line.

Joshua: (reads) X-Z-Q-A-M-W.

Dr. Tanaka: OK. Now the seventh line.

Joshua: (reads) P-S-R-B-N-F.

Dr. Tanaka: Hmm. OK. Now the bottom two lines. Look carefully. They make a sentence.

Joshua: (reads) "Night was falling in Dodge City. The gunslinger walked down the street, wearing

_____."

7. (a hat that holds ten gallons)

Dr. Tanaka: Very good! I think I understand. It sounds like you have what we call

_____. You're anxious about being asked to perform, and

8. (anxiety induced by performance)

you expect to read poorly aloud, so you do. But you just showed me you can read fine when

you're not thinking about it. I distracted you when I told you I wanted to test your eyes.

Joshua: Wow! No kidding?

Dr. Tanaka: That's right. It's not going to be that hard to help you, either. I've got

_____ that should have you reading perfectly—if you're

9. (a program that takes two months)

game to try it. What do you think?

Joshua: I sure am. When can we start?

3. Medical School

Jennifer Yu is interested in the complexities of the human mind and is in a postgraduate program in psychiatry at a medical school. She is preparing for an exam. Complete her study definitions by putting the given words in the correct order.

Psychiatric Terms

1. Psychotherapy is ___the treatment___ of ___mental disorders___ through ___psychological methods___ .

    methods/treatment/disorders/the/psychological/mental

2. A phobia is _____

    _____ .

    thing/fear/an/particular/a/of/irrational

3. Repression is ___a___ ___psychological process___ in which ___bothersome, things___ are kept from ___conscious awareness___ .

    things/awareness/process/a/conscious/psychological/bothersome

4. Multiple personality is ___a mental disorder___ in which ___several different personalities___ exist in ___a single mind___ .

    mind/disorder/single/a/personalities/mental/a/different/several

5. A neurosis is ___a nervous disorder___ having ___no apparent physical cause___ .

    disorder/cause/no/nervous/physical/a/apparent

4. Party Expectations

Bill and Nancy, a young married couple, are going to attend a party at the home of Nancy's new boss. They are trying to dress for the occasion and aren't sure what is expected, and Nancy is very worried about making a good impression. Unscramble the sentences in their conversation.

Bill: This is _____ a formal office party _____, isn't it? What if I wear
1. (party / office / formal / a)

_____?
2. (tie / my / silk / new)

Nancy: That's fine, but don't wear _____ with it. People will
3. (shirt / pink / ugly / that / denim)

think you're _____ with no taste.
4. (class / uneducated / lower- / an / hippie / middle-)

Bill: Why not? Why should I pretend I have taste when I don't?

Nancy: Because there are going to be _____ there, and I have
5. (people / business / a lot of / important)

to make _____. It's my job, remember? I don't want
6. (impression / a / well-rounded / , / good)

people to think I have _____, which you're not, of
7. (husband / a / uncultured / , / brash)

course. Humor me just this once, OK, Sweetie? Hmm. . . . I wonder if I should wear

_____ or
8. (round / my / earrings / sapphire / blue)

_____.
9. (green / oval / ones / emerald / the)

(Later, at the party)

Nancy: Hi, Paul. This is Bill, my husband.

Paul: Welcome. Bill, I'm glad to know you. You two are _____.
10. (guests / two / first / our)

Help yourselves to snacks. There are _____. Please
11. (pastries / excellent / some / miniature / ham-and-cheese)

make yourselves at home. You know, Nancy, I'm sorry I didn't make it clear that this isn't

_____. You two really look great, but I hope you
12. (elegant / party / dress-up / , / an)

won't feel out of place.

Bill: Thanks. By the way, Paul, I really like _____ you're
13. (beautiful / shirt / purple / denim / that)

wearing. Where did you get it?

5. Editing

Every week or two, medical student Jennifer Yu writes in her computer diary.
A computer problem has scrambled some of her words, resulting in eighteen
modification errors. Find and correct these errors.

Dear Diary:

It's 12:00 midnight, the end of ~~day a long~~ *a long day* . My two first weeks of

school medical are over, and I'm exhausted but exhilarated! I'm so glad

I decided to go to medical school. It was definitely right the decision. I'm

not completely sure yet, but I think I want to go into psychiatry child

clinical because I love working with children.

Yesterday child class our psychology visited local a hospital where

children disturbed many go for treatment. I expected to see a lot of boys

and girls screaming, but most of them were pretty quiet. They just

looked like they needed personal some attention.

Today in class medical our surgery we had a teacher student, male

young a intern who was filling in for usual our professor. It was really

interesting to get viewpoint a student on things.

only The thing I don't like about medical school is food the cafeteria

tasteless! I'm going to have to start taking lunch own brown-bag my.

Well, Diary, it's time for me to get some sleep. I hope program this

computer new works correctly. I'll write again soon.

COMMUNICATION PRACTICE

6. Practice Listening

▪▪ *Joshua Murray is working on his reading program with Dr. Tanaka.*
Listen to their conversation on the tape.

Comprehension

Now listen again and mark the following statements true, false, or I don't know,
based on what you hear on the tape.

	True	False	I Don't Know
1. The first session will last only thirty minutes.	✔	☐	☐
2. Joshua likes his own voice.	☐	☐	☐
3. A growth spurt often occurs during adolescence.	☐	☐	☐
4. Joshua is thirteen years old.	☐	☐	☐
5. Joshua is afraid of reading orally.	☐	☐	☐
6. The phrase that Joshua will say to distract himself will not be difficult to remember.	☐	☐	☐
7. In the story Joshua reads, people feel lonely.	☐	☐	☐
8. The people in the story have three dogs.	☐	☐	☐
9. Large, warm, and furry dogs can keep you warm on a cold night.	☐	☐	☐

Optional Dictation

Now listen again and fill in the blanks. Place commas between adjectives when the
speaker pauses, and be sure to hyphenate compound modifiers.

1. Our first meeting is only going to be ____a thirty-minute session____.

2. We don't want to make this ___a brain beater___.

3. I feel like ___a total complete idiot___.

4. And I feel like I have _____.

5. You're just going through _____.

6. It happens to _____.

7. The key to getting you over this _____ is to distract you

   from thinking about how well you're doing.

8. Let's think of _____ that you can keep in the back of your

   mind.

9. "It was _____."

(continued on next page)

10. "It promised to be one of _____."

11. What's _____?

12. It's a night that's so cold that you need _____ to sleep with to keep you warm.

7. Tape Discussion

How do developmental problems like Joshua's affect a person's life?

8. Role Play in Pairs

Work with a partner. Choose one of the following situations and role-play it. Then reverse the roles and play it again.

1. Two friends are talking, and one of them suffers from an inferiority complex (feelings that one is not good enough). The other friend tries to convince the first friend that it's the feelings of inferiority that are causing a particular problem.

   Example:
   A: Are you going to try out for the volleyball team?
   B: Nah, they'd never choose me.
   A: What do you mean? You play pretty well. You know, your inferiority complex is getting in the way again.
   B: What do you mean? . . .

2. Two friends are talking, and one of them suffers from the "poor-me," or self-pity, syndrome. The other friend tries to convince the first friend that it's the feelings of self-pity that get in the way of happiness and well-being.

3. Two friends are talking, and one of them suffers from some kind of phobia, such as fear of speaking in public or some other performance-based anxiety. The other friend gives the first friend advice on dealing with the problem.

9. Essay

Write an essay of two or three paragraphs about a phobia or fear you have. If you can, explain where the fear came from and tell when you first had it. Use modifiers to describe your fear.

10. Picture Discussion

One person who likes to draw volunteers to go to the chalkboard. (This person does not look at the picture.) The other students study the picture of the dining room and describe it in as much detail as they can to the student standing at the board. The student at the board draws the dining room, based on the descriptions of the others.

Example:
There's an **oval glass** table in the room. . . .

INTRODUCTION

▶▶ *Read and listen to an editorial that recently appeared in* Thrift *magazine.*

Questions to Consider

1. What is your opinion of credit cards? Do you have any?
2. What are the benefits of credit cards? What are the disadvantages?

THRIFT

Don't Be a Credit-Card Junkie

You're driving by a music store, and it occurs to you that you might just check and see if the store has received **any** new CDs or audiotapes. You'll just drop in and browse for **a few** moments. Once in the store, you're delighted to discover **a number of** new audiotapes and **several** CDs that you absolutely must have. You could buy them some other time, of course, but you're already here, so why not? In the checkout line you wonder whether to write a check or pay with a credit card. **Either** way would be OK, you suppose. The trouble with writing a check, though, is that you don't have **much** money left in your checking account. Sure. Just use the credit card. You won't have to pay for at least a month, and when you do pay, you'll only have to pay **a little** bit **each** month. So you blithely hand the salesperson your piece of plastic, and the sale of $71.44 is rung up.

Does this sound familiar? Does it sound like something you might do? If so, you may well be a credit-card junkie, addicted to **one** of the newest drugs of choice: the credit card.

There are **a few** good things about credit cards. For **one** thing, it's almost impossible to rent a car without one. For another, they're helpful if you're in a situation where you don't have your checkbook or you have **little** cash with you. Also, we can't deny that **many**, if not **most**, establishments will accept credit cards for payments these days, so credit cards are convenient.

What are the disadvantages? One is that relatively **few** adults, and even **fewer** teenagers, have the discipline to use their credit cards wisely. Instead, **many** fall into the buy-now-pay-later trap. **Plenty of** us become "addicted to plastic." Another disadvantage is that credit cards are more abstract than money or checks and thus contribute to our having **less** control over our money. Bank notes are physical things, and you have to reconcile your checking account **every** month when you pay with a check. This takes **a bit of** work, and although it's painful, it's more realistic. Credit cards represent the ultimate abstraction, lending a certain air of unreality to the arena of managing your finances.

All you do is sign your name; someone else does the math for you.

The most serious disadvantage is that **much of** the time credit cards encourage us to <u>live beyond our means</u>. They <u>lull</u> us into the belief that we have money we don't really have. When we first get a credit card, we may not pay **much** attention to **the amount of** money we're spending, so we charge **lots of** purchases. Pretty soon, though, the charges add up, and before we know it we owe **a lot of** money on which we will have to pay **a great deal of** interest.

Our recommendation to our readers is this: Use your credit card only for convenience and not for credit. Otherwise, you may fall into a pit so deep that not even membership in Credit Card Junkies Anonymous will be able to help you crawl out of it. Start doing **a little** saving. Get the credit-card monkey off your back.

QUANTIFIERS OF NOUNS

QUANTIFIERS USED WITH SINGULAR COUNT NOUNS

Every time you borrow money you have to pay interest.
Each bank has its own policies.
Either course of action is OK.
Neither plan seems realistic.

QUANTIFIERS USED WITH PLURAL COUNT NOUNS

Credit cards have **a few** advantages.
Few people can use credit cards wisely.
There are **fewer** banks in this city than there used to be.
There are **many** advantages to saving money.
It can take **a great many** years to pay off a credit-card debt.
Alice made **several** financial miscalculations.
We made **a number of** purchases.
I have **a couple of** suggestions for you.
She owns **three** houses.
Either of the plans is workable.
Neither of the choices is attractive.
Both (of the) businessmen went bankrupt.
Certain (of the) policies are ridiculous.
We had **a bunch of** people over for a party last night.

(continued on next page)

QUANTIFIERS USED WITH NON-COUNT NOUNS

I have **a little** money to spend.
I have **little** patience with finance.
I have **less** money than I used to.
Jack has invested **a great deal of** money in the stock market.
When we're in debt, we are forced to use **much of** our income unproductively.
Reconciling your checking account takes **a bit of** work.

QUANTIFIERS USED WITH NON-COUNT NOUNS AND PLURAL COUNT NOUNS

NON-COUNT NOUNS	PLURAL COUNT NOUNS
I owe **a lot of (lots of)** money.	She has **a lot of (lots of)** friends.
I have **no** time for foolish pursuits.	We have **no** new ideas to offer.
I have **more** energy than I used to.	I have **more** opportunities as well.
I've lost **most of** my patience.	I paid back **most of** my debts.
You need **some** advice.	The country needs **some** honest politicians.
Lisa has **plenty of** time to help us.	**Plenty of** us are credit-card junkies.
None of the work is finished.	**None of** the bills have been paid.
Did you save **any** money?	Do you have **any** solutions?
All (of) the gold has been mined.	**All (of)** my children are in college.
I don't have **enough** money.	I have **enough** friends.

Grammar Notes

1. Quantifiers state precisely or suggest generally the amount or number of something. English has many expressions to quantify nouns and pronouns. These are comprised of phrases or single words that come before the noun or pronoun.

2. Certain quantifiers are used with singular count nouns; others are used with plural count nouns; others are used with non-count nouns; and still others are used with count and non-count nouns.

   a. *Each, either, every,* and *neither* are used with singular count nouns.

      Each problem is unique.
      Neither solution is acceptable.

   b. *Both (of), a bunch (of), certain (of), a couple (of), either of, neither of, a few (of), few (of), fewer (of), a great many (of), many (of), a number of,* and *several (of)* are used with plural count nouns.

      Either of the plans may succeed.
      There have been **many** technological advances.

   c. *A bit of, a great deal of, less, a little (of), little (of),* and *much (of)* are used with non-count nouns.

      We had **a bit of** luck on our trip.

   d. *All (of), any (of), enough (of), half of, a lot of, lots of, most of, no, none of,* and *some (of),* and *(ten) percent (of)* are used with non-count nouns and plural count nouns.

      All (of) my friends came to the party.
      We ate **all (of)** the food.
      Most of my problems have disappeared.
      We spent **most of** our money the first day.

3. Note that many quantifiers appear in phrases with the preposition *of.* The *of* is used when the speaker or writer is specifying particular persons, places, things, or groups.

All of the students passed the exam. However, **none of** them answered question 5 correctly. (The speaker has a particular group of students in mind.)

When speakers or writers make general statements, having no particular persons, places, or things in mind, they use quantifiers without *of.*

   Most students like to learn new things.
   Few students like exams. (The speaker has no particular group of students in mind.)

4. In spoken affirmative sentences, native speakers usually prefer *a lot of* to *much* and *many,* which sound more formal. However, *much* and *many* are often used in negative sentences and in questions.

   A: Does he have **many** friends?
   B: He doesn't have **many** friends here, but he has **a lot of** friends back in San Antonio.

5. Note the characteristics of *some* and *any.* Use *some* with plural count nouns and non-count nouns in affirmative statements.

   Melina has made **some** interesting observations.

Use *any* with plural count nouns and non-count nouns in negative statements.

   We don't want to change **any of** the procedures.
   There are people who avoid taking **any** responsibility for themselves. (The verb **avoid** makes the sentence negative.)

Both forms appear in questions.

   Do you need **some** help?
   Does Frank have **any** debts?

6. Note that when *any* is used in affirmative statements, it doesn't quantify. It refers to an unspecified person, place, or thing.

   Any native-born citizen can become president.

(continued on next page)

7. Be careful! Do not confuse *any more* with *anymore* or *any one* with *anyone*.

> Do you want **any more** soda? (e.g., another glass)
> I don't drink soda **anymore**. (any longer)
> **Any one** of the candidates would make a good president. (any particular one of them)
> I don't see **anyone** I know. (There's no person here whom I know.)

8. Note the difference between *less* and *fewer* and between *amount* and *number*. *Less* and *amount* are used with non-count nouns, while *fewer* and *number* are used with count nouns.

> We have **less money** than we used to, but we also have **fewer problems.**
>
> **The amount of effort** put into law enforcement has grown. In spite of this, **the number of** violent **crimes** has continued to increase.

Usage note: Some native speakers do not make a distinction between *less/fewer* and *amount/number* and use the forms *less* and *amount* to refer to both count and non-count nouns. You will hear statements such as

> I have **less problems** than before.
> OR
> An incredible **amount of people** came to the party.

Many native speakers do not accept these usages, however, and they are not appropriate for writing or careful speech.

9. Note the difference between *a few* and *few*, *a little* and *little*.

> Jennifer has **little** patience. (Jennifer doesn't have much patience.)
> Stanley has **a little** money. (Stanley has some money: not a great deal of money, but enough to put to some use.)

> **Few** environmental problems have been solved. (Not many have been solved.)
> I've paid off **a few of** my bills and plan to pay off **a few** more next month. (I've made progress in paying off my bills.)

10. Be careful! The quantifiers *some of, any of, most of, half of, (10) percent of,* and *none of* can be followed by a singular or a plural verb, depending on the noun before the verb.

> **Some of** the milk **has** spoiled. (non-count noun)
> **Some of** my friends **are** actors. (count noun)
> **None of** the money **was** counterfeit. (non-count noun)
> **None of** the sisters **is** going to inherit the money.

Usage note: The form *none of* is increasingly felt by many native speakers to be plural in meaning. The last sentence above would normally be said in conversation as

> **None of the sisters are** going to inherit the money.

However, some native speakers do not accept this usage and insist on a singular verb after *none*.

Usage note: The forms *either of* and *neither of* are considered singular in formal English. However, many native speakers use a plural verb after *either* or *neither,* especially in conversation. Not all native speakers accept this plural use.

> FORMAL:
> **Neither of** the boys **has** arrived.
> **Either of** the solutions **is** acceptable.
>
> CONVERSATIONAL**:**
> **Neither of** the boys **have** arrived.
> **Either of** the solutions **are** acceptable.

FOCUSED PRACTICE

1. Discover the Grammar

Listen to financial expert Jane Vieira's radio show. Then listen again as you read the script of her talk. Circle all quantifying expressions. Do not circle ordinal numbers or comparative words. Include the word **of** *as part of the quantifying expression if it appears.*

Good evening. I'm Jane Vieira with this week's edition of "We're in the Money."

We've had (a lot of) requests to do a program similar to the broadcast we did (several) months ago on getting out of debt and learning to manage your money wisely, so tonight we're going to cover (all) the points we made in that original program and add (a few) new ones.

First and foremost: Pay yourself before you pay anyone else. Regardless of what your regular income is, save at least (a little of it) each week, even if it's only a dollar or two. Do it first, before you pay your bills, and before you spend the money on something you don't really need.

Second, pay your bills regularly and on time. (Many of us) put off paying our bills until we're sent a second notice, thinking that we'll have (plenty of) money next month to take care of them. That's foolish, and it will only get you into trouble.

Third, make an honest, serious attempt to keep from buying things you don't need. (Most of us) spend (a great deal of) money on unnecessary things, which may be all right if we've got (lots of) cash but not if we're trying to get out of debt. (Many of the) books we buy we can borrow from the library. The same holds true for videos and even CDs, which are free to anyone who has a library card.

Finally, take control of your credit cards. (None of us) are permanently immune to their temptations. There's (little) justification to use credit cards for anything other than convenience, and (few of us) are really aware of just how crushing those interest charges can be. When you get your credit card bill (each) month, make sure you pay more than the minimum required, even if it's only a little more. Otherwise, it will take you (a great many) years to pay off the balance. Above all, if you owe (a lot of) money on credit cards, don't make (any) new purchases with them. Shop around for the lowest interest rate you can find. Sometimes it's worthwhile to get a new credit card with a lower interest rate and pay off the balance on your old one.

Well, folks, that's this week's program. Tune in next week for another edition of "We're in the Money," and in the meantime, we wish you (much) good luck in your financial adventures.

2. The Household Budget

Married couple Ron and Ashley Lamont are trying to figure out their budget for next month. Fill in the blanks in their conversation with expressions from the box. You will use each phrase once.

some	the amount of	plenty of	most of
both of	a lot of	the number of	~~fewer~~
~~less~~	either one of	both	much
neither one of	many	every	

Ashley: Honey, we're still spending _____a lot of_____ money on things we don't really need.
1.

After I pay the bills, we're going to have _____less_____ cash left over than we did last
2.

month. And we were supposed to be saving, remember?

Ron: What have we bought that we don't need?

Ashley: That new exercise machine, for one thing. _____Neither one of_____ us has used it more than
3.

two or three times since we bought it. We could get a year's membership at the athletic club for

_____the amount of_____ money it cost.
4.

Ron: You mean _____either one of_____ us could get a membership?
5.

Ashley: No, _____both of_____ us could. That's what I'm saying. The machine cost $320, and
6.

memberships are $150 each. Let's sell the thing and start going to the athletic club.

Ron: Hmm . . . maybe you're right. What else?

Ashley: Well, we're spending more than ten dollars a month extra on those premium cable channels.

We'd have _____fewer_____ channels to choose from if we cut back to the basic
7.

coverage, but we don't watch _____much_____ TV anyway.
8.

Ron: Yeah, you're right. . . . And based on _____the # of_____ times we've actually used it, I'd
9.

say we could get rid of call-waiting on the phone. Even though it hasn't happened very

_____many_____ times, _____most of_____ my friends say they hate it when they
10.   11.

call and then another call comes in while we're talking.

Ashley: Uh-huh. Let's cancel it, then. And one more suggestion. We should _____both_____
12.

start taking a brown-bag lunch to work instead of going out at noon. If we did these four things,

we'd have _____plenty of_____ money left over _____every_____ month.
13.   14.

Ron: Oh, no! Not my lunches with the guys! Lunchtime is when I get to see them.

Ashley: Invite them over to play _____some_____ volleyball instead!
15.

3. "Telling It Like It Is"

Read the following excerpt from the president's speech to the nation. Fill in the blanks in the speech, choosing from the alternatives given.

My fellow citizens. We're at a time in our history when people are tired of empty promises—a time when we need to make _____*some*_____ real sacrifices. Recent presidents have made
1. (any / some)
_____ pledges that they didn't keep. You may not like everything I tell you tonight, but I
2. (much / many)
think you deserve to hear the truth.

On the economy, we've made _____ progress, but we still have
3. (a little / little)
_____ more to do, so there are _____ things I'm proposing. First, I
4. (a great deal / a great many)   5. (much / several)
want to raise taxes on the wealthy because _____ of them are really paying their share.
6. (few / a few)
Second, _____ middle-class people shouldering an unfair share of the tax burden is far
7. (the amount of / the number of)
too great, so I'm asking for a tax cut for the middle class. If I'm successful, _____ you in
8. (most of / any of)
the middle class will be paying 10 percent _____ money in income taxes next year,
9. (less / fewer)
though _____ of you in the higher-income brackets might see your taxes rise
10. (few / a few)
_____.
11. (a little / little)

Now: You will ask how I intend to make up the lost revenue. The problem with the national income tax is
that there are _____ loopholes in the current law which allow _____
12. (much / many)   13. (some / any)
people to avoid paying _____ taxes at all. My additional plan is to replace the lost
14. (some / any)
revenue with a national sales tax, which is fairer because it applies to _____ people
15. (all / some)
equally. Third, we have _____ money to finance health-care reform, and we've made
16. (no / any)
_____ progress in reducing pollution and meeting clean-air standards. Therefore, I am
17. (little / a little)
linking the two problems and asking for a fifty-cent-a-gallon tax on gasoline. That should encourage
_____ more people to use mass transit, and with _____ additional
18. (a great deal / a great many)   19. (the amount of / the number of)
revenue that we will take in, we will be able to finance our new health-care program and help the
environment at the same time.

4. Test Time

Look at an essay test from an economics class. Find and correct the ten errors in quantifiers.

Question: Discuss the national debt problem and suggest some solutions.

Answer:

Simply put, the national debt is caused by the fact that the government takes in ~~fewer~~ *less* revenue than it pays out, and it borrows from banks and even ~~any~~ *some* foreign countries to make up the difference.

We've had the national debt problem for a great deal of *many* years, at least since 1870. At that time it was only $2.4 billion, an average of about $61 for all *each* person in the country. The number *amount* of debt began to accelerate strongly during World War II, increasing from $43 billion in 1940 to a few *little* less than $259 billion in 1945. It has grown steadily since then; in 1992 it was $4 trillion, meaning that some *each* man, woman, and child in the country would owe about $16,000 if we spread the debt around equally. That year the government had to pay more than $293 billion just in interest charges on the debt, which was more than 21 percent of the national budget.

The government is spending too many *much* on interest and not enough on essentials, so less *fewer* and less *fewer* programs get enough funding. Clearly, we must do something about this problem. I think there are two main things we could do to solve it. First, we should support a balanced-budget amendment to the Constitution. That would keep the government from spending more money than it has. The second thing I would suggest is to pass a national sales tax of 1 percent on every purchases. We would use that money to start paying back the national debt.

COMMUNICATION PRACTICE

5. Practice Listening

Jack Andrews, who is three months behind on his loan payments, is talking on the telephone with Nancy Grant, the loan officer at his credit union. Listen to their conversation on tape.

Comprehension

Now listen again and respond true (T) or false (F) to the following statements.

___T___ 1. Jack can't pay the credit union right away.

___F___ 2. Jack has always made his payments on time.

___T___ 3. Jack will earn more money in his new job than he did in his old job.

___T___ 4. At first, Nancy doesn't want to recommend an extension of Jack's time to pay.

___T___ 5. Jack has to pay something right away, or Nancy will turn his account over to a collection agency.

___F___ 6. Nancy says Jack has to make his full payment immediately.

___F___ 7. Jack asks for a lot of time to come up with some money.

___F___ 8. Nancy can help Jack a lot even if he doesn't make a payment.

Optional Dictation

Now listen once more and fill in the blanks in the text.

Grant: Stanford Credit Union. This is Nancy Grant speaking. May I help you?

Andrews: Hello, Ms. Grant? This is Jack Andrews. I wanted to ask if I could have

_____a little more time_____ on this month's payment.
    1.

Grant: Hello, Mr. Andrews. Let me just look at your file. Hmm . . . well, we've received

____no payments____ for three months, and your file shows that ___few of your payments___
    2.   3.

have been made on time since you took out the loan. I'm sorry, but I can't recommend

___any more extensions___.
    4.

Andrews: I know, Ms. Grant, but I just started a new job. I'll be earning ___much more money___ than I
                                                  5.

did in my last position, but I won't be getting paid for a month.

Grant: Well, Mr. Andrews, we try to be helpful here, but we do have ___certain policies___ that we
                                                  6.

have to uphold. There's ___little___ I can do at this point. In fact, I'm going to
                          7.

(continued on next page)

have to turn your account over to a collection agency if you don't pay at least

_____a little_____ on your outstanding balance.

8.

Andrews: Could I have just _____a few more days_____ to try to come up with _____some money_____?

9.   10.

I'm sure I can arrange something if I can have just _____a bit more time_____.

11.

Grant: _____How much more time_____ would you need?

12.

Andrews: How about five days?

Grant: All right, Mr. Andrews. If you can make a payment within five days, we'll reopen your account.

I can't do _____much_____ for you otherwise.

13.

Andrews: Thank you, Ms. Grant.

6. Small Group Discussion

Work in small groups. Discuss how you could spend less and save more. Use the prompts for suggestions about saving.

Example:
fast food
I eat lunch at a fast-food restaurant **every** day and spend **a lot of** money there.
I could save **a great deal** if I took a brown-bag lunch to school.

credit cards	household expenses
utility bills	movies
vacations	carpooling
clothing	coupons
entertainment	a savings account

7. Role Play in Pairs

Work with a partner and role-play one of the following situations. Then reverse the roles and do the role play again.

Example:
A bank customer and a loan officer are discussing mortgage financing.
Customer: Good morning, Mr. Adams. I'm Andrea Prieto and I'm interested in buying a house. Louise Sellers, my realtor, suggested I talk to you about getting mortgage financing.
Loan officer: Good morning, Ms. Prieto. I'm sure we'll be able to help you. First I need to have you fill out these forms. . . .

1. One friend wants to borrow a rather large sum of money from another friend.
2. One spouse is very irresponsible with the household finances. Husband and wife are discussing this.
3. A son or daughter wants a raise in allowance and is discussing this with a parent.
4. A son or daughter has a credit card, has charged a great deal of money on it, and cannot afford the monthly payments. A parent is discussing this with the child.
5. A bank customer and a loan officer are talking about financing for buying a house. The customer has almost no money for a down payment.
6. A bank customer owes a great deal of money, is behind in the payments, and is talking with a loan officer at a bank.

8. Letter

Choosing one of the following topics, write a letter of two or three paragraphs to a politician you know of—mayor, member of Congress, governor, legislator, prime minister, or president. In your letter, state your opinion and suggest a course of action that you would like to see the politician support.

Topic 1. Taxes should be raised.
Topic 2. Taxes should be lowered.
Topic 3. Persons under twenty-one years of age should not be allowed to have **credit cards**.
Topic 4. The use of credit cards should be discouraged.
Topic 5. Debit cards should be encouraged.
Topic 6. Debit cards should be discouraged.
Topic 7. Bouncing a check should be a misdemeanor.

9. Picture Discussion

Ambassador Gorkon has been asked to visit Earth for a period of a year. He has to rent and fill a house with necessary supplies. Form groups of four or five students, with one student taking the role of Gorkon. First decide among yourselves what Gorkon looks like in order to help determine his needs. Then discuss with him what he should buy in this supermarket to stock his completely empty house. Answer his questions and make suggestions.

Example:
> **A:** You need **some** sponges.
> **Gorkon:** What do I need those for?

Students have arrived from Asia and South America for 4 winter months in Canada. Will rent own apartment. What does s/he need?

I. *Fill the blanks with a/an or the, or leave it blank where no article is needed.*

Cyclones

According to ___the___ National Weather Service, _____ cyclones are
        1.   2.

_____ areas of circulating winds that rotate counterclockwise in _____
 3.   4.

Northern Hemisphere and clockwise in _____ Southern Hemisphere.
                                              5.

They are generally accompanied by some kind of _____ precipitation and
                                                                6.

by _____ stormy weather. _____ tornadoes and _____ hurricanes are
   7.   8.   9.

_____ types of cyclones, as are _____ typhoons, which are _____
 10.   11.   12.

storms that occur in _____ western Pacific Ocean.
                 13.

    _____ hurricane is _____ cyclone that forms over _____ tropical
    14.   15.   16.

oceans and seas and has _____ winds of at least seventy-four miles
                            17.

_____ hour. _____ hurricane rotates in _____ shape of _____ oval or
 18.   19.   20.   21.

_____ circle. _____ hurricanes can cause _____ great environmental
 22.   23.   24.

damage. _____ Hurricane Andrew, which hit _____ coasts of Louisiana
     25.   26.

and southern Florida in August 1992, caused _____ extreme devastation.
                                      27.

In terms of _____ environmental damage, _____ Hurricane Andrew was
         28.   29.

one of _____ most devastating hurricanes ever to strike _____ United
    30.   31.

States. Fourteen people died because of _____ Andrew's effects.
                                     32.

II. *Correct the following sentences by providing a phrase that makes each non-count noun countable.*

1. Let me give you an advice: Don't go out with him.

   Let me give you a piece of advice: Don't go out with him.

   _____

2. The last thing I remember hearing before I was knocked out was a thunder.

   _____

   _____

3. I want this room so clean that I don't see a dust anywhere!

   _____

   _____

4. We bought several beautiful and inexpensive furniture at the yard sale.

   _____

   _____

5. Astrophysics is an astronomy dealing with the properties of stars and planets.

_____

_____

6. I love having a tea every afternoon about five o'clock. It's such a civilized custom.

_____

_____

7. We saw several lightning above the forest before the fire started.

_____

_____

8. I heard an interesting news yesterday afternoon.

_____

_____

III. *Complete the conversations by putting the noun modifiers in the correct order.*

1. **A:** It feels like _____a sweltering summer day_____ here, even though it's spring. What's the
   a. (sweltering / a / summer / day)
   weather like where you are?

   B: Here it feels like _____. I envy you.
   b. (chilly / a / winter / late / day)

2. **A:** What do you think of _____?
   c. (satin / pink / new / my / tie)

   B: It makes you look like _____.
   d. (European / upper-class / handsome / a / businessman)

3. **A:** We were finally able to build_____. It's just what we've always

   wanted.
   e. (brick / own / our / new / house)

   B: It sounds great. Maybe we could do the same. We feel like we're living in

   _____.
   f. (old / little / dirty / a / hovel)

IV. *Complete the conversations with the correct quantifiers, choosing from the items given.*

1. **A:** Let's get off this freeway. There's just too _____much_____ traffic.
   a. (much / many)

   B: Yeah, let's. The _____ of people driving is incredible. I've never seen this
   b. (amount / number)

   _____ cars.
   c. (much / many)

2. **A:** Can you bring soda to the picnic? I don't have _____.
   d. (some / any)

   B: Yeah, I think I've got _____ soda left over from the party.
   e. (some / any)

3. **A:** How do you feel about your new job? Do you have as _____
   f. (much / many)

   responsibilities as you used to?

   B: The job is great. I have about the same _____ of work in general to do as
   g. (amount / number)

   before, but I have _____ stress and _____ problems.
   h. (less / fewer)   i. (less / fewer)

(continued on next page)

4. **A:** How do you think you did on the test? I think I did _____ better than last time—
j. (little / a little)

maybe even _____ better. What about you?
k. (a lot / many)

B: Well, I think I made _____ mistakes, but I have the feeling I did well overall.
l. (few / a few)

5. **A:** Mr. President, do you think _____ of your proposed legislation will be passed
m. (much / many)

by Congress during this session?

B: Yes, I think _____ our proposals will be approved. We're not taking
n. (a great deal of / a great many of)

_____ for granted, though. We still have _____ work to do.
o. (nothing / anything)   p. (a great deal of / a great many of)

A: The polls say that there's _____ support nationwide for your welfare reform
q. (little / a little)

program. Isn't that going to hurt you?

B: Not in the long run, no. _____ of the voters actually
r. (Few / A few)

support the welfare system the way it is now. I think we'll be successful.

V. *Each of the following sentences contains four underlined words or phrases, marked A, B, C, or D. Circle the letter of the one word or phrase in each sentence that is not correct.*

1. The journey from Los Angeles to San Diego is a
A   B
three-hours trip if the traffic isn't heavy.
C   D
    A   B   Ⓒ   D

2. The chief executive officer of the company I work for lives
A   B
in beautiful condominium in a ten-story building.
C   D
    A   B   C   D

3. Plan to build a comprehensive monorail system is a citizen-initiated
A   B   C   D
proposal.
    A   B   C   D

4. One of the most famous inventions in the history of humankind is
A   B   C
a wheel.
D
    A   B   C   D

5. The two first films shown in last weekend's film series were
A   B
the most popular ones in the series.
C   D
    A   B   C   D

6. The extinction of the dinosaurs is still a matter of debate in
A   B   C
scientific community.
D
    A   B   C   D

7. Vancouver, the largest city in Canadian Southwest, is
A   B
the closest major Canadian port to the Orient.
C   D
    A   B   C   D

8. When Sarah was a child, she disliked peas, carrots, a bean, and
A   B   C
most other vegetables.
D
    A   B   C   D

9. <u>The Wheelers'</u> <u>ten-years-old daughter</u>, Melanie, was born in   **A**   **B**   **C**   **D**
      A   B

    <u>the city of Rotterdam</u> in <u>the Netherlands</u>.
          C   D

10. Ralph is in <u>the intensive-care ward</u> of <u>the city hospital</u> after being   **A**   **B**   **C**   **D**
                A   B

    struck by <u>a lightning</u> on <u>a camping trip</u>.
              C   D

From Grammar to Writing

Subject-Verb Agreement

▼

1.

Every sentence in English can be divided into two parts, the subject and the predicate. The subject is a person, place, or thing about which a statement is made. The predicate is the statement, and it always contains the verb. (Remember that the subjects and verbs of English sentences agree in person.) In the following sentences, the complete subject is underlined once, and the complete predicate is underlined twice.

> <u>Birds</u> <u>chirp</u>.
> <u>Koalas</u> <u>live in Australia</u>.
> <u>The men at Ron's office</u> <u>like to play volleyball</u>.
> <u>Ron and Ashley Lamont</u> <u>are trying to save money</u>.
> <u>The danger of credit cards</u> <u>is that they encourage us to live beyond our means</u>.

2.

To determine the complete subject of a sentence, ask a *who* or *what* question. The answer to that question will be the complete subject.

> **The man on the train** reminded Penny of her father.
> Who reminded Penny of her father? **The man on the train.** (complete subject)
>
> **The increasing extinction of plant and animal species** is alarming.
> What is alarming? **The increasing extinction of plant and animal species.** (complete subject)

A. *Underline the complete subject in each of the following sentences.*

1. <u>Five of my best friends</u> are coming over tonight to play volleyball.
2. Far too many individuals are addicted to credit cards.
3. The Siberian tiger and the spotted owl are endangered species.
4. That man who is sitting at the mahogany desk is our loan officer.
5. Relatively few adults or teenagers are able to handle credit cards wisely.
6. The expectation that we will like well-known works of art, literature, or music can detract from our appreciation of them.

3.

There is one word in the complete subject that controls the verb (or auxiliary) in the sentence. To determine this main subject, find the word that the other words modify. In the following sentences, it is underlined.

> My blue silk <u>necktie</u> is gorgeous.
> Our first three <u>attempts</u> were unsuccessful.

Note that the main subject of a sentence is never located in a prepositional phrase (a phrase beginning with a preposition and ending with a noun or pronoun, e.g., *on the table*).

In the following sentences, the prepositional phrases are underlined, the main subject is circled, and an arrow is drawn between the main subject and its verb.

One of my best friends has five credit cards.

Both of my brothers are behind in their car payments.

The fate of the spotted owl is unclear.

Either of the plans is worthwhile.

None of the proposals has much merit.

Neither of the skaters is expected to win a gold medal.

B. *Circle the main subject in each of the following sentences and draw an arrow between it and the verb.*

1. Far too few of us have financial discipline.
2. A list of available jobs was posted on the office bulletin board.
3. Much of what you were told was inaccurate.
4. Neither of those two environmentalists is in favor of the clear-cutting of forests.
5. The number of species on the Endangered Species List is increasing.
6. None of the work has been completed satisfactorily.
7. Very little of this work can be done by a single person working alone.
8. That clever little Canadian fox terrier is near and dear to my heart.
9. The singing of that famous Australian opera star is uplifting.
10. More and more old-growth forest is being cut down.

4.

Even though the word *there* is often the grammatical subject of a sentence, it is linked to a word later in the sentence that controls the verb. In the following sentences, an arrow connects the word *there* and the noun it is linked to. Note the underlined verb.

There <u>are</u> hundreds of animals on the Endangered Species list.

There <u>have</u> been many environmental disasters in the last twenty years.

There <u>is</u> a large, fierce dog guarding the house.

C. *Choose the correct verb to complete each sentence.*

1. There _____has_____ never been an environmental disaster of this magnitude.
   (has / have)
2. There _____ many reasons why I am against the use of nuclear power.
   (is / are)
3. There _____ always a rational explanation for his behavior.
   (isn't / aren't)
4. There _____ been fewer business mergers this year than last.
   (has / have)
5. There _____ a lot of demonstrators present at the environmental rally.
   (was / were)
6. There _____ a lot of instances when we put roadblocks in our own path.
   (is / are)
7. There _____ any elegantly dressed people at the party. Everyone was wearing blue jeans.
   (wasn't / weren't)
8. There _____ lots of chances to do worthwhile and ethical things.
   (is / are)

5.

Compound subjects are those in which the subject is composed of more than one item. They are often connected by *and*.

> **Ron and Ashley** are going to join a health club. (two subjects: Ron, Ashley)
> **The spotted owl, the Siberian tiger, and the whooping crane** need our
> protection. (three subjects: owl, tiger, crane)

Some subjects appear to be compound subjects, but they really constitute a single phrase made up of two items acting as a unit. These take a singular verb.

> **Bacon and eggs** is a high-cholesterol but nourishing meal.
> (Bacon and eggs is a single dish.)
> **The owner and manager** of the bank is Mr. Bates.
> (Mr. Bates is one person who has two functions.)

D. *Choose the correct verb to complete each sentence.*

1. Both the whale and the manatee _____need_____ federal protection.
   (needs / need)

2. Multiple personality and schizophrenia _____ two serious mental disorders.
   (is / are)

3. The founder and owner of the franchise _____ Mr. Paul Trudeau.
   (was / were)

4. Liver and onions _____ a meal detested by many children.
   (is / are)

5. The *Exxon Valdez* oil spill and the Three Mile Island nuclear reactor problem _____ as two
   (qualifies / qualify)
   major environmental disasters.

6. Mathematics _____ often considered a difficult subject.
   (is / are)

6.

Subjects connected by *either . . . or* or *neither . . . nor* behave differently from compound subjects. The subject that is closer to the verb determines whether the verb is singular or plural.

> Either the **president** or his cabinet **members are** responsible for this
> environmental policy. (two subjects: **president, members; members**
> is closer to the verb and forces the plural verb **are.**)

> Neither the **members** of the city council nor the **mayor supports** more
> real-estate development. (two subjects: **members, mayor; mayor** is closer
> to the verb and forces the singular verb **supports.**)

Note that if we reverse the order of the sentences above, the verb changes.

> Either the cabinet **members** or the **president is** responsible for this
> environmental policy.
> Neither the **mayor** nor the **members** of the city council **support** more
> real-estate development.

E. *Choose the correct verb in the following sentences.*

1. Either Bob Ashcroft or the Mendozas _____*are*_____ going to host this year's party.
   (is / are)

2. Neither pollution nor other atmospheric phenomena _____ thought to be related to the
   (is / are)
   unusual weather we've been having.

3. Neither the local environmentalists nor the mayor _____ a plan that will satisfy everyone.
   (has / have)

4. Either a major credit card or a check _____ an acceptable means of payment.
   (is / are)

5. Neither Venus nor the outer planets _____ a breathable atmosphere.
   (has / have)

F. *The following letter to the editor of a newspaper has nine errors in subject-verb agreement. Find and correct the errors.*

Editor, The Times

Many parts of our once-beautiful city ~~is~~ *are* starting to look like mini garbage dumps. You will recall that legislation requiring recycling within the city limits were passed last year, and the mayor and other local politicians encourages us to recycle, but in my apartment complex there is no bins for recycling. Neither the manager of the complex nor the owners of the building has a reasonable explanation. Meanwhile, trash cans in the downtown area is overflowing with garbage, and vacant lots all around the city is littered with soda cans, broken glass, and paper. Trash from rock concerts and weekend picnics in the city parks are rarely cleaned up. The owner and publisher of your newspaper, Stanford Black, have always been a supporter of a clean environment. I urge your paper to take leadership in solving this problem.

III

Passive Voice

INTRODUCTION

Read and listen to the article "Circles of Mystery," which recently appeared in Innovation magazine.

Questions to Consider

1. Do you agree or disagree that there is a need for mystery in life, for things to remain unexplained?
2. Do you know of any mysteries?

Circles Of Mystery

In an age when everything **can** supposedly **be explained** by science and rational thought, many of us yearn for the opposite. We don't want everything to **be explained**. We want to **be puzzled, baffled,** and **intrigued.** We seek mystery.

Consider, for example, the mysterious crop circles that have appeared around the world in the last fifteen years or so. These formations **have been reported** in more than twenty countries, including the United States, Canada, and Australia, but the vast majority **have been found** in grain fields in southern England. These circles—large, flat patterns which are often circular but appear in other geometric figures—**are caused** by a force which flattens the grain but does not destroy it. Since the initial discovery of the circles, more and more individuals **have gotten excited** by their existence and have sought explanations. What are they? How **were** they **made,** and by whom?

Explanations abound. According to one theory, electrically charged particles **get picked up** by spinning air currents and flatten the crops below them in a sort of whirlwind. Another explanation holds that the circles **are formed** by the interaction of mysterious forces involved in the testing of new "star wars" weapons, a theory that **has been rejected** by many scientists. Some observers maintain that the circles **have been made** by spirit creatures such as fairies. Perhaps the most intriguing explanation is that the circles are arti-

facts or messages that **have been left** by extraterrestrials visiting our planet.

A nonmysterious explanation comes from the testimony of David Chorley and Douglas Bower, two British painters who claim to have made the English crop circles over a period of several years by using wooden planks and wire. Chorley and Bower say they made the circles as a joke. Supposedly, people in other countries **have been inspired** by the efforts of Chorley and Bower to make more circles in copycat fashion. However, Pat Delgado, a retired engineer who **got attracted** to the investigation by the mysterious allure of the circles, says, "These two gents may have hoaxed some of the circles, but the phenomenon is still there, and we will carry on research." Delgado **is being supported** by many others who don't want to believe that the origin of the circles has such a prosaic explanation.

In fact, maybe the fascination with the circles **is** best **expressed** by Joan Creighton, a researcher in UFOs, who said, "We all have an inner sense that there is a mystery behind the universe. We like mysteries. It's great fun."*

*"It Happens in the Best Circles," by Leon Jaroff, reported by Anne Constable in *Time*, September 23, 1991, p. 59.

THE PASSIVE: REVIEW AND EXPANSION

SIMPLE PRESENT

SUBJECT	*BE* (OR *GET*)	PAST PARTICIPLE	
The circles	**are**	**caused**	by an unknown force.

PRESENT PROGRESSIVE

They	**are being**	**discussed**	everywhere.

(continued on next page)

SIMPLE PAST

Subject	*Be* (or *Get*)	Past Participle	
The engineer	was	attracted	to the project.

PAST PROGRESSIVE

The public	was getting	fooled	by the publicity.

PRESENT PERFECT

These formations	have been	seen	in more than twenty countries.

PRESENT PERFECT PROGRESSIVE

The discoveries	have been getting*	reported	every day.

PAST PERFECT

The story	had been	told	many times before.

PAST PERFECT PROGRESSIVE

They knew they	had been getting*	paid	too much.

FUTURE

She	will be	intrigued	by our findings.
We	are going to be	advised	by an agricultural expert.

FUTURE PERFECT

We	will have been	told	by this time tomorrow.

FUTURE PERFECT PROGRESSIVE

He	will be getting*	driven	there by a group of local farmers.

MODALS AND MODAL-LIKE EXPRESSIONS

The circles	can be	explained	in a number of ways.
They	have to be	examined	carefully.
Their existence	must have been	known	for a long time.

*Note that *get* is more common with perfect progressives.

Grammar Notes

1. Passive sentences are formed with the verbs *be* (*am, are, is, was, were, be, been, being*) or *get* (*get, gets, got, gotten, getting*) plus a past participle.

   > New laws **are written** every day.
   > If you touch a hot stove, you'll **get burned.**

   Be careful! Only transitive verbs, those that take one or more objects, can be made passive. Intransitive verbs cannot be made passive.

2. In general, the active voice is considered stronger than the passive voice. Writers often prefer the active to the passive voice. In academic writing, however, the passive is frequently used.

   In writing and speaking, there are three instances in which the passive voice is recommended.

   a. When we don't know or don't care who performed the action.

   > My furniture **was made** in Portugal. (The furniture was made by workers, but the speaker or writer probably doesn't know or care exactly by whom.)

   b. When we wish to avoid mentioning who performed the action.

   > We **were given** some incorrect information about our insurance. (Perhaps, to be polite, the speaker or writer wishes to avoid saying who gave the incorrect information.)

   c. When we want to focus on the receiver rather than the performer of the action.

   > *Murder at the Gallop* **was written** by Agatha Christie. (The speaker or writer wishes to focus on the work rather than on its author.)

3. Note that the *by* phrase is usually omitted in passive sentences when the speaker or writer considers it undesirable or unnecessary to mention the performer.

   > We **were given** some incorrect information. (by someone whom I choose not to mention—mention is undesirable)
   > Two of my friends **got hurt** in the crash. (by the impact of the collision—mention is unnecessary)

4. The use of the verb *get* to form the passive is considered more informal than the use of the verb *be*. The *get*-passive is conversational and is characteristic of informal writing. The *get*-passive also sometimes seems to focus more on the action than on the result.

   > Politicians don't **get reelected** if their views are unpopular. (more informal; action is emphasized)
   > Politicians **aren't reelected** if their views are unpopular. (more formal; action is not emphasized)

   The *get*-passive is used more often in speech than in formal writing.

5. *Get* and *have* are used to form the passive causative. Use the passive causative to talk about services arranged by one person for himself or herself or for another. They can occur with or without a *by* phrase, but the *by* phrase is often omitted.

   > I ought to **have** the phone **disconnected.**
   > I need to **get** my hair **done.**
   > We **got** our property **appraised by an expert.**

6. Review the formation and the use of the passive in modal constructions.

   > The crop circles **could have been made** by extraterrestrials.
   > Not all mysteries **can be unraveled.**

FOCUSED PRACTICE

1. Discover the Grammar

🔊 *Listen to the excerpt from the radio mystery show "Phantasma." Then listen again as you read the script. Circle all* **be-** *or* **get-***passive constructions.*

Narrator: Midnight. Earlier, the city (was blanketed) by a nearly impenetrable mist, the perfect environment for a crime to be committed. Now the streets are getting pelted by violent raindrops. No one is about.

On the sixty-seventh floor of a massive office building, the door to an executive suite of offices is ajar. Inside, the main room is dimly lit. A man lies crumpled near the windows. An hour ago he had the misfortune to get bludgeoned by a heavy object. The carpet around him is slowly getting stained by blood. A perfect crime has been committed.

Or has it? The perpetrator is now far from the scene, sure that he is going to get paid handsomely for his work. He is certain that the man was killed by the blow to his head and is convinced that his murderous actions haven't been noticed. He believes that his whereabouts are a mystery. He is wrong! A spark of life remains in the man. His life can be saved if help arrives soon. Phantasma knows who the perpetrator is and where he is. Phantasma knows all! Ha ha ha ha ha ha ha!

2. Three Famous Mysteries

Fill in the blanks in the following article with passive constructions with **be** *and the indicated verbs. Add the relative pronoun* **who** *or* **that,** *if possible.*

Three Unsolved Mysteries Continue to Fascinate

So you think there are no more mysteries, that all mysteries _____*are solved*_____ in time? Think
1. (solve)
again. The pages of history teem with mysteries that

_____.
2. (have/never/crack)

Consider, for example, the case of Billy the Kid,

_____ Henry McCarty at birth but
3. (name)
also known as William Bonney. Young Bonney went west in the 1870s and established himself as a force in Lincoln County in the New Mexico territory. Along with several other young men, he _____
4. (befriend)
by John Tunstall, an immigrant shop owner from England. When Tunstall _____ in a frontier
5. (shoot and kill)
feud in the Lincoln County War, Billy and his friends retaliated by forming a gang and killing Tunstall's murderers. For years Billy and his gang

_____ by the law. Finally, Pat
6. (pursue)
Garrett, formerly Billy's friend,

_____ sheriff of Lincoln County.
7. (elect)
As the record tells it, Billy _____ by
8. (gun down)
Garrett on July 13, 1881, in Fort Sumner, New Mexico, and

_____ there.
9. (bury)

Or was he? Some individuals believe that the Kid didn't die in Fort Sumner at all and that someone else

_____ in the grave. In fact, some
10. (inter)
reports claim that Billy escaped and took another identity. One report insists that an old man who was believed to be

Billy_____ walking along a
11. (see)
highway in New Mexico in 1947. What is the truth?

Another puzzling case involved the brigantine ship *Mary Celeste.* She had left New York for Italy in 1872 and

_____ floating erratically east of
12. (later sight)
the Azores. No one_____ on board,
13. (find)
though everything else on the ship

_____ to be in order, and there was
14. (determine)

no indication why the *Mary Celeste*

_____. In fact, tables
15. (have/abandon)
_____ for afternoon tea. One
16. (have/apparently/set)
theory speculates that the ship_____
17. (threaten)
by an impending explosion that

_____ by fumes from her cargo of
18. (cause)
alcohol. That theory, however, _____.
19. (has/never/prove)

A third perplexing mystery is the case of Amelia Earhart, the famous aviator who in the twenties and thirties was considered the quintessential example of the rugged female individual.

Earhart flew across the Atlantic in 1928 and set a record for a cross-Atlantic flight in 1932. In 1937 she embarked on her most ambitious plan, a flight around the world. Earhart began her flight in Miami in June and

_____only by Fred Noonan, her
20. (accompany)
navigator, They reached New Guinea and left for Howland Island in the South Pacific on July 1. After that, no radio reports or messages of any kind

_____. No remains of her plane
21. (receive)
_____ by naval investigators.
22. (locate)
Did she simply attempt the impossible?

_____ she and Noonan

_____when her plane ran out of
23. (simply kill)
fuel and crashed in the Pacific? Historian William Manchester holds his own view. He believes that Earhart and Noonan saw evidence of the illegal Japanese military buildup in the Mariana Islands. Manchester says, "She

_____ almost certainly

_____ ." Or could something else
24. (force down and murder)
have happened? No one really knows.

For the time being, at least, the fate of Amelia Earhart, along with that of Billy the Kid and the *Mary Celeste,* will have to remain mysterious.

Adapted from Kenneth C. Davis, *Don't Know Much About History* (New York: Avon Books, 1990).

3. Joyce's Diary

*Read the following diary entry. Fill in the blanks with forms of the **get**-passive.*

March 15

Dear Diary,

This has been a strange day. I ___got woken up___ by a
      1. (wake up)
phone call at five o'clock this morning. When I answered the

phone, I heard music in the background, and there was just the

click of someone hanging up. I wouldn't think anything of it except

that this is the fifth time I've _____ out of
      2. (roust)
bed like this. It has me worried. Am I just _____
      3. (harass)
by someone like my friend Harriet is? She _____
      4. (bother)
periodically by practical jokers. Or am I going to _____
      5. (rob)
by someone who's been watching me and my apartment?

Tomorrow I'm going to _____ on the
      6. (the locks / change)
doors just in case. I'm also going to call the telephone company. I

just hope I don't _____ again tomorrow
      7. (disturb)
morning. I need a good night's sleep!

4. Editing

*Read the following script for a radio bulletin about a hit-and-run accident. In order to strengthen the writing, you decide to change the underlined sentences from passive to active or from active to passive. You will change seven sentences. Eliminate the **by** phrase in a passive sentence if it would contain the word **people**.*

A hit-and-run accident occurred this evening at approximately 8:45 P.M. <u>The intersection of Fourth and Madison was being crossed by an eight-year-old boy.</u> <u>A blue Toyota Corolla hit him.</u> <u>Massive injuries were</u>
<u>sustained by the boy.</u> <u>Paramedics took him to Harborview Medical Center.</u> <u>People are caring for him in the</u>
<u>intensive-care ward.</u> His condition is critical. <u>People ask anyone with information about the accident to</u>
<u>contact the sheriff's office at 444-6968.</u> <u>People are offering a reward.</u>

1. _____An eight-year-old boy was crossing the intersection of Fourth and Madison._____

2. _____

3. _____

4. _____

5. _____

6. _____

7. _____

COMMUNICATION PRACTICE

5. Practice Listening

Some animals have been stolen from the city zoo. Listen to the conversation between police detective Sadler and zoo administrator Akimura. Then listen again. Circle the letter of the sentence that explains the meaning of certain sentences.

1. (a.) The janitor found the keeper.

   b. The keeper found the janitor.

2. a. Akimura examined the keeper.

   b. A physician examined the keeper.

3. a. The keeper had been drugged.

   b. The keeper had been hit.

(continued on next page)

4. a. It takes two weeks to see turtles.

   b. Two turtles were taken two weeks ago.

5. a. The police were notified about the first theft.

   b. The police weren't notified about the first theft.

6. a. The zoo expansion has been completed.

   b. The zoo expansion hasn't been completed.

7. a. Voters haven't yet approved the zoo expansion.

   b. Voters have already approved the zoo expansion.

8. a. First the animals eat. Then the food preparation area is cleaned.

   b. First the food preparation area is cleaned. Then the animals eat.

9. a. Detective Sadler will check the janitor's references himself.

   b. Detective Sadler will ask someone else to check the janitor's references.

6. Role Play in Pairs

Work with a partner. Choose one of the following situations and role-play it. Then reverse the roles and play the situation again.

1. A patient was prescribed some medicine which caused a severe reaction. The patient is discussing the situation with a nurse practitioner.

   Example:
   Nurse practitioner: What seems to be the problem?
   Patient: Well, I **was given** a prescription for my shoulder pain, and it made me really sick.
   Nurse practitioner: What was the medicine?
   Patient: It was Tylenex, but I didn't realize it until I had already taken it. The trouble is that I **wasn't** even **asked** whether I have had any adverse reactions to certain medicines. . . .

2. A parent feels that his or her child was given some bad advice about taking a course in school, a course which the child is now failing. The parent is discussing the issue with a school counselor.

3. A teenager has been arrested for shoplifting. The child's parent feels that the child is innocent and is discussing the problem with a police officer.

4. An employee in an office had a wallet or purse stolen. The employee feels that someone in the office might have stolen it but doesn't want to accuse anyone and is discussing the situation with the boss.

7. Essay

Write an essay in which you unravel a mystery in your own life. Describe what the mystery is and how it might have been caused. Offer some possible solutions to the mystery.

8. Picture Discussion

These are pictures of Amelia Earhart and Billy the Kid. Form groups of two. One partner tells all he or she knows about Earhart and the other about Billy the Kid. Then, as a class, discuss the similarities and differences between the two mysteries.

Example:
The remains of Earhart's plane **have never been found.**

Reporting Ideas and Facts with Passives

INTRODUCTION

Read and listen to the story about Atlantis.

Questions to Consider

1. Can myths and legends ever be reflections of truth?
2. Why does Atlantis continue to fascinate us today?

Atlantis **was believed** to be a rich and important island nation that **was located** along the edge of the Atlantic Ocean near the Strait of Gibraltar. Its existence was first described by Plato in his work *Timaeus*. Plato said that Atlantis **was known** as a great empire and **was believed** to be the most powerful nation in the world. It had developed an impressive civilization and had had great military success. Its armies **were said** to have defeated nations in both Europe and Africa before failing in their attempt to subdue Athens.

It **is believed** that the end finally arrived for Atlantis approximately thirteen thousand years ago when the nation was struck by a massive series of volcanically generated earthquakes. Enormous waves **are thought** to have battered the coastline and swept inland, inundating all major cities and drowning most of the people. It **is conjectured** that a few hardy souls escaped to nearby Spain and Portugal before volcanic eruptions in the country's central

mountain range destroyed the remainder of the land and caused the subcontinent to sink into the ocean. It **is** even **claimed** by some that the escapees, if there were any, **might be regarded** as the ancestors of the present-day Basques, a people whose language **is** not provably **related** to any other language on the globe. It must be kept firmly in mind, however, that this is only a theory.

Did Atlantis ever actually exist? Or is its story merely a fanciful tale of Plato's? For some time, the Russians have been studying the Atlantic Ridge near the Azores and the Canary Islands. It **is thought** that the huge undersea land mass adjacent to these islands and consisting of submerged plateaus and mountaintops might be evidence of the existence of Atlantis, a prehistoric eighth continent.

It **has been suggested** by some that the destruction of Atlantis was a form of punishment by a Creator angry about the sinful behavior of the Atlanteans. **Could** their fate **have been deserved?** Or was it merely the result of an unfortunate union of circumstances?

The answer to these questions **may** never **be known.**

REPORTING IDEAS AND FACTS WITH PASSIVES

PASSIVE

Atlantis **was considered** a powerful nation.
It **was said** to be the most powerful nation in the world.
It **is suggested** that an earthquake may have destroyed Atlantis.

STATIVE PASSIVE

Atlantis **was located** along the edge of the Atlantic Ocean near the Strait of Gibraltar.

Grammar Notes

1. In the news and in academic discourse, passive voice is widely used for reporting the ideas, beliefs, findings, and knowledge of others. The passive creates an impartial and objective impression by removing the speaker or writer somewhat from the idea.

> Water contains minute solutes that **are thought** to have important health benefits. (The speaker does not claim responsibility for this belief.)

2. Speakers and writers create an even greater distance between themselves and the idea by beginning the sentence with *It*.

> The Pueblo people **are said** to be the descendants of the Anasazi.
> **It is said** that the Pueblo people are the descendants of the Anasazi.

3. Some verbs commonly used to report the ideas, beliefs, and opinions of others are *think, consider, regard, say, allege, believe, claim*, and *suggest*.

Be careful! Passive sentences using these verbs are made from *be*, not *get*.

4. Passive sentences that express the opinions and beliefs of others are often followed by infinitives.

> Atlantis **was said to be** a powerful nation.

5. Stative passives are made from *be* + past participle and are frequently used to state facts: *be located* (*in, at*, etc.), *be found* (*in, at*, etc.), *be made up of, be divided* (*into, by*, etc.), *be related to*.

> Atlantis **was located along** the edge of the Atlantic Ocean near the Strait of Gibraltar. Chicken pox **is related to** herpes zoster.

Stative passives cannot be used with a *by* phrase because there is no performer of any action.

FOCUSED PRACTICE

1. Discover the Grammar

Listen to the news bulletin. Then listen again and circle the eleven passive constructions that report ideas, beliefs, findings, knowledge, or facts.

We interrupt our regularly scheduled program to bring you this news bulletin. A massive series of earthquakes has struck the nation, causing extreme damage to most major cities. The earthquakes are said to have registered a nine on the Richter-scale, though this information is considered preliminary. The minister of science has stated that the epicenter of the quakes was located in the Atlantic Ocean some forty miles west of the Pillars of Hercules. According to unconfirmed reports, vast sections of the coastline are reported to be underwater as a consequence of a gigantic tidal wave that hit the coastal areas in the aftermath of the earthquakes. The exact number of casualties of the tidal wave is not known, though it is estimated that more than 200,000 people have drowned. Serious flooding is believed to have occurred in cities farther inland. The president, who had been vacationing at his mountain retreat, has returned to the capital. Looting is alleged to be taking place in most major cities, and martial law is expected to be declared within hours. It is assumed that the president will be speaking to the nation shortly to announce the details of the imposition of military government. As he was boarding a plane for the flight to the capital, the president did say, "A tragedy has struck our nation. It is hoped that the citizens of Atlantis will conduct themselves in a calm, gentle, and moral manner in our time of need." In the meantime, Atlanteans should gather provisions and head for the highest ground that they can find. Stay tuned for further bulletins.

2. Myth, Legend, or Reality?

Read the following article, which recently appeared in World Review, *about past cultures. Complete the blanks with passive constructions, using the indicated verbs.*

Where do we draw the lines between myth, legend, and reality? How much is true and how much invented? What happens to groups or cultures when they disappear? What happens to their people? We decided to explore some of these questions.

First let's consider the saga of the ancient Pueblo people of the U.S. Southwest. They _____*were called*_____ the Anasazi
1. (call)
by the Navajo people, a term that means "ancient ones," and though their origin

_____ , they
2. (not / know)
_____ to have settled in
3. (think)
the Four Corners area about A.D. 100. They

_____ to have developed
4. (know)
subsistence agriculture and to have built impressive cities and spectacular cliff dwellings. About the year 1300, however, something happened to the Anasazi. They abandoned their dwellings and migrated to other locales such as the Rio Grande Valley in New Mexico and the White Mountains in Arizona.

Today it _____ by many
5. (assume)
anthropologists that the Anasazi are the forebears of present-day Pueblo peoples in the Southwest. The question remains, however: What brought an end to their flourishing culture? Drought? Incursions by unfriendly tribes? _____
certain present-day Native Americans of the Southwest really _____ as the
6. (can / regard)
descendants of the Anasazi? Or did the Anasazi actually disappear?

Next, let's turn our attention to the story of Atlantis, the famed "lost continent" which

_____ to have existed in
7. (say)
the Atlantic Ocean. Atlantis

_____ west of the Strait of
8. (supposedly / locate)
Gibraltar, which _____ the
9. (call)
Pillars of Hercules by the Greeks. Is Atlantis a myth, or does it have a basis in reality?

Plato wrote about Atlantis in two of his dialogues, describing it as a fabulous island larger than Libya and Turkey put together. Atlantis

_____ to have existed
10. (believe / by Plato)
about nine thousand years before his era. The

Atlanteans _____ to have
11. (repute)
conquered many lands around the Mediterranean but

_____ to have become
12. (also say)
evil and greedy in the process. Their island, or

continent, _____ to have
13. (think)
sunk into the sea after being hit by earthquakes.

Was there really an Atlantis? Were the survivors of the catastrophe really the ancestors of the present-day Basques, as _____ by
14. (claim)
certain twentieth-century tale-spinners? Is the Atlantis story just an entertaining legend invented by Plato? Or, if Atlantis was real, is the problem simply that it existed so long ago that wisps of its memory are all that remain? The legend of Atlantis

_____ by many present-
15. (think)
day scholars to have been influenced by reports of the disaster on the island of Thira, north of Crete in the Mediterranean Sea. Thira was destroyed about 1500 B.C. by volcanic eruptions and accompanying earthquakes, which also devastated civilization on nearby Crete.

Is the Thira disaster the basis for the Atlantis legend, or do the descendants of Atlanteans walk among us? The answer _____ .
16. (not / yet / know)

3. Editing

Read the following student essay about places that may or may not have been real. Find and correct the thirteen errors in passive constructions. Some passive constructions have more than one error.

Fact or Fancy?

Did such places as the Fountain of Youth, the Seven Cities of Cibola, and the Mystic Village of Mount Shasta really exist, or are they just mysterious and fun stories that people concocted to entertain themselves? In my opinion, they are just legends that are believe because people want strange things to be real.

Take the Fountain of Youth, for example. In the early 1500s it thought to exist somewhere in the southeastern United States and was allege to contain waters that would give eternal youth. Ponce de León looked for it to no avail but found and named Florida in the process. The point is that people wanted to believe that there was such a thing because perpetual youth regarded by sixteenth-century Europeans as a wonderful thing.

Then there was the case of the Seven Cities of Gold, or the Seven Cities of Cibola, as they popularly called. Supposedly, they were locate in the Southwest, somewhere along what known today as the Zuñi River in the state of New Mexico. The famed Spanish explorer Coronado searched valiantly for Cibola, inspired by legends of fabulous cities whose streets said to be paved with gold, but he found only poor Indian villages. Other explorers also tried to find the Seven Cities, but they were doomed to failure because it was the European lust for gold that created the legends.

Finally, there is the case of the mysterious village that in the early part of the twentieth century thought to exist on the slopes of Mount Shasta in California and to be inhabited by a group of people call Lemurians. It was claim that they were descendants of the survivors of the ancient nation of Lemuria, a civilization that was supposed to have sunk beneath the Pacific Ocean after a prehistoric geological disaster. The Lemurians were report to be living in a pristine village on the mountain and to be conducting strange rituals. They were say to engage occasionally in trade with the "normal" inhabitants of the region. It seems to me, though, that the story of the Lemurians was invented by people who wanted to believe that there could be a group of people who were untainted and unspoiled by modern civilization.

The stories of the Lemurians, the Fountain of Youth, and the Seven Cities of Cibola ought to be taken for what they really are: pleasant and entertaining tales that people created because they needed to believe in fancy.

Adapted from E. Randall Floyd, "Mount Shasta's 'Mystic Village'," *Great American Mysteries* (Little Rock: August House Publishers, Inc., 1990).

COMMUNICATION PRACTICE

4. Practice Listening

▣ *Listen to the TV quiz game as you read the script.*

Quizmaster: All right, contestants, are you ready to begin? Here we go. A revolutionary leader from Venezuela, he was called the Liberator and is considered the father of South American democracy.

Contestant 1: Simón Bolívar?

Quizmaster: That's correct, for $500. Next question: He is thought to have been the author of the *Iliad* and the *Odyssey*. However, it is not known for certain whether he was one specific person or a composite of many.

Contestant 3: Aristotle?

Quizmaster: I'm sorry. That is incorrect.

Contestant 2: Homer.

Quizmaster: Yes, that is correct, for $500. Now, for $800: She was a famous French military leader of the fifteenth century who was said to hear the voice of God. Later, however, she was found to be a heretic and was burned at the stake. Now she is regarded in the Roman Catholic faith as a saint.

Contestant 2: Joan of Arc?

Quizmaster: Absolutely correct. For another $800: It was known as the land where wine berries grew. The tiny villages established there by Leif Eriksson and others are presumed to have been the first European settlements in the New World.

Contestant 1: Vinland?

Quizmaster: Yes, correct. Now for the last question. Contestant 2 is in the lead. For one thousand dollars: One of the daughters of the ruling royal family in Russia, she was thought to have been murdered in the 1917 revolution that brought the Bolsheviks to power. In the years since then, however, it has been persistently rumored that this one daughter somehow survived the assassination attempt and eventually made her way to America.

Contestant 2: Anastasia Romanov?

Quizmaster: Absolutely right. Congratulations, Contestant 2. You are the winner.

Comprehension

Now match these items to complete each statement.

__e__ 1. Homer   a. was thought to have been murdered in the 1917 Russian revolution.

_____ 2. Vinland   b. is presumed to be the site of the first European settlements in the New World.

_____ 3. Simón Bolívar   c. was said to hear the voice of God.

_____ 4. Anastasia Romanov   d. is considered the father of South American democracy.

_____ 5. Joan of Arc   e. is thought to have been the author of the *Iliad* and the *Odyssey*.

Optional Dictation

Now listen again, completing the sentences with passive constructions.

He _____was called_____ the Liberator and ___was considered to be___ the father of South
   1.   2.
American democracy.

He _____was_____ the author of the *Iliad* and the *Odyssey*. However, it
   3.
___is not known___ for certain whether he was one specific person or a composite of many.
   4.

She __was said to have heard__ the voice of God. Later, however, she ___was found to be___ a
   5.   6.
heretic and was burned at the stake. Now she ___is regarded___ in the Roman Catholic faith as
   7.
a saint.

It __was known__ as the land where wine berries grew. The tiny villages established there by
   8.
Leif Eriksson and others __are presumed to have been__ the first European settlements in the New World.
   9.

She __was thot to have been__ in the 1917 revolution. It ___has been___ persistently
   10.
___rumored___ that this one daughter somehow survived the assassination attempt and
   11.
eventually made her way to America.

5. Group Guessing Game

*Divide into groups of four to six. Using passive constructions, prepare five or more
statements about any famous figure you choose: a political or religious leader, an
author, an explorer, an inventor, and so on. The other students in your group will
try to guess who the figure is. Make the first statements less obvious than the later
ones.*

Example:
1. He **was called** "great soul" by his followers and admirers.
2. In his time, he **was revered** for, among other things, his efforts in favor of the untouchables.
3. He **is known** today as the father of the nonviolent movement called passive resistance.
4. He **is regarded** as the principal force behind the achievement of India's independence.
5. In the world today he **is considered** one of the greatest religious leaders of all time.

Answer: Mahatma (Mohandas) Gandhi

She was very rich, had many opportunities, but had a sad life
She was the most photographed woman in the world
She was called the "Princess of Hearts."

6. Essay

Write an essay of three or four paragraphs about a world-famous person, present or historical, whom you admire. This person might be the individual you used for the quiz game in the preceding exercise but needn't be. It can be someone from any country.

7. Picture Discussion

Divide into several groups and study this map of the Mediterranean region. Discuss what you know about the history, culture, peoples, and geography of this region. Then, as a group, prepare a set of questions with passive voice about some of the facts you discussed. Each group should take a turn asking questions of the other groups. Score points.

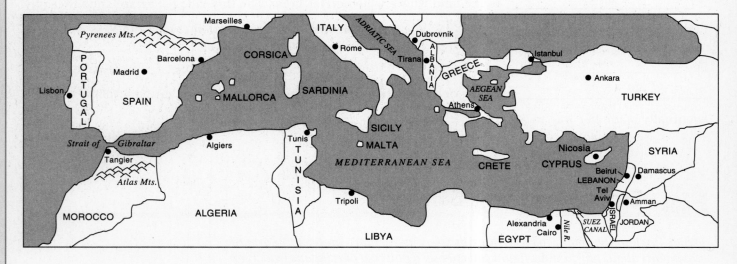

I. *Complete the conversations with* **be-** *or* **get-***passive forms and the indicated verbs. Use* **be** *unless* **get** *is specified.*

1. **A:** Where <u>was the missing child found</u> ?
   a. (the missing child / find)
   B: She _____ walking barefoot along
   b. (discover)
   Stinson Beach.

2. **A:** How do you think the team is going to do this year?
   B: Pretty well, except that I'm sure they'll
   _____ by Central University.
   c. (get / beat)

3. **A:** What happened to your car?
   B: It _____ by a truck—a small one,
   d. (get / hit)
   fortunately.

4. **A:** Mary, _____ for six months.
   e. (we / have / getting / overcharge)
   B: I think we ought to _____ . I've heard the
   f. (have / the company / investigate)
   same thing from the neighbors.

5. **A:** Why are these floors so dirty? _____
   g. (they / not / clean)
   every day?
   B: Normally, yes, but somehow the cleaning
   _____ this morning.
   h. (not / get / do)

6. **A:** Please don't give food to the animals. They
   _____ a special diet.
   i. (be / feed)
   B: OK. Will we be able to see the animals
   _____ while we're here at the zoo?
   j. (getting / feed)
   A: Yes. _____ at four o'clock today.
   k. (They / will / feed)

II. *Read the newspaper article. Rewrite the six numbered sentences, changing passive verb forms to the active and active verb forms to the passive. Eliminate all* **by** *phrases in passive sentences. Do not change intransitive verbs, and do not change the quotation.*

<u>It is said by local citizen Ronald Mason that his lesson has been learned</u>
1.
<u>by him.</u> On Tuesday, Mason was in a hurry to get to a job interview.

<u>His motorcycle was parked by him in a handicapped-parking space.</u>
2.
<u>When Mason came out of the interview, it was discovered by him that</u>
3.
<u>someone had removed his motorcycle from the handicapped spot.</u>

<u>Someone had placed it upside down in the pool of the adjacent fountain.</u>
4.

129

(continued on next page)

People had noticed no one in the area. After recovering his motorcycle, it was said by Mason, "I'll
             5.   6.
never do that again. I deserved what I got."

1. _____ Local citizen Ronald Mason says that he has learned his lesson. _____

2. _____

3. _____

4. _____

5. _____

6. _____

III. *Fill in the blanks in the paragraph with passive forms of the indicated verbs.*

Consider the situation of the mysterious "lost colony" established by Sir Walter Raleigh in 1585 on
the Outer Banks of what is now North Carolina. It _____ is felt _____ today that the plan for the
                                                       1. (feel)
settlement, which _____ on Roanoke Island, was ill conceived from the start.
                                         2. (locate)
Geographical conditions were not favorable, and the local tribes were not friendly. In 1590 all of the
colonists _____ by explorers to have vanished, leaving behind only some refuse
                              3. (find)
and the word *Croatoan*, the name of a nearby island, written on a tree. What happened to the colonists?
No one knows for sure, but today they _____ to have been killed or carried away
                                  4. (assume)
by neighboring peoples.

Today it _____ by some that at least a few of the colonists were absorbed into
                          5. (believe)
local tribes. In fact, descendants of the original native inhabitants of the area claim Raleigh's colonists
as their ancestors. If this is true, the people of the lost colony _____ lost at all, for
                                  6. (not / should / consider)
their genes live on in those descendants.

IV. *Read the sentences in the news broadcast. Each sentence has four underlined words or phrases. The four underlined parts of each sentence are marked A, B, C, or D. Circle the letter of the one underlined word or phrase that is not correct.*

This is news to the hour on KXYZ.

1. The Hawaiian island of Kahoolawe <u>has</u> just <u>being</u>

          A   B
   <u>hit</u> <u>by</u> a tsunami, or tidal wave.

C   D

         A   Ⓑ   C   D

2. The tidal wave <u>were</u> <u>caused</u> <u>by</u> an earthquake

                A   B   C
   <u>centered</u> in the Pacific Ocean, south-southeast

   D
   of Midway Island.

         A   B   C   D

3. Damage on Kahoolawe <u>is</u> <u>say</u> <u>to</u> <u>be</u> major.

                  A B   C D

         A   B   C   D

4. In Central Africa, a breakthrough <u>is</u> <u>being</u>

                                A   B
   <u>report</u> involving resumption of the <u>stalled</u>

   C   D
   peace talks.

         A   B   C   D

5. These talks <u>were been</u> <u>held</u> <u>last week</u> <u>between</u>

          A   B   C   D
   the leaders of Tintoria and Illyria.

         A   B   C   D

6. They <u>have been</u> <u>broken off</u> <u>when</u> the president

    A   B   C
   <u>stormed</u> out of the first face-to-face meeting.

   D

         A   B   C   D

7. It <u>is</u> <u>rumored</u> that the talks <u>are be</u> <u>resumed</u> next

  A   B   C   D
   week in Switzerland.

         A   B   C   D

8. The new space station that <u>is being</u> <u>sponsored</u> by

                          A   B
   the seven-nation consortium <u>will</u> <u>launching</u> next week

                          C   D
   from Woomera Field in Australia.

         A   B   C   D

9. The station <u>will</u> <u>be</u> <u>staff</u> by astronauts from each of the

          A   B   C
   seven <u>participating</u> nations.

       D
   That's news to the hour from KXYZ.

         A   B   C   D

From Grammar to Writing

Parallelism

▼

1.

Parallelism (also called parallel structure) is an important feature of English that makes our speaking, and especially our writing, easier to understand. To make speech or writing parallel, put all items in a series in the same grammatical form.

Over the weekend I **bought a new car, painted the living room,** and **planted a garden.** (All three verbs in the predicate are in the simple past and in the active voice.)

The prisoner **was arrested, was taken** to the police station, and **was booked and fingerprinted.** (All three verb phrases are in the passive voice.)

My favorite hobbies are **skindiving, reading,** and **playing the guitar.** (All three subject complements are gerunds or gerund phrases.)

Children in this program are not allowed **to watch television** or **to eat junk food.** (The two complements are infinitive phrases.)

We will concentrate in this unit on parallelism with nouns and articles and with active or passive voice. See From Grammar to Writing after Part IV, page 160, for a discussion of parallelism with gerunds and infinitives.

2.

In writing sentences which contain a series of nouns and articles, you can place the article before each noun or before the first noun only. However, it is more common to place the article before each noun.

On her shopping trip, Mrs. Figueroa bought **a** book, **a** dress, and **a** CD.

OR

On her shopping trip, Mrs. Figueroa bought **a** book, dress, and CD.

NOT

~~On her shopping trip, Mrs. Figueroa bought a book, dress, and a CD.~~

A. *Read the following paragraph and correct the five errors in parallel structure with nouns and articles.*

Rolleen Laing poured herself a second cup of coffee as she ate her breakfast, which consisted of a fried egg, *an* orange, and a piece of dry toast. She was sixty-two years old and had been successful as a university professor, writer of detective fiction, and an amateur detective. Just then the telephone rang. It was Harry Sadler, a local police detective. Ever since Rolleen had helped Harry crack a murder case several years previously, she had been called in as an unofficial consultant on several cases. She had helped Harry solve cases involving a hit-and-run victim, a murdered television executive, and, most recently, koala stolen from the city zoo.

"Hi, Rolleen. This is Harry. You're needed on another case. It's a robbery this time. Some thieves broke into the art museum and stole a Van Gogh, Picasso, Gauguin, and a Matisse. Meet me at the museum at ten, OK?"

3.

In sentences with several items in the passive voice, the auxiliary may be repeated each time or used before the first item only. Both styles are equally common.

The prisoner **was arrested, was tried,** and **was found innocent.**

OR

The prisoner **was arrested, tried,** and **found innocent.**

NOT

~~The prisoner was arrested, tried, and was found innocent.~~

Notice the following nonparallel sentence with two phrases with the passive voice and one with the active.

The evidence was taken to the crime lab, a team of biochemists analyzed it, and used in a criminal trial.

To put this sentence in parallel structure, change the middle item to the passive voice, eliminating the word *it*.

The evidence **was taken** to the crime lab, **analyzed by a team of biochemists,** and **used** in a criminal trial.

B. *Each of the following sentences contains an error in parallelism involving active or passive voice. In each case, one item is nonparallel with the others. Correct the nonparallel item.*

1. The crop circles in the English countryside have been photographed, written about, and ~~have been~~ scientifically analyzed.
2. According to historical records, Billy the Kid was hunted, killed in a gunfight, and was buried.
3. Anthropologists speculate that the Anasazi might have been attacked by unfriendly tribes, decimated by crop failures, or drought might have driven them away.
4. After Amelia Earhart's airplane was lost, naval investigators searched for debris, interviewed residents of South Pacific islands, but no trace of Earhart and Noonan was found.
5. According to legend, the continent of Atlantis was struck by devastating earthquakes, inundated by floods, and the ocean swallowed it up.

C. *Read the following paragraph about the Judge Crater mystery. Correct the three errors in parallelism with active or passive voice.*

On the evening of August 6, 1930, Judge Force Crater, a wealthy, successful, and good-looking New York lawyer, disappeared without a trace. Earlier in the evening he had been seen with friends at a Manhattan restaurant. At 9:10 P.M. he left the restaurant, hailed a taxi, and ~~was driven~~ *drove* away. No one ever saw or heard from him again. It was ten days before he was even reported missing. On August 16, his wife called his courthouse, the secretary was asked about his whereabouts, and learned that he was probably off on political business. This news reassured Mrs. Crater somewhat, but when he still hadn't turned up by August 26, a group of his fellow judges started an investigation. A grand jury was convened, but its members could not come to any conclusion as to what had happened to Judge Crater. They theorized that the judge might have developed amnesia, run away voluntarily, or been a crime victim. His wife disagreed with the first two theories, holding that he had been murdered by someone in the Tammany Hall organization, the political machine that controlled New York City at the time. The mystery remains unsolved to this day. He could have been killed by a Tammany Hall hiree, a girlfriend could have murdered him, or kidnapped by an organized crime group. He might in fact have suffered from amnesia, or he might have planned his own disappearance. Reports of his whereabouts have continued to surface over the last sixty years.

Adapted from E. Randall Floyd, *Great American Mysteries* (Little Rock: August House Publishers, Inc., 1990).

IV

▼

Gerunds and Infinitives

INTRODUCTION

Brenda Matthews, an anthropologist and family counselor, recently completed a series of lectures on dealing with the challenges of modern life. Read and listen to this excerpt from one of her speeches.

Questions to consider

1. Do you think a fast pace of life is negative, that it causes stress? Or is it merely an unavoidable characteristic of modern life?
2. What aspects of modern life are governed by our watching the time and keeping to schedules?

I want to begin this evening by **asking** all of you: How many of you live your life by the clock? Are you guilty of any or all of the following: **Speeding? Skipping** a meal? **Frequenting** fast-food restaurants? **Ordering** meals over the phone? **Getting** angry in a traffic jam? **Honking** your horn if that terrible person in the car ahead of you waits more than two seconds to resume **driving** when the light changes to green? **Becoming** impatient if some idiot in the supermarket is moving his cart too slowly? **Dividing up** your day into small blocks, like half hours or even quarter hours? **Carrying around** a daily planner in which you've got everything scheduled, including parties and entertainment, for the next several weeks?

I, too, used to be guilty of **overscheduling** my life and **charging** through everything I did, but fortunately I saw the light. My **having changed** my basic relationship with time is probably the best thing I ever did. I'm an anthropologist, and about six years ago I did some field work on group relationships among the Navajo people in Arizona and New Mexico. My work included **spending** time with Navajo elders, **observing** their activities, and **recording** many of the things they said. One thing I learned very quickly was that the notion of **hurrying** is basically foreign to the Navajo.

I was assigned to an elderly man named Mr. Begay. I would spend my days with him and watch what he did. I loved **being allowed** to participate in Navajo culture, but at first I was irritated by Mr. Begay's **taking** so long to do things, and I'm sure he was amused at my **becoming** so impatient with him. Gradually, though, I started **slowing down** and **entering** into the Navajo lifestyle. For many Navajos, **starting** and **finishing** things at prescribed times is basically alien. **Accomplishing** something takes as long as it takes. Eventually I started **looking** at things in a new way, and today I'd say that my **having been given** this opportunity to see how another culture deals with time probably taught me more than any other single thing.

I remember **going** to pueblo dances later on and **being amused** by tourists who were impatient for the dancing to begin. I'd hear irritated voices saying things like, "When are they going to start the dance? It was supposed to start at 11:30. If they don't hurry, we're going to miss our lunch reservation."

But at those pueblo dances, Native Americans start **dancing** when they're ready to start. Things take as long as they take. Now it wouldn't be a bad idea if we in the mainstream culture gave some thought to **adopting** part of that lifestyle. Too many of us want everything to be instantaneous: fast food, micro-wavable meals, instant money from automatic tellers, instant credit. When things don't go according to schedule, we feel stress, and stress can kill us. And it keeps us from **enjoying** things as we experience them.

OK. Now let's take a break—a leisurely break. When we come back, I'll give you some suggestions for **slowing** things **down.**

GERUNDS

GRAMMATICAL FUNCTIONS:

GERUND AS SUBJECT

Living life in the fast lane is unhealthy.

GERUND AS OBJECT

Americans like **eating** in fast-food restaurants.
Many people are guilty of **overscheduling** their lives.
Native Americans give **dancing** an important place in their culture.

GERUND AS SUBJECT COMPLEMENT

My favorite activity is **dancing**.

FORMS:

VERB + GERUND

	VERB	GERUND
The phone rang before I	**finished**	**eating.**

PERFECT FORM

My **having slowed down** my life is the best thing I ever did.

PASSIVE FORM

Being given the opportunity to participate in another culture taught her more than any other experience.

Grammar Notes

1. A gerund (also called a verbal noun) is derived from a verb by adding *-ing* to the base form of the verb (and making any necessary spelling changes). Gerunds perform the same functions as nouns do: They act as subjects, direct and indirect objects, and objects of prepositions.

   subject
   Dancing is healthful.
   direct object
   Many people love **skiing.**
   indirect object
   Inconsiderate skiers give **skiing** a bad name.
   object of preposition
   The French are accustomed to **eating** their salad after their main course.

   Gerunds also function as subject complements. A subject complement is a word or phrase which refers to the same person, place, or thing as the subject and further identifies or describes it.

   subject complement
   My favorite activity is **dancing.**

   See Appendix 17 on page A21 for spelling rules.

2. Gerunds can be used in perfect form (*having* + past participle). This form suggests the past in relation to some other time.

   You might remember **having seen** or **heard** about that TV program. (You heard about the program before now.)
   I remembered **having met** her before. (I had met her before then.)

3. Gerunds can occur in passive form with *being* or *getting* + past participle or *having been* or *gotten* + past participle.

   I enjoyed **being allowed** to participate in Navajo culture.
   Most of us hate **getting cheated** by unscrupulous salespersons.

   Having been selected to do research on Native American culture pleased me immensely.

4. Use a possessive noun or pronoun, not a regular noun or an object pronoun, before a gerund.

   possessive pronoun
   Mr. Begay was amused at **my** getting annoyed with him.
   possessive noun
   At first I was irritated by **Mr. Begay's** taking so long to do things.

   Usage note: In informal conversation and writing, native speakers often use a regular noun or an object pronoun (instead of a possessive) before a gerund or gerund phrase.

   object pronoun
   She objects to **me** smoking.
   noun
   We enjoyed **Jennifer** taking the time to visit us.

5. Be careful! Do not confuse gerunds with verbs in the progressive form or with present participles.

   progressive
   Mr. Ramos was **singing** in the shower.

   present participle used as an adjective
   His singing was **annoying.**

   present participles used in an adverbial phrase
   Sitting and **doing** nothing, Jack took stock of his life.

   See Unit 15 for a discussion of adverbial phrases.

6. Remember that some verbs are followed only by gerunds or infinitives. Others are followed by either gerunds or infinitives. See Appendices 10, 11, and 12 on pages A17, A18, and A19, for listings of all these categories.

FOCUSED PRACTICE

1. Discover the Grammar

Read the next part of Brenda Matthews's TV show "Slow Down!" Circle all gerunds or gerund phrases. Consider a possessive part of a gerund phrase. Do not circle present participles or verbs in the progressive form.

OK, folks, we're back. Now for some suggestions on improving the quality of your life by slowing it down. I'm going to be describing some hypothetical situations and giving you a recommendation for each one. Now let's talk first about driving. You're on your way to work, and you're running late. As you approach an intersection, you see that the light is turning yellow. Adrenaline starts coursing through your system, and you feel the churning of your stomach and the tightening of your muscles. Stop! Instead of speeding up and charging through the intersection, force yourself to slow down. Count to twenty and breathe deeply. Let your neck muscles relax. Say to yourself, I will not hurry. Miss the light. Having missed the light, ask yourself, Why does it matter? Now concentrate on being in the moment and enjoying that moment. How much time would you have saved by barreling through that intersection, anyway? Thirty or forty seconds?

2. All Work and No Play

Brian Hansen is constantly tired and isn't satisfied with his life. He has gone to a doctor to see if there is anything physically wrong with him. Fill in the blanks in the conversation with gerunds or gerund phrases. Use a possessive before a gerund where indicated.

Doctor: Well, Brian, what seems to be the problem?

Brian: Well, it's the rat race, I guess. I feel like I'm on a treadmill. Some nights when I come home from

work I'm so exhausted I don't feel like _____ *doing* _____ anything but

1. (do)

_____ on the sofa and _____ in front of the TV. Is there

2. (collapse) 3. (vegetate)

anything physically wrong with me?

Doctor: No, I've looked at the test results, and you're healthy. How long have you been feeling like this?

Brian: Oh, two or three months, I guess. Long enough so that I've started _____ about

4. (worry)

_____ any energy. Basically I'm not doing anything besides

5. (I / never / have)

_____ a time clock.

6. (punch)

Doctor: How much are you working?

Brian: Well, I'm putting in a lot of overtime—all in all at least sixty hours a week, I'd say.

Doctor: Why are you doing this? Are you trying to kill yourself?

Brian: Well, _____ overtime gives me the chance to pay off my bills. The other thing is
7. (work)

that I only recently moved here, and I hardly know anyone, so I figured I'd concentrate on

_____ money for a while. I like _____, but I don't know quite
8. (make)   9. (socialize)

how to go about _____ new people.
10. (meet)

Doctor: You're not married, then?

Brian: No, I'm not.

Doctor: Well, _____ bills is one thing, but _____ yourself is another. I
11. (pay off)   12. (kill)

think you need to stop _____ so much and start _____ a
13. (work)   14. (play)

little—to put things in balance. Have you considered _____ a singles group?
15. (join)

There are lots of them around.

Brian: Well, I've actually thought about _____ that, but I just haven't gotten around to it.
16. (do)

Doctor: I'd recommend _____ one out. A very good friend of mine was depressed and
17. (you / try)

unhappy until several months ago. She joined a group and has been having a lot of fun. In fact, I think

_____ that group is the best thing she's done in a long time.
18. (she / join)

Brian: What kinds of things do they do?

Doctor: Oh, I think they do a lot of _____, _____,
19. (dance)   20. (play cards)

_____ to the theater and movies—that sort of thing. Her name is Jane Travanti.
21. (go)

I'll give you her number. You can call her and find out about _____ a member.
22. (become)

Forgive me for _____ so, but all work and no play makes Brian a dull boy.
23. (say)

Brian: OK, thanks a lot. I guess I needed to hear that.

3. Wisdom Proverbs

Test your knowledge of proverbs. Match the following English-language proverbs with their definitions. Use gerunds to complete the definitions. How many of the proverbs do you agree with?

_____ 1. Haste makes waste.

_____ 2. A stitch in time saves nine.

_____ 3. A bird in the hand is worth two in the bush.

_____ 4. Pride goeth before a fall.

_____ 5. All that glitters is not gold.

_____ 6. Don't count your chickens before they're hatched.

_____ 7. Absence makes the heart grow fonder.

_____ 8. A fool and his money are soon parted.

a. _____ apart from someone makes
   (Be)
   you like that person better.

b. ____Doing____ things too hastily can lead to
   (Do)
   trouble.

c. _____ you have something before
   (Assume)
   you actually have it is dangerous.

d. _____ in a proud manner often
   (Act)
   leads to failure.

e. _____ the time to do something
   (Take)
   right the first time will save a lot of time later.

f. _____ your money too quickly is
   (Spend)
   foolish.

g. Beware of _____ things that shine
   (pursue)
   or glow. They may not be what you expect.

h. _____ satisfied with one thing
   (Be)
   that you already have is better than

   _____ two things that you might
   (pursue)
   not be able to catch.

4. Good or Bad Timing?

Read the following article, which recently appeared in Pocket Digest, *about historical situations of fortunate and unfortunate moments of action. Fill in the blanks with gerund phrases containing a possessive and* **having** *+ past participle.*

TIMING *Is Everything*

Is there such a thing as good or bad timing—a moment in time when events and currents combine fortuitously or unfortuitously to cause major changes? Apparently there are such moments, though of course the labels "good" and "bad" depend heavily on one's viewpoint.

On August 3, 1492, for example, Christopher Columbus set sail for what would later become known as the New World. __His having persuaded__ the Spanish
1. (He / persuade)
monarchs, King Ferdinand and Queen Isabella, to sponsor his voyage at a moment when they were disposed to help him is a classic example of historical good timing—from the European viewpoint, that is.

Another example of good timing occurred on March 30, 1867, when the United States purchased Alaska from Russia for $7.2 million as a result of the efforts of U.S. Secretary of State William H. Seward.

_____ the potential worth of
2. (Seward / perceive)
Alaska later disproved the criticisms of his detractors, who called the territory "Seward's Icebox" and the purchase "Seward's Folly."

A momentous example of good timing occurred on December 5, 1955, in Montgomery, Alabama, when Rosa Parks, a black woman, refused to give up her seat and move to the back of a city bus out of deference to white people. The U.S. Supreme

_____ school segregation a
3. (Court / outlaw)

year and a half previously had set the stage for the event.

_____ in advance not to give
4. (Parks / decide)
up her seat and _____ her
5. (she / carry out)
plan in a resolute manner set in motion the Montgomery Bus Boycott, a movement that brought to prominence the pastor of Parks's church, Martin Luther King, Jr., and immeasurably affected the U.S. civil rights movement.

_____ to make a political
6. (John F. Kennedy / agree)
trip to Dallas, Texas, on November 22, 1963, the day of his assassination, is a tragic example of bad timing, especially in light of _____ by several
7. (he / be / warned)
advisors not to go to Dallas at that time.

Another example of bad timing occurred in 1968 in Prague, when the brief experiment with the democratization of the Communist regime in Czechoslovakia ended with Warsaw Pact forces invading the country and quashing the hopes of the reformers.

_____ the resolve of the
8. (They / misjudge)
Soviets apparently paved the way for the invasion. In November 1989, however, amidst the tide of revolt that was sweeping Eastern Europe,

_____ new elections led
9. (protestors / seize the moment / and / demand)
to the resignation of the Communist leadership and to the end of communism in Czechoslovakia. Their timing was certainly right the second time around.

5. Editing

There are nineteen missing gerunds and two missing possessives in this letter from a visitor to a dude ranch in New Mexico. Find and correct them.

Dear Adam,

I've been here for three days and am having a great time, but I
               wishing
can't help ~~with~~ you were here too. Tell your boss I'm really angry at
him. He not let you take any vacation time qualifies him for the
Jerk-of-the-Year Award. (Just kidding. Don't say that!)

Believe it or not, the first night I missed hear all the city noises,
but I haven't really had any trouble get used to the peace and quiet
since then. It's all so relaxed here—there's no rush around or write
things down in your daily planner. Get out of New York City was
definitely what I needed, even if it's only for two weeks. The ranch
has lots of activities for the guests—horseback ride, river raft on the
Rio Grande, hike in the wilderness—you name it. The ranch
employees do everything for you here—get taken care of is nice, for
a change, and I love be chauffeured around Santa Fe in the ranch
limousine.

Tonight a bunch of us are going to do some country western dance
at a place called Rodeo Nites in Santa Fe, so I have taken those
Texas Two-Step lessons last summer will come in handy. It's just too
bad you couldn't come along so we could both do some kick up our
heels. Tomorrow we're all going to Taos Pueblo to watch some weave
being done and to see some Native American dance, which is great
because I'm really interested in learn more about Native American
culture. And I'm looking forward to see The Magic Flute at the
Santa Fe Opera on Saturday.

I'll write again in a day or two. Miss you lots.

Love,
Louise

COMMUNICATION PRACTICE

6. Practice Listening

Brian Hansen and Jane Travanti are having a telephone conversation. Brian is asking Jane about the singles group she belongs to. Listen to the conversation. Then listen again and mark the following statements true, false, or I don't know, based on what you heard about the group.

	True	False	I Don't Know
1. Brian is looking for a singles group to join.	✔	☐	☐
2. The club has about fifteen activities a month.	☐	☐	☐
3. Brian likes playing cards.	☐	☐	☐
4. Everybody in the group goes to the movies every month.	☐	☐	☐
5. Dr. Stephanopoulos says Brian is addicted to making money.	☐	☐	☐
6. Dr. Stephanopoulos wants Brian to stop working.	☐	☐	☐
7. People in the club are interesting.	☐	☐	☐
8. The club suggests attending three events before joining.	☐	☐	☐
9. The members of the club date each other.	☐	☐	☐
10. The club's purpose is matchmaking.	☐	☐	☐

7. Tape Discussion

What are some ways to meet new friends in a new place?

8. Role Play in Pairs

Work with a partner. Role-play one of the following situations. Then reverse the roles and play the situation again.

1. A student is ten minutes late to class. The teacher is angry. They are discussing the problem.
   Example:
   Teacher: You're late again, Kate. **Being** late hurts your grade—you know that.
   Student: I'm sorry, Mr. Adams. I had a good reason.
   Teacher: OK, what's your reason? I hope it's a good one. I'm tired of **hearing** excuses.
   Student: I got caught in a traffic jam on the way to class. . . .

2. Employees in a company are allowed a fifteen-minute break in the morning and one in the afternoon. An employee is fifteen minutes late returning from the break. The boss and the employee are discussing the lateness.

(continued on next page)

3. A parent wants to start having family meals together. A teenager insists that his or her schedule prevents that. They are discussing the issue.

4. A police officer has arrested a driver for speeding. The driver feels there was a good reason for speeding. They are discussing the problem.

9. Small Group Discussion

Divide into small groups. Discuss one or more of the following pairs of proverbs. Each pair contains two statements with somewhat opposing meanings. First talk about what the proverbs mean. Give an example of each proverb. Then discuss the extent to which you believe in it.

1. Haste makes waste. vs. Strike while the iron is hot.
   Example:
   A: "Haste makes waste" means that **trying to do** things too quickly can lead to trouble. For example, I did some grocery **shopping** yesterday, and when I got home I was really in a hurry to get the groceries unloaded. I tried to carry too many things at once and dropped one whole bag. All the food in that bag got smashed.
   B: "Strike while the iron is hot" means that **knowing** when to do something and **acting** fast can lead to success. . . .

2. Absence makes the heart grow fonder. vs. Out of sight, out of mind.

3. Pride goeth before a fall. vs. You've got to toot your own horn because nobody else is going to do it for you.

4. A stitch in time saves nine. vs. He who hesitates is lost.

10. Essay

Are you satisfied with the pace of your life, or do you think you need to slow down? Are you trying to do too many things? Write an essay of three or four paragraphs on your relationship with time. Explain your viewpoint.

11. Picture Discussion

Look at this picture for several minutes. What feelings does it convey to you? Then form small groups. Imagine what circumstances led to this scene and what will happen next. Each group will create its own story about the picture.

Example:
She's afraid of **crossing** the bridge.

Edvard Munch: *The Scream*. Woodcut.
Foto Marburg/Art Resource, NY

INTRODUCTION

◧ *Read and listen to the story and think about the questions.*

Questions to Consider

1. What are the dangers of procrastination?
2. Do you ever put things off until it is too late?

I Meant to Call...

The clock radio boomed on at 8:30 and jarred Carolyn Reynolds awake. It was a Saturday morning, and as Carolyn rolled over she caught a glimpse of heavy thunderheads in the sky outside the window. It looked like it was going **to be** another one of those rainy, sleepy days. Even though it was Saturday, she needed **to go** to work later, and she'd arranged **for** the office **to be opened** by one of the security people so that she could use the computer **to work** on that awful annual report. The report was supposed **to have been completed** and **left** on her supervisor's desk three days ago. Carolyn sighed and snuggled back down under the covers. **To sleep** for just a few more minutes wouldn't hurt, would it?

When Carolyn woke up the second time, the clock read 10:35. She'd better get rolling if she was going **to get** anything done today. She went into the kitchen and put a cup of coffee in the microwave **to heat up.**

She glanced at two pieces of mail that had been lying on the counter for more than a week now. One was a postcard from her veterinarian reminding her that Omar, her pet cat, was **to have been given** his distemper and feline leukemia shot a month ago. The other piece of mail was a letter from her mother, who lived in a nursing home in a town thirty miles away. The letter was actually three weeks old; Carolyn hadn't spoken to her mother recently, and she was sure her mother expected her **to have written** or **called** by now, though of course she hadn't said anything about it. She really should give her mother a call, though—perhaps when she came back from work tonight. She sat down at the dining room table and glanced at the newspaper while she drank her coffee and ate a doughnut. Omar jumped up into her lap, but she pushed him off, annoyed. "Not now, Omar—I don't feel like holding you right now."

147

When Carolyn arrived home at 6:30 that evening, she was drained and irritable. The message light on her answering machine was blinking, but Carolyn thought she'd wait until later **to listen** to the messages. Feeling too tired **to cook** a regular meal, Carolyn called and ordered some Chinese food **to be delivered.**

The next day was Sunday. Carolyn got up at nine feeling refreshed and spent a leisurely hour reading the Sunday paper. She'd arranged **to meet** her friend Hal for brunch at a new restaurant that was rumored **to have** excellent omelets.

* * *

The brunch was delicious, and Carolyn enjoyed Hal's company. She felt good, so she decided **to stop** at a nearby shopping mall **to get** her mother a birthday present. Her mother's seventy-fifth birthday had actually occurred a month previously, but they had agreed that it wasn't important **to celebrate** the precise day; the important thing was the thought, no matter when the gift came. Carolyn had said, "Mom, I want **to get** you the right thing, something really nice. I don't want **to be rushed** into it." Her mother had agreed, saying, "Of course, honey. I'm long past the age when I expect **to be fussed over** for a silly birthday or **be given** a birthday party."

When Carolyn walked into her apartment, she noticed that the red phone message light was still blinking, and she realized that she had forgotten **to listen** to her messages the evening before. She pressed the play button and heard the first message:

Hi, honey, this is Mom. I just wanted **to tell** you that I'm going into the hospital for a couple of days. I just haven't been feeling well these last two weeks or so, and the doctor thinks I need **to have** some tests. Maybe you could give me a call later if you have time. My number at the hospital is 688-9294.

The machine beeped, and then the second message came on.

Carolyn, this is Doctor Stephenson at Parkland General Hospital. Please give me a call right away at 688-9299.

Carolyn's heart was racing now, and she quickly dialed the number. The phone was answered by an aide, and it took several minutes **for** Dr. Stephenson **to be tracked down.** Finally she heard his voice on the other end: "This is Mark Stephenson."

"Hello, Dr. Stephenson. This is Carolyn Reynolds. I got a message on my machine this morning from my mother. She said she was going to the hospital. Then I got your message. Is everything OK? She's all right, isn't she?"

"Ms. Reynolds, I'm sorry **to have to be** the one to tell you this, but I have some very sad news. Your mother passed away this morning at 11:15."

INFINITIVES

GRAMMATICAL FUNCTIONS:

INFINITIVE AS SUBJECT

> **To live** a long and healthy life is my ideal.

INFINITIVE AS OBJECT

> I don't want **to do** anything that might hurt you.

INFINITIVE AS SUBJECT OR ADJECTIVE COMPLEMENT

> Her idea was **to get** to the hospital before it closed.

> She was anxious **to hear** about her mother.

FORMS AND USES:

VERB + INFINITIVE

	VERB	**INFINITIVE**	
Carolyn	**expected**	**to go**	to the office.

VERB + OBJECT + INFINITIVE

	VERB	**OBJECT**	**INFINITIVE**	
Why didn't her superiors	**ask**	**her**	**to do**	anything creative?

PERFECT FORM

> A nursing home in the vicinity was reported **to have set up** an excellent new care and treatment plan.

PASSIVE FORM

> She had passed the age when she expected **to be fussed over** on her birthday.

INFINITIVE OF PURPOSE

> The doctor's office was always sending out notices **to get** patients to make appointments.

ELLIPSIS OF FULL INFINITIVE

> I haven't read that book yet, but I'm planning **to.**

Grammar Notes

1. An infinitive is *to* plus the base form of a verb. Infinitives and infinitive phrases often substitute for nouns, performing the same functions that regular nouns do: They act as subjects, objects, and complements.

> subject
> **To sleep** a few minutes longer wouldn't hurt anything.

> direct object
> Carolyn expected **to go** to the office.

> subject complement
> His job was **to help** the other employees.

> adjective complement
> Carolyn was eager **to try** the new restaurant.

2. Remember that certain verbs are followed only by infinitives, some only by gerunds, and some by either infinitives or gerunds. Some verbs are followed directly by the infinitive, and some are followed by an object and the infinitive. Certain adjectives are followed by the infinitive. See Appendices 10, 11, 12, and 13 for listings of all these categories.

3. An infinitive of purpose explains the purpose of an action. It often answers the question "why?"

> The doctor's office was always sending out notices **to get** patients to make appointments.

An infinitive of purpose can also be stated in the longer form *in order to*. This form, however, is more formal and less common in speech and informal writing than *to* plus the base form.

> The doctor's office was always sending out notices **in order to get** patients to make appointments.

Use *in order not to* to express a negative purpose.

> She wrote a reminder to herself **in order not to forget** to call.

A negative purpose can also be expressed without *in order*.

> She wrote things down **not to forget** them.

Be careful! Never use *for* directly before an infinitive of purpose.

> Carolyn intended to leave that afternoon **to see** her mother. NOT ~~Carolyn intended to leave that afternoon **for to see** her mother.~~

4. Infinitives can be used in perfect form (*to* + *have* + past participle). This form suggests the past in relation to some other time.

> He seems **to have left.** (He left before now.)
> He seemed **to have left.** (He had left before then.)

5. Infinitives can occur in passive form (*to* + *be* or *get* + past participle).

> We expect **to be paid** by Friday. (Someone will pay us.)
> This letter seems **to have been opened** already. (Someone opened it.)

6. When verb + infinitive constructions refer to a verb mentioned earlier, it is not necessary to repeat the base form of the preceding verb. The *to* alone is sufficient and is understood to stand for the earlier verb. This process is called <u>ellipsis</u>.

> A: Have you written your essay yet?
> B: No, but I'm planning **to** this evening. (= planning to write it)

Ellipsis is also made with the *to* of the modal-like expressions *have to, have got to, had to, ought to, be supposed to, be about to*, and *be able to* and with the future with *be going to*.

> A: Are you leaving right now?
> B: No, but we're going **to** in a few minutes. We have **to.** (= going to leave and have to leave)

7. Usage note: Some native speakers of English object to splitting an infinitive—inserting modifying words between *to* and the verb that follows. However, split infinitives are common in English speaking and writing, even in relatively formal writing.

> It takes courage **to boldly go** where no one has gone before.

The general rule in formal written English is to avoid splitting an infinitive unnecessarily, especially if the modifier that is inserted consists of more than one word.

> The officers were ordered by the lieutenant **to** as quickly as possible **recapture** the escaped prisoner. (awkward sentence)
> The officers were ordered by the lieutenant **to recapture** the escaped prisoner as quickly as possible. (corrected sentence)

Be careful! Avoid splitting an infinitive with *not* or *never*.

> I asked you not (never) to do that. NOT ~~I asked you to not or never do that.~~

FOCUSED PRACTICE

1. Discover the Grammar

Listen to the on-the-spot news coverage of the collapse of a bridge. Then listen again and circle all infinitives and infinitive phrases, including the word **to** *if it represents the ellipsis of a preceding verb.*

Good afternoon. I'm Jan Arthur with live minicam coverage of the collapse of the Inland Causeway Floating Bridge. As we have been reporting, damage to the structure caused by gale-force winds prompted the highway department to close the bridge early this morning; fortunately, no one was on the structure when it collapsed and sank.

    The one-mile bridge spanned the Inland Waterway and was built in 1954 to handle increasing traffic between Centerville and the peninsula. As population grew, traffic increased much more rapidly than highway planners had expected it to, and a year and a half ago engineers determined that the bridge needed to be structurally reinforced and repaired. County officials asked voters to approve a bond issue to finance the repairs, which they did, and the bridge was scheduled to be closed for a six-month period for this renovation to be done.

    According to the original schedule, the renovation was to have been completed by February of this year. Unfortunately, disagreement and haggling between the state highway department and the governor's office forced the project to be delayed; no actual work had yet been started. In an angry statement to the press, the chief engineer of the state blasted the governor, saying, "To ask for additional time for safety's sake is one thing, but to let petty jealousies and inertia get in the way of completing this

(continued on next page)

renovation is criminal. This is a case of sheer procrastination and stonewalling and nothing more." There has been no response from the governor's office.

Meanwhile, motorists and onlookers are urged not to travel on any of the roads near the disaster area. To get regular updates on highway conditions, call 724-1919. Station WKSK will interrupt regular programming to bring you breaking developments.

2. Philosophical Infinitives

Read the following paraphrases of certain philosophical sayings or quotations.
Then match them with the sayings, filling in the blanks with infinitive structures.

_____ 1. Life and death is the fundamental question.

_____ 2. Loving someone and losing that person is better than never having loved anyone.

_____ 3. A risky life in which you uphold your honor is superior to a safe life in which you give up your will.

_____ 4. Making a mistake is a normal human thing, but forgiving another's mistake is heavenly.

_____ 5. The journey is more important than the destination.

_____ 6. Doing one small thing positively is better than complaining about the unfairness of life.

a. It is better _____ on your feet
(die)
than _____ on your knees.
(live)
(attributed to Emiliano Zapata)

b. It is better _____ one candle
(light)
than _____ the darkness.
(curse)
(the motto of the Christophers)

c. ____To be____, or ___not to be___:
(be)　　　　　　(not be)
that is the question. (Shakespeare)

d. It is better _____ than
(seek)
_____ .
(find)

e. _____ is human,
(err)
_____ divine.
(forgive)

f. It is better _____
(have + *past participle of love and lose*)
than _____ at all.
(never have + *past participle of love*)
(English poet Alfred, Lord Tennyson)

3. Seize the Day

Writer Jessica Taylor has again interviewed neurophysiologist Robert Stevens for an article in Pocket Digest *magazine. Read this excerpt from her interview about the basis of procrastination. Complete the blanks in the conversation by supplying active or passive infinitive structures of the indicated verbs. Supply the correct object pronoun where necessary.*

Pocket Digest: Dr. Stevens, the last time we talked, you spoke about the expectation syndrome. This time I wanted ___to ask___ you if there's such a thing as a
1. (ask)
procrastination syndrome.

Stevens: Well, I don't know if we could go so far as to call it a syndrome, but for many people procrastination is a very serious problem.

Pocket Digest: Yes, that certainly seems _____
2. (be)
the case for a lot of individuals. What causes

_____ , anyway? Laziness?
3. (they / procrastinate)

Stevens: That's a popular notion, but I'd have to say that laziness is a relatively minor cause at best. No, I think that fear is really the most important force that motivates people _____
4. (put off)
doing something until later.

Pocket Digest: Fear? Not laziness? You'll have to explain that to me a little bit.

Stevens: Well, it's actually somewhat related to the expectation syndrome. A lot of people feel they have to live up to other people's expectations. They're afraid _____ . Many times
5. (fail)
they fear they won't be able to do something perfectly or well. They're afraid _____
6. (make)
mistakes, or maybe they don't want _____
7. (reject / passive)
or _____ no. They let fear
8. (tell, passive)
take control of them, and they put off any action.

Pocket Digest: What would be an example of that?

Stevens: Well, suppose someone wants _____
9. (invite)
people to a party—let's say it's a young woman named Blanche. She's never been very good at these kinds of things, and she expects, either consciously or

unconsciously, _____ , so she
10. (turn down, *passive*)
delays calling people until the very last moment. The party is going to take place at such short notice that few people are likely to be able to accept the invitation. And that's what happens. Hardly anyone can come. In an ironic way, Blanche's fear has caused things _____ like this.
11. (turn out)

Pocket Digest: Uh-huh. Well, what if someone is a procrastinator and wants _____ ?
12. (change)
What would you advise that person _____ ?
13. (do)

Stevens: Well, there are three principles I try _____
14. (adhere)
to. The first is _____ until
15. (never put off)
tomorrow what needs _____
16. (do, *passive*)
today. The second comes from Eastern philosophy, and that's _____ the
17. (not resist)
needle—in other words, don't try _____
18. (avoid)
pain or painful things. The third comes from Western philosophy and is summed up in the Latin phrase *carpe diem*: Seize the day. Consider everything that comes before you an opportunity. If it seems like a good and proper thing _____ , do it, regardless
19. (do)
of whether it's going to provide pain or pleasure. Don't even think about whether it causes you fear or not. You've heard the phrase "Just do it"? It's generally good advice. I'm not advising people _____
20. (take)
unnecessary or foolish risks, but I am urging _____

_____ living. They may not get
21. (they / not put off)
another chance.

Pocket Digest: Well, Dr. Stevens, thanks for another stimulating discussion.

4. On the Loose

A dangerous fugitive has escaped from prison. Read this transcript of the police bulletin and fill in the blanks with the infinitive structures indicated.

Official Transcript

Here is a bulletin from the Mason County Sheriff's Office. Death row prisoner Charles Gallagher

__is reported to have escaped__
1. (be / report / have / escape)

from the maximum security facility at Grandview. Gallagher and two other prisoners

_____ out
2. (be / think / have / be / smuggle)

of the prison in a laundry truck. Prison authorities are noncommittal as to how the break could have taken place, but according to usually reliable sources, the three men

_____ in
3. (be / believe / have / be / aid)

their escape by a confidant within the prison.

Ironically, a new state-of-the-art security system was supposed _____
4. (have / be / install)

two months ago, but because of unexplained delays and apparent bureaucratic problems, it is not yet operative. Listeners should be aware that the three prisoners

_____ and
5. (be / think / be / arm)

_____
6. (be / believe / be)

traveling in the direction of Aberdeen. Listeners

_____
7. (be also / warn / not / approach)

the fugitives and

_____
8. (be / ask / contact)

the Mason County Sheriff's Office or call the toll-free number, 1-800-555-3232, if they have any information.

5. Editing

Bob Jacobs, an inveterate procrastinator, has decided to reform. Read his diary entry. Find and correct the fourteen errors in infinitive structures.

My Diary

April 15

How are you supposed to begin a diary if you've never written one before? I'm tempted ʌsay "Dear Diary."

OK. Dear Diary. For about ten years now I've wanted keep a diary or journal, but my procrastinating tendencies got in the way. From now on I'm reforming. It's a significant date, too—April 15. This year, for the first time in memory, I managed get my tax return done three days in advance! Some little voice in my head warned me to not put if off, so I just sat down and did it. For me, get it done in advance was really an accomplishment.

So what else have I done for to stop procrastinating? For one thing, I finished my annual self-evaluation at work and submitted it. It was supposed to turned in on Friday of last week, but I gave it to the boss on Thursday! The other thing is that I summoned up my courage call Mary talk about our relationship, which hasn't been going anywhere. For the first time, I took the initiative. We went out to dinner and talked about things, and we agreed it would be better not see each other anymore. I feel sad, but maybe there's some truth in that saying, "It's better to loved and lost than to never have loved at all." I've started feel better.

OK, Diary, that's all for today, but I swear keep writing every day.

COMMUNICATION PRACTICE

6. Practice Listening

■● *Kenny Anaya is a junior in high school and has difficulty getting his work done. Listen to the conversation on tape between Kenny and his mother.*

Now listen to certain of the sentences again. Circle the letter of the choice that correctly explains the meaning of each sentence you hear.

1. a. Kenny hopes Mom will be able to write his paper for him.
   b. Kenny hopes Mom will be able to type his paper for him.

2. a. Mom won't have time to type the paper.
   b. Mom won't have time to go to the party.

3. a. Kenny thinks Mom should turn in the paper.
   b. Kenny thinks Mom should type the paper.

4. a. Kenny promises to get his work done on time in the future.
   b. Kenny promises to type the paper himself.

5. a. Mom is not going to bail Kenny out of his difficulties.
   b. Mom is not going to attend the party.

6. a. Kenny may need to get a snack.
   b. Kenny may need to stay up all night.

7. Small Group Discussion

Divide into small groups, and look back at exercise 2 on page 152. Examine the six sayings. Discuss the degree to which they are true or false. Illustrate each situation with an example.

Example:
It is better to seek than to find.
   A: I agree that it is better **to seek** than **to find.** In my senior year of high school I wanted **to be** class president. I worked really hard **to win** the office and made a lot of friends. It was a great period. When I won the office, though, I found out that it was no big deal **to be** president. Getting there was more important.
   B: I agree that it's important **to seek** things, but I think it's more important **to find** them. In high school I worked twenty hours a week **to buy** my own car, which was a good experience, but I was much happier **to buy** the car and **to have** it.

8. Essay

All of us have procrastinated at one time or another. Write an essay of from three to five paragraphs about a time when you put off doing something and the results were bad. Speculate about the reasons for your procrastination and discuss the consequences.

9. Picture Discussion

This is a picture of the aftermath of a plane crash into the Potomac River in Washington, D.C., during a cold, snowy winter day. The survivors of the crash desperately tried to stay afloat in the icy waters as passing motorists risked their lives by jumping into the river to save them. As a class, discuss your beliefs about an individual's responsibilities when faced with a situation when other people are in danger. What would you have done if you had been at this scene? How much of a risk would you be willing to take to save someone else's life, especially a person you don't know?

Example:
I would be willing **to try to . . .**

I. *Choose the correct form to complete the conversations.*

1. **A:** What do you want _____to do_____ tonight?
   a. (doing / to do)

   B: I feel like _____ to a movie.
   b. (to go / going)

2. **A:** It's not so bad _____ a white lie, is it?
   c. (telling / to tell)

   B: I don't think _____ is ever right.
   d. (lie / lying)

3. **A:** It isn't wrong _____ yourself, is it?
   e. (to defend / defend)

   B: I think _____ yourself is the right thing to do if
   f. (defend / defending)
   you have a good reason.

4. **A:** How did you end up _____ in forestry?
   g. (to major / majoring)

   B: I've always loved _____ outdoors.
   h. (be / being)

II. *Fill in the blanks in the conversation with possessive + gerund forms.*

Lois Walker: I saw your "Slow Down!" show a few weeks ago, and I

wanted to ask your advice about

_____families' eating meals_____ together. I remember
1. (families / eat meals)

_____ you thought it was a
2. (you / say)
good idea for families to do that.

Brenda Matthews: Yes, I certainly do. Do you have any meals together

now?

Lois: No, we don't. _____ different
3. (Everybody / have)
schedules makes that really difficult.

Brenda: Well, I understand the difficulty, but I'd say that

_____ at least once each day
4. (a family / get together)
is crucial for their relationship. Isn't there one meal

when you could do that?

Lois: Well, possibly, but I know what our teenagers would

say—they'd resent _____ to
5. (we / try)
"control their lives," as they put it.

Brenda: I don't think _____
6. (you / insist on)

_____ once each day is
7. (the family / sit down together)
unreasonable. Just tell the kids this is the way things

are going to be. I'd recommend

_____ a different person to
8. (you / assign)
be responsible for dinner each night—you and your

husband included, of course.

III. *Complete the traffic report with gerund or infinitive forms of the indicated verbs.*

You'll have a hot and heavy commute this afternoon, folks. Interstate 5 is blocked for two miles north and south of 80th Street, so I suggest _____taking_____ an alternate route if possible.
1. (take)

Construction on the Factoria interchange has caused _____ on I-405, so use caution there.
2. (slow)

Repairs on the Evergreen Point Bridge _____ by today, but the bridge is still closed.
3. (expect / have / be / complete)

The Highway Department issued a statement apologizing for _____ further inconvenience
4. (have / cause)

to motorists, but the repairs are taking longer than planned. They are expected _____ by
5. (be / finish)

5:00 A.M. Tuesday. An accident involving an overturned van in the left lane on the 509 freeway isn't

expected _____ for at least half an hour, so avoid the 509 northbound. You can improve
6. (be / clear)

your commute by _____ Highway 99, where traffic is smooth and relatively light. This is
7. (take)

Hank Simmons for KAJK Traffic Watch.

IV. *Complete the conversations, using ellipsis.*

1. **A:** Why didn't Alex and Anna come to the party?

   B: They _____were going to_____, but they got called to the hospital.
   a. (be going)

2. **A:** Wasn't Gabe going to bring hot dogs to the picnic?

   B: He _____, but I don't see any. I don't think he did.
   b. (be supposed)

3. **A:** Are you going to attend the university?

   B: I _____, but I have to earn some money first.
   c. (plan)

4. **A:** Doesn't Amanda know how to cook?

   B: She _____. She's worked in a restaurant for over a year.
   d. (ought)

5. **A:** Why didn't you type my paper? It's due tomorrow!

   B: I _____. I had my own work to do.
   e. (not have time)

6. **A:** Aren't you going to buy that house?

   B: No, I _____, after all. It doesn't have a view.
   f. (not want)

V. *Circle the letter of the correct answer to complete each sentence.*

1. We are in favor of _____ the bridge.   A Ⓑ C D
   A. build
   B. building
   C. to build
   D. having built

2. I asked Juanita _____ the proposal.   **A**   **B**   **C**   **D**
   A. review
   B. reviewing
   C. to review
   D. having reviewed

3. "Mom, can you type my paper?"   **A**   **B**   **C**   **D**
   "I don't have time _____ right now. Maybe later."
   A. to
   B. to do
   C. to doing
   D. to have done

4. _____ my lifestyle is the best thing I ever did.   **A**   **B**   **C**   **D**
   A. My having changed
   B. Having changing
   C. Me having changed
   D. My change

5. You're expected _____ well prepared for a job   **A**   **B**   **C**   **D**
   interview.
   A. be
   B. to be
   C. being
   D. having been

6. "The report was supposed _____ completed by   **A**   **B**   **C**   **D**
   March 1. What happened?"
   A. being
   B. be
   C. have been
   D. to have been

7. The sign warned pedestrians _____ on the grass.   **A**   **B**   **C**   **D**
   A. not walking
   B. not to walk
   C. not walk
   D. not to have walked

8. Ms. Francis was said _____ the article.   **A**   **B**   **C**   **D**
   A. to write
   B. writing
   C. to have written
   D. write

From Grammar to Writing

Parallelism of Gerunds and Infinitives

▼

Remember that in parallel structure all items in a series are in the same grammatical form: singulars with singulars, plurals with plurals, actives with actives, passives with passives, etc. Parallelism makes our speaking and writing more communicative. Mixing gerunds and infinitives in the same series is a common parallelism error.

               gerund   gerund   gerund

My summer hobbies are **hiking, boating,** and **mountain biking.**

                           NOT

               gerund   gerund   infinitive

~~My summer hobbies are hiking, boating, and to go mountain biking.~~
(All of the subject complements in this series should be presented in the same form.)

                                      infinitive

As Pam started college, her goals were **to make** new friends and

    infinitive

to become well educated.

                           NOT

                              infinitive

~~As Pam started college, her goals were to make new friends and~~

    gerund

~~becoming well educated.~~

2

A series of infinitives or infinitive phrases may be presented with the word *to* before each item or before the first item only.

Helen loves **to read, to write,** and **to attend the opera.**

                   OR

Helen loves **to read, write,** and **attend the opera.**

                  NOT

~~Helen loves to read, write, and to attend the opera.~~

Remember that in any series a common element can either be used before each item or before the first item only. See From Grammar to Writing after Part III, on page 132, for a discussion of this feature of parallel structure.

If a sentence is long, it is often best to include the word *to* before each infinitive phrase.

In his sensitivity training, Bob learned **to listen** carefully to other people, **to consider** their feelings, and **to imagine** himself in their situations.

Gerunds or gerund phrases containing a possessive and/or *having* + past participle should also be presented in parallel structure.

I want to thank everyone for making this party a success. I especially appreciate **Sarah's having invited** the guests, **Jack's having cooked** the food, and **Jennifer's having organized** the whole thing.

4.

Similarly, long infinitive phrases should be presented in parallel structure.

> Applicants to the university are expected **to have completed** a
> college preparatory program, **to have graduated** in the upper third
> of their high school class, and **to have participated** in extracurricular
> activities.

A. *Each of the following sentences contains an error in parallelism with gerunds
or gerund phrases. Correct the nonparallel items.*

1. Kenneth loves camping, ~~to~~ collect͏ing stamps, and playing baseball.
2. Lately I've been able to stop speeding in traffic, to schedule too many activities, and rushing through each day like a crazy person.
3. To live a happier life, we should all focus on eating meals together, on airing our problems and concerns, and, in general, on to slow down the pace of our lives.
4. Mr. Matthews's planning the agenda, Ms. Bono renting the hall, and Mrs. Tanaka's arranging for the guest speakers made the conference a success.
5. My life is vastly changed because of my having stopped working so hard, joined a singles group, and having found some interesting new hobbies.

B. *Each of the following sentences contains an error in parallelism with infinitives or infinitive phrases.
Correct the nonparallel items.*

1. On our vacation this year we want to see the Butchart Gardens in Victoria, to camp near Great Slave Lake, and to drive up the Alaska Highway.
2. "[We are] . . . strong in will
   To strive, seek, to find, and not to yield."
   (The conclusion to Alfred, Lord Tennyson's poem "Ulysses")
3. I'm advising you not to sell your property, take out a loan, and not to buy a new house right now.
4. Most presidents want to be reelected to a second term, taken seriously by other world leaders, and to be remembered fondly after they leave office.
5. To be hired in this firm, you are expected to have earned a bachelor's degree and having worked in a bank for at least two years.

C. *Read the following paragraph about speech anxiety. Find and correct the ten
errors in parallelism with gerunds and infinitives.*

What are you most afraid of? Are you worried about being cheated, ~~to lose~~ losing your job, or contracting a deadly disease? Well, if you're like the vast majority of Americans, you fear standing up, to face an audience, and to deliver a speech more than anything else. A recent survey found that anxiety about public speaking terrifies Americans more than dying does. Somehow, people expect to be laughed at, ridiculed, or to be scorned by an audience. Many college students fear public speaking so much that they put off taking a speech class or even to think about it until their last term before graduation. Speech instructors and others familiar with the principles of public speaking stress that the technique of desensitization works best for overcoming speech anxiety. This idea holds that people can get over their fear of speaking in public by enrolling in a course, to attend the class faithfully, and to force themselves to perform the speech activities. Once they have discovered that it is rare for people to die, making fools of themselves, or to be laughed at while making a speech, they're on their way to success. Consequently, their anxiety becomes a little less each time they get up and talk in public. It may take a while, but eventually they find themselves able to stand up willingly, speaking comfortably, and expressing themselves clearly.

Adverbials and Discourse Connectors

INTRODUCTION

📼 *Read and listen to the following interview from* World Review *magazine.*

Questions to Consider

1. What effects does television have on people? Are they positive, negative, or both?
2. Can TV watching cause violence?
3. What other possible causes of violence and crime can you identify?

What Does the Expert Say?

Part I

World Review recently spoke with Dr. Krishna Das, a United Nations expert on crime and violence, particularly as they relate to the structure of families. Here is the first part of the interview.

World Review: Dr. Das, people used to say that violence was just an American problem, but today we see it **wherever we look.** Crime and violence aren't just American problems anymore, are they?

Das: No, not at all. Violence exists nearly everywhere in the world, and it's spreading; it's much more prevalent today **than it was even ten years ago. While it used to be fashionable to say it was strictly an** American problem, that is no longer true, **if it ever was true.**

WR: Why is this happening? What are the causes?

Das: Well, there are many complex causes. One, of course, is the shortage of jobs. **If people are employed in meaningful work activities,** they are much less likely to be involved in crime. Some say the easy availability of guns is another. And there's evidence to suggest that television promotes violence **because there's so much of it on TV** and **because certain people who watch it**—children especially—**apparently can't tell the difference between reality and the situations they see on TV programs.**

WR: Yes, we've heard a lot about the pervasive violence on TV, **although we could say the same thing about movies,** couldn't we? Aren't they just as violent as certain TV shows, if not more so?

Das: Yes, sometimes, but there are some key differences. For one thing, movies have gotten **so expensive that people are seeing fewer of them.** And **since we usually watch television in our own living rooms at home,** it seems like a "normal" rather than a special activity, part of the daily range of things we do. **If we see enough violent acts on TV**, we may become desensitized to the violence. But **when we go out to see a film,** we may

164

unconsciously regard what we're seeing on the screen as somewhat out of the ordinary. **If we see someone shoot someone else in a film,** we tend on some level to recognize this as a kind of "performance" as we would a theatrical play. Another reason that movies contribute less to violence is that the film ratings establish some control over what children can see—**provided that they are enforced.**

WR: OK. But **even if it's true that TV watching causes violence,** what can we do about it?

Das: I think we will have to accept the notion that we can't have total freedom in everything. You may remember that in the early nineties, the U.S. attorney general suggested that TV networks in America must "clean up their act" and that, **unless they do it themselves,** the government will have to do it for them.

WR: What would that mean—cleaning up their act?

Das: A clearly defined code of decency would have to be established for television programs. Networks and producers would have to agree not to show material that violated this code, at least during the hours of the day when children would be likely to be watching. But that leads me to a second major cause of societal violence today: the breakdown of family structure. Actually, I've run out of time. We'll have to save the discussion of that for the next interview.

ADVERB CLAUSES*

CLAUSE OF REASON
Television violence may influence crime **because there is so much violent behavior on TV.**

CLAUSE OF CONTRAST
We've heard a lot about violence on TV, **although we could say the same thing about movies.**

CLAUSE OF CONDITION
If we see enough violent acts on TV, we may become desensitized to violence.

CLAUSE OF TIME
When we go out to see a film, we regard it as a special activity.

CLAUSE OF PLACE
Today we see violence **wherever we look.**

CLAUSE OF COMPARISON
Violence is much more prevalent today **than it was even ten years ago.**

CLAUSE OF RESULT
Movies have gotten **so** expensive **that people are seeing fewer of them.**

*Adverb clauses of manner with *as if* and *as though* are discussed in Unit 20.

Grammar Notes

1. A clause is a group of words that contains at least a subject and its verb. Clauses can be either <u>independent</u> or <u>dependent</u>. Independent clauses (also called main clauses) can stand alone as complete sentences. They do not need another clause to be fully understood. Dependent clauses (also called subordinate clauses), on the other hand, do need another clause to be fully understood.

INDEPENDENT CLAUSE

Violence is increasing today

DEPENDENT CLAUSE

because children watch too much TV.

2. Adverb clauses are dependent clauses that answer questions such as *why, where, how,* or *when* in the same way that single adverbs do.

> **Wherever there are gangs,** there is violence. (answers the question "Where is there violence?")

Speakers and writers use adverb clauses to combine thoughts and show connections between ideas. They also use them to vary their writing style. Compare these two ways to convey an idea.

> Television violence may promote crime. The reason for this is that there is a lot of violence on TV. (two sentences)
> Television violence may promote crime because there is a lot of violence on TV. (one sentence made up by combining an independent clause and a dependent adverb clause)

Sentences made up of an independent clause and a dependent clause introduced by a subordinating conjunction are called <u>complex sentences</u>. In a complex sentence the main idea is usually in the independent clause.

3. Following are seven important types of adverb clauses, listed with the subordinating conjunctions and expressions that can introduce each type of clause (see Appendix 21 on page A24 for a more complete list of subordinating conjunctions):

a. Adverb clauses of reason: introduced by *because, since, on account of the fact that.* These clauses answer the question "why?"

> **Since we watch TV at home,** we tend to regard it as a "normal" activity.
> Some teenagers get into crime **on account of the fact that they don't have enough to do.**

b. Adverb clauses of contrast: introduced by *although, though, even though, while, in spite of the fact that.* These clauses present a contrast with the idea expressed in the independent clause.

> TV has some very serious negative qualities, **though it has some positive qualities as well.**
> **In spite of the fact that there have been many protests,** there is still a lot of violence on TV.

c. Adverb clauses of condition: introduced by *if, unless, in case, provided (that).* These clauses answer the question "under what condition?"

> **If children watch too much TV,** they may lose the ability to distinguish fantasy from reality.
> TV violence won't be reduced **unless viewers protest.**

d. Adverb clauses of time: introduced by *when, whenever, before, after, as, as soon as, while, since, until.* These clauses answer the question "when?"

> We need to recognize the problem **before we can solve it.**
> **When we reduce the amount of TV violence,** we will begin to see a decline in violent crime.

(continued on next page)

e. Adverb clauses of place: introduced by *where, wherever*. These clauses answer the question "where?"

> We need to place the blame **where it belongs.**
> **Wherever there are gangs,** there is violence.

f. Adverb clauses of comparison: introduced by *than, as much as, as many as*. These clauses make comparisons of quantity.

> There is far more gang activity today **than there was even ten years ago.**
> Today there are probably **as many** violent crimes committed in a month **as there used to be in a year.**

g. Adverb clauses of result: introduced by *so (that)* or containing the expressions *so + adjective + that* or *such + noun phrase + that.* These clauses present the result of a situation stated in the independent clause.

> The networks will have to clean up their act **so (that) the government won't have to do it for them.**
> Crime is increasing **so** fast **that we will have to build more prisons to hold the criminals.**
> Some children have **such** terrifying experiences at school **that they refuse to go.**

4. Except for clauses of comparison and result, most adverb clauses can come either before or after the independent clause. When the adverb clause comes first, we place a comma after it. When the adverb clause comes second, we generally do not place a comma before it.

> **Because there is so much violence on TV,** many people want more government control of programming.

Many people want more government control of programming **because there is so much violence on TV.**

We place a comma before a dependent clause, however, if the dependent clause sets up a contrast.

> We can deal with the problem of violence**, though it won't be easy.**

5. Unlike the other adverb clauses, adverb clauses of comparison and result cannot normally be moved. This is because their meaning is linked to or dependent on a particular element in the independent clause.

> There is far **more** gang activity today
> **than there was even ten years ago.**

> Today there are probably **as many** violent crimes committed in a month
> **as there used to be in a year.**

> Crime is increasing **so** fast
> **that we will have to build more prisons to hold the criminals.**

> Some children have **such** terrifying experiences at school
> **that they refuse to go.**

Be careful! Note the difference between *so* and *such. So* occurs before an adjective or adverb with no following noun. *Such* occurs before a noun or noun phrase.

> so fast
> so incredibly fast
> such terrifying experiences
> such a happy couple

FOCUSED PRACTICE

1. Discover the Grammar

In each of the following sentences, underline the dependent clause once and the independent clause twice.

1. <u>Police confiscate illegal weapons</u> <u>wherever they find them</u>.
2. We won't be able to correct the problem of violence unless we treat its underlying causes.
3. Some cartoons contain as much violence as R-rated movies do.
4. Though the drug problem has worsened, there are some positive signs.
5. Some parents curtail their children's TV watching because they think it encourages passivity.
6. There are so few programs of quality on television that some people have gotten rid of their TV sets.
7. Whenever there is an economic downturn, there is a corresponding increase in crime.

2. Why Sports?

Read the essay, which contains twelve adverb clauses. Underline all of the adverb clauses. Determine the role each clause plays in the sentence. Write **where, when, why,** *or* **under what condition** *above the clauses that answer those questions. Write* **result, comparison,** *or* **contrast** *above the clauses that present results, comparisons, or contrasts.*

WHY SPORTS?
by Jamal Jefferson

A lot of people are criticizing school sports these days. Some say there's too much
emphasis on football and basketball and not enough on education. Others say the idea
of the scholar-athlete is a joke. Still others say sports are a way of encouraging violence.
I think they're all wrong. If anything, school sports help prevent violence, not
encourage it. Why do I think sports are a positive force?

For one thing, sports are positive because they give students opportunities to be
involved in something. Every day on TV we hear that violence is increasing. I think a
lot of people get involved in crime on account of the fact that they don't have enough to
do to keep themselves busy. After two or three hours of basketball, baseball, or any
other kind of sports practice, you're so tired that it's hard to commit a violent act.

Second, sports teach people a lot of worthwhile things, especially at the high school
level. By playing on a team, students learn to get along and work with others. When
their team wins, they learn how to be good winners; when their team loses, they find
out they have to struggle to improve. They discover that winning a few and losing a few
are part of the normal ups and downs of life. Also, there's no doubt that students
improve their physical condition by participating in sports.

Finally, sports are positive because they give some students, especially poor ones, an
opportunity to get out of a difficult situation and improve their chances for a successful
life. If a young basketball player from a poor village in Nigeria can get a scholarship to
play for, say, UCLA, he will have a chance to get an education and make his life better
than it ever was. If a young woman coming from a ghetto is accepted on the University
of Missouri swim team, she'll have the chance to permanently leave that ghetto and be
successful wherever she goes. In spite of the fact that some school sporting programs
have deficiencies that need to be ironed out, their benefits outweigh their disadvantages.
I should know because I'm one of those students. School sports must stay.

3. Crime Prevention

A panel of experts has been investigating the causes of crime. Write their conclusions by combining each of the following pairs of sentences into one sentence with a dependent clause and an independent clause. Place the idea that seems more important in the independent clause. Use the indicated subordinating conjunctions. Do not add words.

1. We can begin to solve the crime problem. We must look at the underlying causes of violence. (before)

   Before we can begin to solve the crime problem, we must look at the underlying causes of violence.

2. Many citizens support gun control. They believe that the easy availability of guns is a key ingredient in violent crime. (because) _____

   _____

3. Many citizens do not support gun control. They recognize that guns are part of the crime problem. (although) _____

   _____

4. Teenagers have meaningful activities. They are likely to get involved in crime. (unless)

   _____

   _____

5. There is potential danger. We go. (wherever) _____

   _____

6. Criminals commit three serious crimes. They will be sent to life in prison without possibility of parole. (if)

   _____

   _____

7. The Brady Law to control handguns was finally passed. Its supporters had lobbied for years for its passage. (after) _____

   _____

8. Politicians argue about the war on drugs. The drug problem continues to grow. (while)

   _____

   _____

4.   Traffic Court

Stan Everly was involved in an automobile accident and is explaining his side of the story to the judge of the traffic court. Fill in the blanks in their conversation, using the subordinating conjunctions and expressions from the box to complete the dependent clauses.

as much . . . as	in spite of the fact that
more . . . than	on account of the fact that
so . . . that	such . . . that
if	

Judge: Well, Mr. Everly, your description of the accident is _____ *so* _____ confusingly

written _____ *that* _____ I'm not sure I understand it. Tell me in your own words
             _{1.}

what happened.

Everly: Well, your honor, I had just received a telephone call from the nurse at my daughter's school. I

was speeding _____ *on account of the fact that* _____ she'd been hurt in an accident, and I was frantic to
                              _{2.}

get there.

Judge: OK. What happened next?

Everly: Well, I sideswiped that parked car, and I was in _____ *such* _____ a hurry

_____ *that* _____ I didn't have time to leave a note on the driver's windshield.
      _{3.}

Judge: What? This is _____ *more* _____ serious _____ *than* _____ I thought. You
                                                                   _{4.}

left the scene of the accident without notifying the driver of the other car?

Everly: Yes, your honor.

Judge: Well, Mr. Everly, a crime is a crime, and I don't have _____ *as much* _____ patience with

these kinds of cases _____ *as* _____ I used to. *In spite of the fact that there weren't* there
                                _{5.}   _{6.}

were extenuating circumstances, I can't dismiss these charges. I'm fining you $150.

_____ *If* _____ something like this happens again, I'll revoke your license.
          _{7.}

5.   Editing

Each of the following sentences contains an error in the dependent clause, either in structure or in logical word choice. Rewrite each sentence, correcting the error.

1. We won't make a dent in crime until identify the root causes of violence.

   _____ *We won't make a dent in crime until we identify the root causes of violence.* _____

2. The prison escapee was driving such rapidly that he lost control of the car and was apprehended.
                                        so

   _____

(continued on next page)

3. If *they* get enough attention from their parents, children probably won't turn to crime.

_____

4. Some children watch so *much* a lot of television that they have trouble telling reality from fantasy.

_____

5. The sheriff's office has put more agents on the streets in case *of* there being additional trouble.

_____

6. Provided their governments to appropriate enough money, nations everywhere can gain headway

against crime.

_____

7. Today there is more awareness about the underlying causes of violence than there *was* be in the past.

_____

8. Many juvenile criminals today receive light sentences although *they* commit serious crimes.

_____

9. Today there isn't as much abuse of certain drugs *as* than there used to be. That's a positive sign.

_____

10. In spite of *the fact that* he had exhibited good behavior, the prisoner was denied parole.

_____

COMMUNICATION PRACTICE

6. Practice Listening

◼◼ *Bradley Freeman and Jennifer Strand are having a debate on gun control.*
Listen to their conversation on the tape.

Now listen to certain of the sentences again. Circle the letter of the choice which correctly explains the meaning of each sentence you hear.

1. (a.) Jennifer thinks people are likely to use guns if they have them.

   b. Jennifer thinks people probably won't use guns even if they have them.

2. a. According to Bradley, people don't die because other people have guns.

   b. According to Bradley, people die because other people have guns.

3. a. Bradley thinks law-abiding citizens die because they have guns.

   b. Bradley thinks law-abiding citizens die because a lot of criminals don't get punished.

4. a. Jennifer thinks a person who has a gun probably won't shoot anybody.

   b. Jennifer thinks that in any situation where a person has a gun, it is more likely that someone will be shot.

5. a. Bradley thinks it's true that if we outlaw guns, outlaws will still be able to get them.

   b. Bradley thinks it's true that if we outlaw guns, outlaws won't be able to get them.

6. a. Jennifer thinks outlawing guns is a criminal act.

   b. Jennifer doesn't think outlawing guns is a criminal act.

7. a. According to Jennifer, getting rid of guns won't change the attitude toward violence.

   b. According to Jennifer, getting rid of guns will change the attitude toward violence.

8. a. Bradley thinks we must change the attitude toward punishment before we can change the attitude toward violence.

   b. Bradley thinks we must change the attitude toward violence before we can change the attitude toward punishment.

9. a. According to Bradley, we need to build more prisons to cause violence to decline.

   b. According to Bradley, building more prisons won't cause violence to decline.

10. a. Jennifer thinks incarceration of violent criminals is the real answer to the problem.

    b. Jennifer doesn't think incarceration of violent criminals is the real answer to the problem.

7. Small Group Discussion

Combine each of the following ideas with a dependent clause to express your own ideas.
Then choose one of the topics to discuss with the other members of your group.

1. We won't get control of the crime problem.

   We won't get control of the crime problem until we identify the real causes of violence.

2. We can provide jobs for everyone.

3. Parents should not leave their children home alone.

4. The number of gun-related deaths has increased a great deal in the last decade.

(continued on next page)

5. Parents need to limit their children's television viewing.

_____

6. Some people have proposed legalization of drugs as a solution to the crime problem.

_____

8. Role Play in Pairs

Work with a partner. Look at the four illustrations. Choose one situation and role-play the parts of the two people pictured. Use as many of the words and expressions from the box as you can.

because	✓ as many as	✓ in spite of the fact that
since	✓ than	✓ if
on account of the fact that	✓ so . . . that	unless
although	such . . . that	✓ in case
though	✓ so (that)	✓ provided (that)
as much as	✓ even though	when
whenever ✓	✓ before	after
as	✓✓ as soon as	while
until	✓ where	wherever

9. Essay

Choose one of the following clauses and begin a short essay with it.

Clause 1. Because guns are a key ingredient in the escalation of violence all over the world, . . .
Clause 2. Although guns are a key ingredient in the escalation of violence all over the world, . . .
Clause 3. Because watching television is essentially a passive activity, . . .
Clause 4. Because drugs are so pervasive in today's society, . . .

10. Picture Discussion

Form two teams. Make a list of the positive and negative effects of team sports.
Then have a debate about this issue, with one team taking the positive side and the
other taking the negative side.

INTRODUCTION

Read and listen to the second half of the interview with Dr. Krishna Das.

Questions to Consider

1. Do you think that family structure is declining?
2. Do you think a decline in family structure can promote violence?
3. Would providing people with fewer work hours and more leisure time help reduce violence and crime?

What Does the Expert Say?

Part II

World Review: When we left off the last interview, Dr. Das, you were about to talk about the breakdown of family structure as a factor in violence.

Das: Yes. As I was saying, restricting the amount of violence shown on TV is only the beginning. The real key is to strengthen the role of parents. They should be able to limit the amount of television their children watch and to control what they see. They **even** need to be able to say to their children, "We're not watching any TV **at all** this evening."

But far more important is their need **simply** to be with their children more. **Even** in many well-off families, both parents have to work **just** to make ends meet. **Sadly,** because of this, many parents find it difficult or impossible to have close involvement with their children. **Seldom** do they have enough time for all the things they want and need to do. When working parents come home from work, they are usually tired; **rarely** do they have enough energy to play with their children, read to them, that sort of thing. They often use TV as a babysitter, **unfortunately.** This is understandable because someone has to do the chores. But what happens? They put the children in front of the television set, **perhaps** not **even** supervising what they are watching.

WR: But this is a colossal problem, isn't it? How can we address it?

Das: Yes, it's **certainly** a difficult issue, though solving it is not impossible. There are a number of things that could be done for starters. **At the top of the list** is the need for workplace day care, where parents could see their young children periodically during the workday. Day care personnel would be licensed, supervised professionals who would guide the children in meaningful activities in a caring environment. **Second on the list** is the need to reduce the workweek so that parents would have more time to spend with their children and with each other. **Maybe** we could cut it down to thirty-five or thirty-two hours. And **not only** should we reduce the workweek, but we should also encourage and expand the use of flextime.

WR: How would flextime help the situation?

Das: By allowing employees to work shifts that reflect the demands of their families' schedules so that one parent could always be available when children need care. In these ways, **perhaps,** we would give people some crucial extra time to spend with their families. It could help tremendously.

WR: This all sounds good, but wouldn't it take a lot of money?

Das: Clearly, but that seems a small price to pay. We must strengthen the family structure. **Only** then will we be able to reduce the level of crime and violence.

WR: Well, Dr. Das, you've provided much food for thought. Thank you for your comments. **Perhaps** we can discuss other solutions in a future interview.

Das: Yes, thank you. I would like that.

ADVERBIALS: VIEWPOINT, FOCUS, AND NEGATIVE

VIEWPOINT ADVERBS
Fortunately, quality day care is available.
Crime is **certainly** a serious problem.
Family structure has declined, **clearly.**
Perhaps limiting TV watching will help.
Maybe violent crime will be reduced.

FOCUS ADVERBS
The Millers have **only** one child.
They **only** want the best for her.
They have saved **almost** $20,000.
They have **even** made arrangements for her admission to college.
They **just** want her to be happy.

NEGATIVE ADVERBS
Rarely has the situation been this dangerous.
Seldom do they supervise their children.
Never before have crime levels been so high.

Grammar Notes

1. <u>Viewpoint adverbs</u> give the speaker or writer's viewpoint or comment about the statement made, modifying entire sentences rather than elements within them. They include *fortunately, unfortunately, clearly, obviously, certainly, luckily, surely, evidently, frankly, actually, perhaps,* and *maybe.* Note the difference in the meaning of *sadly* in the following sentences.

> The mother reacted **sadly** to the news.
> **Sadly,** she was unable to do anything to help.

The adverb *sadly* in the first sentence modifies *reacted,* showing the manner in which the mother reacted to the news. The word *sadly* in the second sentence is a viewpoint adverb which shows the speaker or writer's comment about the situation.

Placement: Except for *maybe* and *perhaps,* viewpoint adverbs can appear at the beginning of a sentence, in its middle, or at the end. When they appear at the beginning of the sentence, they often have a comma separating them from the rest of the sentence. When they appear at the end of the sentence, they are always preceded by a comma. If they appear in the middle, they are always close to the verb and are usually enclosed in commas when they precede the verb. In general, writers use the comma when they want to separate the viewpoint adverb from the rest of the sentence.

> **Fortunately,** use of certain drugs is declining.
> Use of certain drugs is declining, **fortunately.**
> Use of certain drugs is **fortunately** declining.
> Use of certain drugs**, fortunately,** is declining.

Usage note: The word *hopefully* is often used as a viewpoint adverb meaning "it is to be hoped that." However, some speakers and writers object to its use.

2. <u>Focus adverbs</u> include *only, just, even, almost, merely, really,* and *simply.* Like viewpoint adverbs, they are flexible words that can appear in many places in a sentence. In writing and in formal speaking, we place focus adverbs just before or after words or phrases that we want to focus on specifically. The following examples show how strongly focus adverbs affect meaning.

> The Millers have **only** one child. The Millers have one child **only.** (Focus on **one** or **one child** = She is all the children they have.)
> They want **only** the best for her. (Focus on **the best** = This is all they want.)
>
> I **almost** called the police. (Focus on **called** = I was about to call but changed my mind.)
> I made **almost** fifty calls yesterday. (Focus on **fifty** or **fifty calls** = I made nearly fifty calls yesterday.)
>
> **Even** Ms. Smith signed the petition. (Focus on **Ms. Smith** = She would not be expected to sign it.)
> Ms. Smith **even** signed the petition. (Focus on **signed** = It was one of many things that she did.)

Placement: In informal speech and writing, the adverbs *only* and *just* usually occur before the verb. In speaking the meaning is made clear through stress and intonation:

> I ONLY asked Mr. Green for his opinion. (Strong stress on **only** = That's all that I did.)
> I ONLY asked MR. GREEN for his opinion. (Strong stress on **only** and **Mr. Green** = Mr. Green is the only person I asked.)
> I ONLY asked Mr. Green for his OPINION. (Strong stress on **only** and **opinion** = I asked him for his opinion, not his support.)

3. <u>Negative adverbials</u> include *never, rarely, seldom, scarcely, not only, only then, neither, hardly, little, on no account.* They often occur in the same position as frequency adverbs. Because negative adverbials are already negative, the verb in the sentence doesn't need the word *not.*

> Parents **rarely** have much energy after work.

Placement: For emphasis, negative adverbs are sometimes placed at the

(continued on next page)

beginning of a sentence, especially in writing or more formal speech. When they come at the beginning, they force the subject and auxiliary to invert.

Seldom have I been so disappointed.
Hardly had we left when the car quit.
Not only is she a good parent, but she is also a good daughter.
Only then will we be able to solve the problem.

In sentences in simple present or simple past, subject-auxiliary inversion forces the appearance of the auxiliary *do/does/did*.

Rarely do parents have much energy after work.

Placing negative adverbials at the beginning of the sentence sounds somewhat formal to most native speakers and is less common in conversation than in writing.

4. Like the negative adverbials, certain other adverbials can be placed at the beginning of a sentence, particularly in descriptive writing. When they are, the subject and verb are inverted if the subject is a noun.

At the top of the list is the need for governments to provide day care in the workplace.
Second on the list is the need to reduce the workweek.

In both formal and informal English, this type of inversion is common if the sentence begins with *here* or *there* and a noun follows.

Here are your **books.** Run and catch the bus!
There goes the **bus!** You missed it.

Be careful! Inversion after *here* and *there* occurs only when the subject is a noun. If the subject is a pronoun, the word order is normal.

Here **they are.**
There **it goes.**

5. Be careful! The adverbial *at all* occurs only in negative and interrogative sentences. It is often used with the indefinite pronouns. It also never begins a sentence.

Is there **anything** we can do **at all?**
Is there **anything at all** we can do?
I don't like television **at all.**

FOCUSED PRACTICE

1. Discover the Grammar

Part 1   *The Martins took a family trip to Disneyland. Circle the focus adverb in each of the following statements about their excursion. Note that the word the adverb focuses on is boxed.*

1. Jim and Helen Martin and their four children took a trip to Disneyland. They had been saving money for (almost) two years.

2. They left for the airport. The traffic was heavy, and they almost missed the plane.

3. The children were keyed up about the trip. Even seventeen-year-old Nancy was excited.

4. They arrived at the park. Eight-year-old Michael had only ten dollars to spend on souvenirs.

5. Only [Eric] had enough money to buy what he wanted.

6. Nancy was in a good mood. She even [lent] her brother Michael twenty dollars.

7. Jim and Helen wanted to watch the parades. The children only [wanted] to go on the rides.

8. Michael wanted to go on only [one] ride: Space Mountain.

9. Sam and Eric, the thirteen-year-old twins, just [wanted] to visit the arcades.

10. At the end of the day, the Martins had just [three] dollars left.

Part 2   *Look again at some sentences adapted from the interview with Dr. Das. Find and circle the fourteen viewpoint, focus, or negative adverbials. One sentence has two adverbials.*

1. But that's (only) the beginning.

2. You can watch just one hour of TV this evening.

3. But far more important is their need simply to be with their children.

4. Even in many well-off families in the United States, both parents have to work just to make ends meet.

5. Sadly, many parents find it difficult or impossible to develop close involvement with their children.

6. Seldom do they have enough time for all the things they want and need to do.

7. Rarely do they have enough energy to play with their children, read to them, that sort of thing.

8. They often use TV as a babysitter, unfortunately.

9. Yes, it's certainly a difficult issue.

10. Not only should we reduce the workweek, but we should also encourage and expand the concept of flextime.

11. Instead of requiring everyone to work from nine to five only, we ought to try to accommodate people's individual situations.

12. Clearly, but that seems a small price to pay.

13. Only then will we be able to reduce the level of crime and violence.

2. Talking to Parents

Dr. Krishna Das is talking with a group of parents who want to know about violence and what they might do about it. Combine the ideas in the following pairs of sentences to create his statements to the parents. Use a viewpoint adverb in each case. Note that a viewpoint adverb can appear in at least three places in a sentence. Write three sentences for each numbered item.

1. Children should not have to go to school in constant fear about crime. That is clear.

   Clearly, children should not have to go to school in constant fear about crime.

   Children should clearly not have to go to school in constant fear about crime.

   Children should not have to go to school in constant fear about crime, clearly.

(continued on next page)

2. Violence has increased in public schools. This is an unfortunate development.

_____

_____

_____

3. Some parents are able to spend a great deal of time with their children. This is a lucky situation.

_____

_____

_____

4. We must be willing to make some sacrifices. I am sure of this.

_____

_____

_____

5. Some young people manage to survive unhappy childhoods. This is fortunate.

_____

_____

_____

6. Some schools have no policies on bringing guns to campus. That is evident.

_____

_____

_____

7. It is important to place limits on your children's behavior. I am being frank.

_____

_____

_____

3. Talking to a Teenager

Shari and Jonathan Hughes are having a discussion with their daughter Alison, who violated her curfew last night. Fill in the blanks in their conversation, using the focus adverbs given. Consider the context carefully in deciding where the focus adverbs should be placed.

Shari: Alison, it was 2 A.M. when you got home last night. _____We were really_____

1. (Really, we were / We were really)

worried. _____ the police, but your father persuaded me

2. (Almost I got up and called / I almost got up and called)

to stay in bed. Who were you out with, and what were you doing?

Alison: I was with Jerry at a restaurant. _____ and drinking coffee.

3. (Only we were talking / We were only talking)

We weren't doing anything bad. I _____ track of time.

4. (just guess we lost / guess we just lost)

Jonathan: But why didn't you _____ us you'd be late?
5. (simply call and tell / call and tell simply)

_____ knows enough to do that.
6. (Your little brother even / Even your little brother)

Alison: I did. I _____ ten times, but the line was busy.
7. (almost called / called almost)

Shari: Busy? The phone didn't ring once, and it wasn't off the hook.

Alison: Well, uh . . .

Jonathan: Alison, we can't monitor your every move. You're old enough now to make some of your own

decisions. I _____ know the difference between right and
8. (just hope you / hope you just)

wrong. There are going to be times when _____ decide that.
9. (only you can / you can only)

In this case, I don't know if _____ be punished. We'd like to
10. (even you should / you should even)

be able to trust you.

Alison: You can, Dad, you can.

4. Families

*Read the following statements about families. Then rewrite them, beginning each
sentence with the negative adverbial provided.*

1. Fathers gain custody of the children in divorce cases. (Rarely)

   Rarely do fathers gain custody of the children in divorce cases.

2. Families eat meals together. (All too seldom)

   _____

3. Domestic violence can be ignored. (On no account)

   _____

4. Young people should start paying their own bills. They will begin to truly appreciate their parents.
   (Only then)

   _____

5. A teenager knows about how difficult it is to be a parent. (Little)

   _____

6. They understand the need for discipline. (Hardly ever)

   _____

5. Editing

Find and correct the ten errors in adverbials in the following letter.

April 15

Dear Mom,

I'm sitting in the train station, waiting for the 5:25 to come along, so ~~just~~ I *I just* thought I'd drop you a quick note.

Tax day is over with, at long last! Almost we didn't get our taxes done on *Focus* time, but Jonathan and I stayed up until midnight last night, and I mailed the forms this afternoon. I hate income taxes! Only once in the last ten years we *we* have gotten a refund, and this time the tax return was so complicated that *even* Jonathan got even upset, and you know how calm he is.

Besides that, we've been having a few problems with Alison. It's probably nothing more serious than teenage rebellion, but whenever we try to lay down the law, she gets defensive. Rarely if ever she takes criticism well. The other *does* night she and her boyfriend stayed out until 2:00 A.M.—this was the second time in two weeks—and when we asked her what they'd been doing she said, "Only we were talking and listening to dance music at the Teen Club. Why can't you leave me alone?" Then she stomped out of the room. Fortunately, Karen and Kenny have been behaving like angels—but they're not teenagers yet!

Meanwhile, Alison's school has started a new open-campus policy. Students can leave the campus whenever they don't have a class. Even they don't have to tell the school office where they're going and when they'll be back. Jonathan and I approve of that policy at all. School is for studying and learning, not for *don't* *neg. sentence grammar notes #5* socializing. Little those school officials realize how much trouble teenagers can *do* get into whenever they're roaming around unsupervised.

Well, here the train comes. I'll sign off now. Write soon.

sentence beginning c here
see grammar notes #4

Love,
Shari

COMMUNICATION PRACTICE

6. Practice Listening 1

Janet Robertson, a member of a newspaper editorial staff, is interviewing Dr. Krishna Das about Bob Brown, a teenager who was arrested for shoplifting. Listen to their conversation on the tape. Then listen again, marking the following statements true (T) *or false* (F), *based on what you hear.*

_____T_____ 1. Dr. Das can be easily understood when he speaks about juvenile delinquency.

_____F_____ 2. Robertson thinks that jail is an appropriate punishment for shoplifting.

_____T_____ 3. Dr. Das feels that Bob's arrest will have a good effect on him.

_____T_____ 4. Bob's mother felt unhappy when he was arrested.

_____F_____ 5. Bob's mother doesn't think his arrest will have a good effect.

_____F_____ 6. Robertson is certain that Bob can be rehabilitated.

_____F_____ 7. Dr. Das says that Bob's shoplifting was no mistake.

_____F_____ 8. Dr. Das says that Bob will happily serve his sentence.

_____T_____ 9. Robertson is reconsidering her opinion about the case.

7. Tape Discussion

Are people benefited by punishment?

8. Practice Listening 2

Listen to the tape. Pay close attention to the speakers' stress and intonation. Circle the letter of the sentence that explains the meaning of the sentence you hear.

1. (a.) That's all I asked her to do.

   b. That's all I asked her to vacuum.

2. a. That's all I asked Alison to do.

   (b.) Alison was the only person I asked.

3. (a.) I didn't ask her to do anything else to the living room.

   b. I didn't ask anyone else to vacuum the living room.

(continued on next page)

4. a. Jerry is the only person Alison dates.

   b. Alison doesn't go steady with Jerry.

5. a. Jerry is the only person Alison dates.

   b. Alison doesn't go steady with Jerry.

6. a. All I want to do is talk.

   b. You're the only person I want to talk to.

7. a. All I want to do is talk.

   b. You're the only person I want to talk to.

8. a. It's only tonight that I want to talk to you.

   b. It's only you that I want to talk to tonight.

9. a. Jerry is the only person Alison is friends with.

   b. That's all Alison and Jerry are—friends.

10. a. Jerry is the only person Alison is friends with.

    b. That's all Alison and Jerry are—friends.

9. Small Group Discussion

Work in small groups to role-play one or more of the following situations. Try to incorporate some of the adverbs in the box into your role play.

fortunately	actually	even	rarely
unfortunately	almost	only	never

1. You and your spouse both have full-time jobs, but you can't afford day care. You are talking with each other about a solution to the problem.

   Example:
   Spouse 1: Honey, what do you think we ought to do about day care for the kids?
   Spouse 2: Well, I've got a plan, and it might **actually** work. Would your boss let you have one of the weekdays off if you worked on Saturday?
   Spouse 1: I don't know. Why?
   Spouse 2: We could set up an all-day play group for the small kids in the neighborhood. We'd **only** need four other sets of parents. . . .

2. You are a parent and you believe that requiring all students to wear uniforms in schools would improve the school climate. You are trying to convince the school board to accept your idea.
3. Children need to have a sense that their parents care about them. You have just had a terrible argument with your teenage daughter, and she told you that you're always too busy to pay any attention to her. You are talking with her.
4. Your teenage son is "running with a bad crowd." You are talking with him about it.
5. Violence in some schools has become so serious that many children do not feel safe. You are a high school principal and are talking with a group of parents about the issue.
6. Truancy in schools has become more and more widespread. Your ten-year-old daughter has been caught by the truancy officer, and you are talking with her about the problem.

10. Essay

Choose one of the following topics and write an essay of three or four paragraphs about it.

Topic 1. To reverse the breakdown of family structure, we . . .
Topic 2. To communicate better within our families, we . . .
Topic 3. To reduce violence in society, we . . .
Topic 4. Flextime should be encouraged.
Topic 5. The day care system should be vastly expanded.

11. Picture Discussion

Look at this picture of a day care center and consider the impact of day care on society. Then, in groups of four or five, participate in a panel discussion for a TV news program with each person taking one of the following roles: day care administrator, working parent whose child is in the day care center, parent opposed to day care, child psychologist, and moderator.

INTRODUCTION

◖●●◗ *Read and listen to this essay about the automobile in the modern world.*

Questions to Consider

1. Do you think that the automobile has exerted negative as well as positive influences on society? Explain your viewpoint.
2. Suppose it were determined that the only way to curb pollution and solve other car-related problems would be to sharply curtail, if not ban, car use. Would you give up your car?

WOULD YOU

GIVE UP YOUR CAR?

by Helen Moreaux

On October 1, 1908, Henry Ford introduced the Model T to the world, setting in motion the process of making the car available "to the multitude." The rest is history. Ford, of course, didn't invent the car, **but** he did popularize it. **In fact,** today cars are *so* popular and define our world so much that it's worth taking a look at what they have done for us and to us. **Besides** looking at the car's effects, we can also speculate on what we can do to control the car **instead of** letting it control us.

First, cars have vastly increased our mobility. A thirty-mile trip that in the nineteenth century would have taken two days by horse and carriage or three or four days on foot can today be made in an hour or less. **Along with** mobility, **however,** comes stress. The car is available to nearly everyone, **and** monstrous traffic jams are created **as a result.** We get nervous or angry if the car ahead of us isn't moving or if someone cuts in front of us. This causes stress, **and** too much stress can even kill.

Second, cars have allowed people the freedom to live far from their workplaces. **And** when we go shopping, we don't have to buy enough supplies to last a month or two, **for** it's easy just to stop at the supermarket on the way home to get food for supper. **On the other hand,** the car has its negatives. **Despite** giving us freedom, it has also contributed to the decline of community. **Instead of** taking public transportation to work and interacting with other passengers, many of us ride alone in our autos. **Moreover,** we used to buy things at local stores where we knew the proprietors,

but today we largely trade with strangers at vast, impersonal commercial centers. **In addition,** modern neighborhoods are hardly neighborhoods in the old sense of a place where people come into daily contact with each other; **instead,** they are locations accessible above all to the automobile and are **thus** controlled by it. **Consequently,** the concept of the neighborhood has been weakened.

Finally, we know the car industry has created jobs, industries, and companies: rubber, steel, electronics. Jobs aren't everything, **though;** there is a downside. **For one thing,** the economy is dependent on the automobile, perhaps too dependent. In recent years, **for example,** certain car manufacturers have moved their factories for increased profits. **However,** the towns housing the original factories have been devastated by increased unemployment. **And** we must not forget that, **in addition to** dominating the economy, the automobile is the source of much air pollution.

Clearly, the effect of the car on human society has been momentous. **But** we can't now "uninvent" cars or abolish them. They are far too necessary and beneficial to our world. **Nevertheless,** we must get control of the car, develop new fuel sources, and reduce air pollution. These are the challenges that face us.

OTHER DISCOURSE CONNECTORS

COORDINATING CONJUNCTIONS

It used to be common to buy things at neighborhood stores, **but** now we trade at vast, impersonal shopping malls.
The automobile provides jobs, **and** it gives us mobility.
We can take the train, **or** we can drive.
I was spending three hours a day commuting in my car, **so** I switched to the train.

TRANSITIONS

Ford, of course, didn't invent the car. **However,** he probably did more than anyone else to popularize it.
Oil and gasoline won't last forever. **Therefore,** we will have to develop new fuel sources.
In addition to dominating the economy, cars are the source of much air pollution.

Grammar Notes

1. <u>Discourse connectors</u> are words and expressions that tie together the ideas in a piece of writing or in speech. They join ideas both within sentences and between sentences or larger stretches of text.

   joins ideas within complex sentence
   He's a terrible driver **even though** he's had a license for years.

   joins ideas between sentences
   Ford didn't invent the car. **However,** he probably did more than anyone else to popularize it.

   Two important types of discourse connectors are <u>coordinating conjunctions</u> and <u>transitions</u>.

2. The coordinating conjunctions (*and, but, or, nor, for, so,* and *yet*) connect ideas within sentences, joining two independent clauses. Sentences made up of two or more independent clauses joined by a coordinating conjunction are called <u>compound sentences</u>.

   On our vacation we drove our car, **and** we also traveled by bicycle. (**And** adds information.)
   Cars give us freedom, **but** they also cause stress. (**But** presents a contrast.)
   You can drive your car, **or** you can take the bus. (**Or** adds information.)
   Catherine doesn't like taking the subway, **nor** do I. (**Nor** adds information.)
   Nick's driver's license was revoked, **for** he had been convicted of drunk driving. (**For** presents a cause.)
   Catherine's automobile broke down, **so** she had to use public transportation. (**So** presents an effect.)
   I'm glad that James has his driver's license, **yet** I'm nervous about it too. (**Yet** presents a contrast.)

3. Transitions are words and phrases such as *however, therefore, in addition, consequently, in fact, first, second,* and *finally*. We use them to connect ideas between sentences or larger expanses of text.

Cars cause pollution. **In addition,** they create traffic jams. (**In addition** adds information.)
Cars are too prominent in our society to be gotten rid of. **Nevertheless,** we will have to do something to address the problems they create. (**Nevertheless** presents a contrast.)

4. Be careful! Some people object to beginning a written sentence with a coordinating conjunction, particularly in academic writing. However, some writers use coordinating conjunctions to connect ideas from sentence to sentence.

   connects ideas within sentence
   I hate driving, **so** I took the bus.
   connects ideas from one sentence to another
   I hate driving. **So** I took the bus.

5. Punctuation of compound sentences: When coordinating conjunctions are used to join two independent clauses in a compound sentence, these conjunctions are generally preceded by a comma.

   Cars are beneficial, **but** they cause many problems.

6. Placement of coordinating conjunctions: Coordinating conjunctions are placed only at the beginning of a clause, not within it or at the end of it.

   I was hungry, **so** I made a sandwich.
   OR
   I was hungry. **So** I made a sandwich.
   NOT ~~I was hungry, I so made a sandwich.~~
   OR
   ~~I was hungry, I made a sandwich, so.~~

7. Placement of transitions: Transitions can come at the beginning of a sentence, within it, or at the end, depending on what the writer or speaker wants to emphasize. They are usually separated from the rest of the sentence by a comma or commas.

   However, cars are harmful as well as beneficial.
   Cars, **however,** are harmful as well as beneficial.
   Cars are harmful as well as beneficial, **however.**

(continued on next page)

8. Types of transitions:

a. The following transitions add information: *also, in addition (to), additionally, for one thing, moreover, furthermore, plus, besides (that), for example, for instance, likewise, in fact, along with, indeed.*

> Cars have caused people to forsake public transportation. **Moreover,** they've led to the construction of gigantic shopping malls.

b. The following transitions offer contrasting information to an idea presented earlier: *however, still, nevertheless, in contrast, in fact, instead (of), in spite of (this), despite (this), on the contrary, on the other hand.*

> Cars cause many problems. **However,** it would be difficult to live without them.

c. The following transitions present a cause for or a result of an action or situation discussed earlier: *therefore, thus, because (of this), on account of (this), consequently, accordingly, otherwise, as a result.*

> Cars make it possible to live far away from the workplace. **Thus,** more animal and plant habitats are destroyed each year to make way for new homes.

d. The following transitions show the relation of actions, events, or ideas in time: *next, then, afterwards, meanwhile, after that, first, second, third, finally, in conclusion, to sum up.*

> I had a series of disasters. **First,** the car broke down. **Next,** it was impounded by a policeman.

These transitions are also commonly used to show the organization and presentation of a writer's or speaker's ideas.

> **First,** cars have vastly increased our mobility. **Second,** cars have given people more freedom. **Finally,** the car industry provides employment.

Note: Some transitions can function in more than one category. See Grammar Note 11.

See Appendix 22 on page A25 for a more complete list of transitions.

9. Punctuation of transitions: Be careful! Be sure to place a period or a semicolon— not a comma—before a transition when it is the first word in a sentence or clause. A comma in this location is incorrect and creates an error called a <u>comma splice.</u>

> She has a car. **However,** she rarely uses it.
> OR
> She has a car; **however,** she rarely uses it.
> NOT ~~She has a car~~**~~, however,~~** ~~she rarely uses it.~~

See From Grammar to Writing after Part VIII, page 302, for further discussion of comma splices.

10. Be careful! Do not confuse subordinating conjunctions with transitions.

> The train is old and dirty. **However,** it gets me to work. NOT ~~The train is old and dirty.~~ **~~Although~~** ~~it gets me to work.~~

11. *Though* can be a subordinating conjunction or a transition.

subordinating conjunction
> **Though** cars have become increasingly expensive, nearly everyone finds a way to afford them.

transition meaning *however*
> Jobs, **though,** aren't everything.

In fact can both add and contrast.

> I'm very fond of train rides. **In fact,** trains are the most civilized way to travel. (adds)
> Many people believe that planes are unsafe. **In fact,** they're statistically safer than cars. (contrasts)

The coordinating conjunction *or (else)* can have two meanings.

> You can take the metro, **or (else)** you can go by bus. (adds an alternative)
> Make your payment, **or (else)** we'll repossess your car. (suggests a consequence)

FOCUSED PRACTICE

1. Discover the Grammar

Read the newspaper article and underline transitions and coordinating conjunctions if they join independent clauses or sentences. Above each, write what the transition or coordinating conjunction presents: an addition, a contrast, a result, a cause, or a relation in time. You will find seven coordinating conjunctions and sixteen transitions.

The Concord Clarion

Take the Train? Well, Maybe . . .

by John Baca

Readers of our newspaper know that we favor the increased use and development of mass transit over the building of more highways. For years we've supported those who have been calling for the development of a regional transportation network whose components would be heavy rail, using existing tracks that the big trains run on; light rail, which would mean building new tracks that trolleys and small trains could run on; better bus service; and a metro system. Heavy rail tracks are already there, so heavy rail has gotten the most favorable press.

It occurred to our chief editor, however, that maybe someone should be sent to find out whether trains are really as efficient and pleasant as they're cracked up to be. I've written a lot of articles on transportation in the last several years, so I was the logical choice to do the investigation because I was considered an "expert." Therefore, I confidently set out on my journey one rainy Saturday morning.

I took the bus downtown to the train station, bought a ticket for Santa Maria, just 100 miles away, and went out on the platform to wait for the 9:02. That's when the train trip from hell began. Everything that could go wrong did go wrong.

First, the train was an hour late. Also, we were at the height of the tourist season, so when it finally did arrive, there seemed to be at least a million people waiting to board it. The quick rushed on, mercilessly elbowing the slow out of their way. I finally managed to board and tried to find a seat. There wasn't one, though; I had to stand with five other people in the space between two cars. I was right next to the men's restroom, which did not exactly smell like a flower garden. In

fact, to say that it smelled like a garbage dump would have been too charitable.

For half an hour or so the train just sat on the track, not moving. A man standing next to me with extremely bad breath insisted on telling me his life story. I listened politely for a while; then I excused myself, saying that I hadn't eaten breakfast. Meanwhile, the train had started, so I swayed back and forth on my way to the dining car, propelled violently by the motion of the now-moving cars.

As I was entering the dining car, a violent lurch of the train threw me to the left, causing me to lose my balance and land in the lap of a portly woman drinking coffee, which spilled on both of us. I apologized profusely. My apology, however, was apparently not convincing, for the woman just glared at me. I got up and went to order tea and a sandwich, which cost me $8.95, from an impolite attendant. The tea was lukewarm and virtually flavorless, and the sandwich tasted like a combination of sawdust and cardboard. I wended my way back to my starting place, but there still wasn't a vacant seat. I was forced to spend the next hour and a half listening to the same man tell his life history all over again.

By the time the train finally arrived in Santa Maria, two hours late, I had come to several conclusions as to why more people don't take the train, if ours was any indication. First, trains are extremely slow; it had taken four hours to go 100 miles. Second, the train was filthy and uninviting. Third, train personnel were generally surly and unhelpful. Fourth, the tracks were in terrible condition.

So does this all mean that I'm now anti-train and pro-highway? No, I'm still a supporter of mass transit. However, I've learned that the situation isn't nearly as simple as we at the newspaper have been portraying it. All over the country we've allowed trains to deteriorate. We must make them viable again if we expect people to use them. We've got to demand excellent, efficient service. That will take money, perhaps (gasp!) even a tax increase. Nonetheless, it would be well worth it.

2. Disaster

Listen to the following segment of a radio newscast. It was recorded during a thunderstorm, and static makes it impossible to hear some parts of it. Listen again while you read the text. Think about what needs to go into each blank and write in the appropriate connector. Choose words and phrases from the box.

meanwhile	otherwise	first	in fact
however	therefore	and	second
also	next		

_____Next_____ we focus on the aftermath of the recent California earthquake.
1.

Investigators have determined that it will cost billions of dollars to rebuild damaged highways. According to the governor, two actions have to be taken: _____First_____, the federal government will
2.

have to approve disaster funds to pay for reconstruction; _____second_____, insurance investigators will
3.

have to determine how much their companies will have to pay in the rebuilding effort. With luck, the governor says, some key highways could be rebuilt within six months.

He cautioned, _____however_____, that the six-month figure is only an estimate; the process depends on
4.

timely allocation of funds, and certain insurance companies have in the past been notoriously slow to approve such funds. The rebuilding effort could, _____therefore_____, drag on for at least a year.
5.

_____Also_____, bad weather could hamper the speedy completion of the project.
6.

_____Meanwhile_____, it is taking some people as long as four hours to commute to work, and others
7.

haven't been able to get to work at all. Interviewed by our news team, one commuter who works in an office downtown, some forty miles from her home, said, "This has been ridiculous. It took me six hours to drive to work last Friday. I knew I'd have to find some other way of getting there; _____otherwise_____, I'd
8.

never make it. Well, yesterday I took the train and arrived there in fifty minutes. _____And_____ you
9.

know, the trip was really pleasant. I got the chance to read the morning paper. _____In fact_____, I think
10.

I'm going to switch permanently to the train."

3. Public Transportation

A public panel has met and made recommendations for improving the local transportation system. Complete their recommendations by choosing one of the two transitions in parentheses to connect each pair of sentences.

1. Widespread use of public transportation is better for the environment than reliance on the automobile. It will be cheaper in the long run, _____*also*_____. We need to de-emphasize the use of cars.
   (though / also)

2. We must develop better mass-transit systems. _____, we must also find a way to pay for them. An increased sales tax may be the best source of revenue.
   (However / Thus)

3. Many cities around the world are building underground metro systems, but these will take time to construct. _____, citizens will have to depend on bus transport. We need to expand bus service.
   (Moreover / Meanwhile)

4. Mass transit systems must be made attractive and convenient; _____, people will not use them. Our regional system must be pleasing to the patrons.
   (otherwise / on the contrary)

5. Some people are afraid to fly because they believe they have a better chance to survive a car accident than a plane crash. _____, airplanes are much safer statistically than automobiles. Our task force supports expanded air travel and the building of a new airport.
   (In fact / Likewise)

6. In many European cities, the transportation systems make it pleasant, easy, and relatively cheap to get around fast. In Paris, _____, you can buy a metro pass that is good for three days on an underground system that goes nearly everywhere. That's the sort of incentive plan we need in our new system.
   (on the other hand / for example)

7. The cost of digging a subway has increased geometrically in the last twenty years. _____, it will cost far more, proportionately, for cities without subway systems to build them than it would have cost had they been built before 1970. We need to de-emphasize subway construction and push for light rail.
   (Because of this / Afterwards)

8. We will have great difficulty persuading people to use mass transit instead of their cars, for most individuals will make strong arguments in favor of continuing to go everywhere by car. _____, there are compelling reasons for trying to persuade them. Our group feels that we can persuade the public if we mount the right sort of campaign.
   (Nonetheless / Accordingly)

4. Editing

Find and correct the twelve mistakes in the use of discourse connectors, providing a correct connector in each case. You may add or delete words, but do not change word order or punctuation.

MY CAR IS MOVING TO THE SUBURBS
by James Marx

The other day I was driving on the Evergreen Expressway, ~~also~~ *and* a policeman stopped me for speeding. I had to pay a ninety-dollar fine, ~~in spite of~~ *even though / though / after the fact that* I was going only seven miles per hour over the speed limit. That was the last straw. I've decided that I'm going to send my car to a new home in the suburbs.

I used to think that a car was the most wonderful thing in the world. I loved the freedom of being able to come and go to my part-time job or to the college whenever I wanted. A year ago I was in a car pool with four other people, however, I hated having to wait ~~on account of~~ *of the fact that / or not being* my car pool members weren't ready to leave.

~~Although,~~ *However,* I've changed my mind since then. Now it's clear to me that there are just too many disadvantages to having a car in town. For one thing, sitting stalled in your car in a traffic jam is stressful, besides it's a phenomenal waste of time. In addition, it costs me $200 a month to park my car in the city, ~~also~~ there's always the chance it will be vandalized.

~~Because,~~ *therefore; so* I've decided to leave it at my cousin Brent's house in the suburbs, Or, I'll end up going broke paying parking costs. My car will have a good home, ~~also~~ *however* I'll use it just for longer trips. When I'm in the city, ~~although,~~ I'll take the bus or the trolley, ~~otherwise~~ *or* I'll walk. Who knows? They say that you can meet some interesting people on the bus. Maybe I'll find the love of my life.

COMMUNICATION PRACTICE

5. Practice Listening

Alice Wu is a driver's license examiner. Listen to her statements to people about how they did on their exams. Then circle the letter of the sentence that correctly restates her meaning.

1. (a.) Though Mr. Matos could use some practice in parallel parking, he passed the exam.

   b. Because Mr. Matos could use some practice in parallel parking, he passed the exam.

2. a. Mrs. Adams failed the exam because, in addition to handling the car well, she ran a red light.

   (b.) Mrs. Adams failed the exam because, despite handling the car well, she ran a red light.

3. (a.) If Bob had turned his wheels away from the curb, he would have passed.

   b. If Bob had turned his wheels away from the curb, he still wouldn't have passed.

4. (a.) Jan signaled neither to turn left nor to stop.

   b. Jan signaled to stop but not to turn left.

5. a. Dr. Thomas passed the exam, for he scraped the curb.

   (b.) Dr. Thomas passed the exam, but he scraped the curb when he parked.

6. (a.) Because Deborah failed the written exam, she can't take the road test yet.

   b. Because Deborah can't take the road test yet, she failed the written exam.

7. (a.) Ms. Hanai needs to work both on hand signals and parking.

   b. Ms. Hanai needs to work on hand signals but not parking.

8. a. Ambrose's California license expired before he took the written exam.

   (b.) Ambrose's California license expired after he took the written exam.

6. Tape Discussion

Are driver's license requirements strict enough?

7. Small Group Discussion

Divide into small groups. Begin with the statements here and make additional statements, using the transitions given. Write your sentences down and then report them to the class later.

1. Cars give us mobility. (*also, furthermore, however, besides that*)
   Example:
   A: Also, they give us freedom.   **C: However,** they are getting very expensive.
   B: Furthermore, it's difficult to do without a car.   **D: Besides that,** it's hard to find a place to park.

2. Car insurance is quite expensive. (*in addition, moreover, because of this, nevertheless*)
3. Trains are an efficient means of transportation. (*for one thing, therefore, though, plus the fact that*)
4. Flying is a good way to travel. (*for example, in fact, however, consequently*)

8. Role Play in Groups

Work in small groups and role-play one of the following situations. Then reverse the roles and play the situation again.

1. A bystander has witnessed a hit-and-run accident and is talking to a police officer who is investigating the situation.
   Example:
   Officer: OK, ma'am, can you tell me what you saw?
   Bystander: Yeah. I was just starting to cross the intersection when I saw the little girl who was hit start to cross from the other side. We had the walk signal. A red Honda Accord was coming really fast from the opposite direction. It slowed down just before the intersection. **However,** it didn't stop. The driver hit the girl and went on through the intersection. . . .

2. A teenager wants permission to buy a car. The parents can't afford to buy another car, but the teenager is willing to work to pay for it. They are discussing the situation.
3. A married couple are planning a vacation. One spouse wants to drive, and the other wants to go by train. They are trying to come to some agreement.
4. A couple have just gone to a movie. Coming out of the movie theater, they have discovered that their car has been towed. They are convinced that the car was towed illegally and are talking to the head of the towing company.

9. Essay

Choose one of the following topics and write an essay of three or four paragraphs on it.

Topic 1. One way to reduce or eliminate automobile pollution is . . .
Topic 2. To persuade people to use their cars responsibly, we need to . . .
Topic 3. Mass transit isn't necessarily the answer to our transportation problems.

10. Picture Discussion

This painting shows a scene from America's past. The road in the picture was considered a highway. How has transportation changed since that time? As a class, discuss how transportation has changed in other countries around the world.

Example:

In _____, most people ride bicycles. **However,** more and more people are buying cars.

Edward Hopper: *Gas.* (1940) Oil on canvas, 26 ¼ x 40 ¼".
The Museum of Modern Art, New York. Mrs. Simon Guggenheim Fund.
Photograph ©1995 The Museum of Modern Art, New York.

INTRODUCTION

Read and listen to the script of a student's speech to a class.

Questions to Consider

1. What are some serious problems facing the world today?
2. Do you think overpopulation is one of them?

Millions and Millions

Today the population of Planet Earth is more than five and a half billion, an increase of one and a half billion in only eighteen years. There are more of us every minute, and the more people there are, of course, the greater the strain on the world's resources. By the year 2020, the world's population is expected to exceed eight billion. **Observing that population always increases geometrically while the food supply increases arithmetically,** nineteenth-century economist Thomas Malthus gave us an early warning of the problem we now face. There will never be any more water on the earth's surface than there is now, but there will be more people. **By using new methods of farming and newly developed, higher-yield crops,** farmers have been able to increase the amount of available food, but this can't go on forever. Can they continuously expand the food supply to match the population growth? It doesn't seem likely.

How did we arrive at this situation? There are two principal forces operating: a vast increase in the number of people, caused in part by advances in medicine and health; and the revolution of rising expectations. **Having wiped out smallpox,** scientists now contemplate the elimination of polio and other diseases. Infant mortality rates, while still tragically high in many nations, have been declining worldwide. People are living much longer than they used to; in many nations the life expectancy is seventy-five years and rising.

Meanwhile, the increasing trend toward a world economy has made more and more products available to more and more people, **straining the world's resources.** It is reasonable, a natural consequence of a rising standard of living, for people to want what others have. Eventually, however, this desire will have to be controlled. The population will continue to increase, but the amount and number of natural resources won't.

What can we do to solve the problem? Should we (1) colonize other planets? (2) Let "nature take its course" **by allowing wars to reduce the number of people?** (3) Create a world government which controls the world food supply and <u>forcibly</u> limits the number of children a couple can have? These measures seem <u>draconian</u> or fanciful; isn't there a more realistic or <u>humane</u> solution? Some say that, **to prevent a future disaster,** we must achieve Zero Population Growth, or ZPG, everywhere on the planet. How would it work? **Having reached childbearing age,** parents would limit themselves to no more than two children—the replacement level. This procedure would supposedly cause population to eventually stabilize and later decline. But could this really happen? And wouldn't it violate the sincere beliefs, <u>legitimate</u> rights, and religious liberty of many people?

A real-life example illustrates the situation. **Faced with an increasingly large population,** now nearing 1.2 billion, the government of China has for some time had a policy of permitting only one child per family. The effect has been a slower rate of population growth than in the past.

However, the Chinese solution may not be every country's solution. **If presented with proposals to adopt the Chinese program in their own nations,** in fact, many people might object violently, **considering such measures harsh, immoral, and out of the question.** It seems clear, though, that **to prevent major war, outbreaks of disease, and increased poverty,** all nations will eventually have to address the problem of population growth, which I consider our most serious worldwide dilemma today.

ADVERBIAL MODIFYING PHRASES

WITH A PRESENT PARTICIPLE

Recognizing that hunger is a problem, we must take steps to eliminate it.

Not wanting to commit himself, the president declined to be specific.

WITH *BY* + PRESENT PARTICIPLE

By using new agricultural methods and higher-yield crops, farmers have been able to increase the amount of food.

WITH A PAST PARTICIPLE

Given two options, we will choose the one that results in the greatest good for the greatest number.

When asked if he would support the treaty, the president wouldn't give a clear answer.

WITH *HAVING* + PAST PARTICIPLE

Having conquered many deadly diseases, scientists are now trying to develop a vaccine for AIDS.

PHRASES REDUCED FROM CLAUSES

While talking with an expert on homelessness, I learned a great deal.

Grammar Notes

1. In Unit 12, we studied sentences made up of independent clauses and dependent adverbial clauses. We saw how clauses enable speakers and writers to combine thoughts in such a way that precise connections between the ideas become clear.

> adverbial clause
>
> **Because the population of the country had increased dramatically,** there was a severe shortage of adequate housing.

Similarly, we can link ideas clearly by using modifying phrases which modify the ideas and actions in independent clauses.

> adverbial modifying phrase
>
> **Having conquered many deadly diseases,** scientists are trying to develop a vaccine for AIDS.

In this sentence, the adverbial modifying phrase, "having conquered many deadly diseases," modifies the main (or independent) clause, "scientists are trying to develop a vaccine for AIDS." The sentence above can be seen as a combination of the following two underlying ideas:

> Scientists have conquered many deadly diseases. They are trying to develop a vaccine for AIDS.

Remember that a clause contains a subject and a verb. A phrase does not.

2. Two sentences can be combined into one sentence with an independent clause and an adverbial modifying phrase if their subjects refer to the same person, place, or thing. In sentences of this type, the adverbial modifying phrase can come either before or after the main clause, though it more commonly appears first.

> modifying phrase
>
> By taking significant measures now,

> independent clause
>
> we can prevent overpopulation.

> independent clause
>
> We can prevent overpopulation
>
> modifying phrase
>
> by taking significant measures now.

3. There are five main types of adverbial phrases.

a. <u>With a present participle</u>: Use this form when you are talking about two actions or events that occurred in the same general time frame. Place the idea that you consider more important in the independent clause. Then replace the subject and verb from the subordinate idea with a present participle.

> Nineteenth-century economist Thomas Malthus observed that population always increases geometrically while the food supply increases arithmetically.
>
> PLUS
>
> He gave us an early warning of the problem we now face.
>
> BECOMES
>
> **Observing that population always increases geometrically while the food supply increases arithmetically,** nineteenth-century economist Thomas Malthus gave us an early warning of the problem we now face.
>
> OR
>
> Nineteenth-century economist Thomas Malthus gave us an early warning of the problem we now face, **observing that population always increases geometrically while the food supply increases arithmetically.** (Both original actions, **observing** and **giving**, occurred in the same general time frame.)

> The prime minister didn't want to publicize the details of the treaty. PLUS The prime minister refused to speak to the press. = **Not wanting to publicize the details of the treaty,** the prime minister refused to speak to the press.

(continued on next page)

b. <u>With *by* plus a present participle</u>: Use this form when there is a clear sense of intention or purpose—i.e., that one action causes a certain result. Replace the subject and verb with *by* plus a present participle.

The Chinese government encouraged single-child families.

PLUS

The Chinese government attacked the problem of overpopulation.

BECOMES

By encouraging single-child families, the Chinese government attacked the problem of overpopulation.

OR

The Chinese government attacked the problem of overpopulation **by encouraging single-child families.** (The Chinese government used this means to attack the problem.)

c. <u>With a past participle:</u> Use this form when you want to communicate a passive meaning. Replace a subject and auxiliary with a past participle.

People are presented with proposals to adopt the Chinese program in their own nations.

PLUS

Many people might object violently.

BECOMES

Presented with proposals to adopt the Chinese program in their own nations, many people might object violently.

OR

Many people might object violently, **presented with proposals to adopt the Chinese program in their own nations.** (The writer wants to include a passive idea—that people will be presented with certain proposals—in order to focus on their objections.)

d. <u>With *having* plus a past participle:</u> Use this form when you are talking about actions or events that occurred at different times. Replace the subject and verb with *having* + past participle.

past

Scientists **wiped out** smallpox.

PLUS

present

They now **contemplate** the elimination of polio and other diseases.

BECOMES

Scientists now contemplate the elimination of polio and other diseases, **having wiped out smallpox.**

OR

Having wiped out smallpox, scientists now contemplate the elimination of polio and other diseases. (The wiping out of smallpox occurred earlier in time.)

e. <u>Reduced from adverb clauses:</u> Some adverbial phrases are actually a reduced form of an adverbial clause that contained *be* and a subordinating word such as *although, even though, if, though, unless, until, when, whenever, while*. To reduce a clause in this way, delete the subject and auxiliary verb from the adverbial clause.

If they are carried out right, proposals to reduce the population might work.

BECOMES

If carried out right, proposals to reduce the population might work.

When he was asked if he would support the treaty, the president wouldn't give a clear answer.

BECOMES

When asked if he would support the treaty, the president wouldn't give a clear answer.

While I was talking with an expert on homelessness, I learned a great deal.

BECOMES

While talking with an expert on homelessness, I learned a great deal.

Note that in the examples above, the phrase can be further reduced by eliminating the subordinating word as well.

If carried out right, proposals to reduce the population might work.

BECOMES

Carried out right, proposals to reduce the population might work.

4. The infinitive of purpose is often used adverbially. Use this form when there is an infinitive phrase and a sense of purpose involved in the action. Delete the subject and verb.

> We want to prevent war, disease, and poverty.
>
> PLUS
>
> We must do something major and comprehensive.
>
> BECOMES
>
> **To prevent war, disease, and poverty,** we must do something major and comprehensive.
>
> OR
>
> We must do something major and comprehensive **to prevent war, disease, and poverty.** (Note existence of infinitive phrase and clear sense of purpose.)

The sentence with the adverbial phrase can also be written with *in order to*.

> **In order to prevent war, disease, and poverty,** we must do something major and comprehensive.

5. Be careful! If we combine (with an adverbial phrase) two sentences whose subjects are different, we create an incorrect, illogical sentence. This error is called a <u>dangling modifier</u> because the phrase we create "dangles," having nothing in the sentence to modify. The following two sentences cannot be combined.

> subject
>
> The **population** of China had increased tremendously.
>
> PLUS
>
> subject
>
> Government **officials** had to take significant measures.
>
> CANNOT BE COMBINED AS
>
> ~~Having increased tremendously in population, Chinese government officials had to take significant measures~~.

The phrase with *having* is a dangling modifier. It has nothing in the sentence to modify. The government officials did not increase in population, so the sentence is incorrect and illogical. The problem arises from joining two sentences whose subjects are different: *population* and *officials*.

To make sure that two sentences have the same subjects, draw a rectangle around each subject and connect the two rectangles with an arrow. If they refer to the same person or thing, they can be combined logically and correctly.

> Farmers are using new methods. They can increase the amount of available food.

The two subjects, *farmers* and *they*, refer to the same thing, so the combination is clear and logical.

> (By) using new methods, farmers can increase the amount of available food.

FOCUSED PRACTICE

1. Discover the Grammar

Listen to the following newscast on the tape. Then look at the text of the newscast and underline all of the adverbial phrases.

Good afternoon. This is news to the hour from the World Broadcasting Network.

☐ The cease-fire has been broken in Franconia. <u>When asked whether he would attend the upcoming peace conference in Geneva</u>, dissident leader Amalde declined to commit himself, saying that the success of the conference depends on the good-faith actions of Mr. Tintor, the country's president. Mr. Amalde went on to say that Mr. Tintor could demonstrate good faith by agreeing to free and unconditional talks. Interviewed about Mr. Amalde's comments, an aide to President Tintor, speaking on condition of anonymity, said that he did not expect the peace conference to take place as planned.

☐ Meanwhile, researchers from the Global Health Foundation announced plans to test a new vaccine for AIDS. Acknowledging that the current vaccine is ineffective, the researchers claim that their new vaccine is a marked improvement over the old one and believe that it holds great promise.

☐ Scientists at WASA, the World Aeronautics and Space Association, announced plans to launch a new space telescope with four times the magnification power of the existing space instrument. Having conducted successful repairs and identified flaws on Magna Maria, WASA's existing instrument, the agency is confident that the new telescope will be well worth its billion-dollar price tag.

☐ Finally, a new nation comes into existence at midnight tonight. <u>To be known as Illyria</u>, the new nation has been carved out of the eastern portion of Spartania. <u>According to its new president</u>, Illyria will need massive infusions of foreign aid to be a viable state.

☐ That's news to the hour; stay tuned for breaking developments.

2. World Concerns

Draw a rectangle around the subject in each pair of sentences. Connect the pairs of rectangles with an arrow. Then say whether the two sentences can be correctly combined or not.

1. Scientists have eliminated smallpox. They are trying to find a vaccine for AIDS.　　yes　　no

2. The standard of living has risen worldwide. New problems have been created.　　yes　　no

3. The population increases geometrically. The food supply increases arithmetically.　　yes　　no

4. Governments seek to prevent unrest. They must ensure the welfare of the majority.　　yes　　no

5. Many parents want more than two children. These people oppose ZPG.　　yes　　no

6. Governmental leaders feel that they propose workable solutions. Citizens often disagree.　　yes　　no

3. The Problem of Poverty

Writer Jim Lamoreaux has just returned from an assignment in Latin America. He is preparing a talk about his trip to a group of citizens. Shorten his sentences by reducing each adverbial clause to an adverbial phrase. Place the subject in the independent clause, and eliminate the subject and form of the verb **be** *from the dependent clause.*

1. While tourists from wealthy nations are enjoying their vacations in poor nations, they don't realize how desperate the lives of people they see on the streets may be.

   While enjoying their vacations in poor nations, tourists from wealthy nations don't realize how

   desperate the lives of people they see on the street may be.

2. When some tourists are giving money to beggars on the street, they mistakenly think they are doing their part to help the poor.

3. Tourists cannot truly understand the plight of the poor unless they are provided with firsthand knowledge of poverty.

4. If orphans in poor countries are sponsored by people in wealthier nations, they can escape the cycle of poverty.

5. Poor people will not be able to escape poverty until they are given job opportunities.

4. Human Interest

Jim Lamoreaux has sold an article on his trip to Outlook *magazine. Read and carefully study the article. It contains eleven sentences with adverbial modifying phrases. Five are correct; six are wrong because they contain dangling modifiers. Underline all of the incorrect sentences.*

A Helping Hand

BY JIM LAMOREAUX

If you are at all like me, you tire of requests to help others. Barraged by seemingly constant appeals for money to support public television, the Policemen's Benevolent Association, or the Special Olympics, worthy organizations all, I tend to tune out, my brain numbed.

It's not that I'm selfish, I don't think; it's just that there are so many of these requests. Subjected to many stimuli, only the crucial ones stick in my mind. By arguing that I don't have enough money anyway, the request is ignored. At least that was the way I saw the situation until the magazine I write for sent me to a small village overseas to do a human-interest story on homeless children.

Having seen and heard numerous television requests to sponsor a child overseas, I had always said to myself, "I'll bet the money gets pocketed by some local politician." My opinion changed after I got to know Elena and after I saw the reality of her life.

Having landed in the capital city, a taxi took me to my hotel in the center of town, and that's where I met her. Sitting on a dirty blanket on the sidewalk in front of the hotel, my eye was caught by her. She didn't beg; instead she was trying to scratch out a semblance of a living by selling matches. Smiling up at me, she asked, with almost no accent, "Matches, sir?" I bought some matches, and we got to talking. Her parents were both dead, and she lived with an elderly English-speaking great-aunt who had no job but sold firewood for money. I eventually learned from the great-aunt that Elena had suffered from polio at the age of five and now walked with a distinct limp.

While talking later with a nun at a nearby covent that administers gift money from other countries, much worthwhile information was given to me. She proved to my satisfaction that money from sponsors does indeed get to those who need it. Finding that I could sponsor Elena for fifty cents a day, I began to be ashamed; I spend more than that on my dogs. But what remains most vivid in my mind is my vision of Elena. She didn't beg, and she didn't feel sorry for herself. Selling her matches, her spirit shone through, simply trying to scratch out a semblance of a living. So I say to you reading this: The next time you hear an ad about sponsoring a child, pay attention.

5. World Issues

Combine each of the following pairs of sentences into one sentence with an
independent clause and an adverbial phrase, using the form in parentheses.

1. We want to make the world safer. We must outlaw chemical and biological warfare. (infinitive)

   <u>To make the world safer, we must outlaw chemical and biological warfare.</u>

2. We are given the choice between disaster and some kind of restriction on our right to have as many children as we want. We may have to choose the latter. (past participle) *replace subject + aux. c̄ past participle*

   Given the choice ...

   — used when a̶x̶'ing a passive meaning, emphasis on " we may have to ... "

3. The world's population grew slowly between the years 500 and 1700. It then began to accelerate. (*having* + past participle) *actions + events that have occurred at diff. times*

   between the years 500 + 1700,

   Having grown slowly, the world's pop'n ...

4. Farmers all over the world clear more and more land for farms every year. They unfortunately destroy animal habitats. (present participle) *2 actions or events that occur at the same time*

   most NB idea in the independent clause

   Clearing more + more land for farms each year, Farmers unfortunately ...

5. Many governments want to ensure that their citizens are healthy. They provide immunizations to all children. (infinitive) *sense of purpose involved in the action*

   To ensure ...

6. Health officials in some countries provide contraceptive devices to their citizens. They are trying to deal with the problem of overpopulation. (*by* + present participle) *clear sense of intention + purpose*

   By providing contraceptive devices ...

7. We must stabilize the world's population growth. We need to prevent ecological disaster. (infinitive)

   To prevent ...

8. We have witnessed two devastating conflicts in this century. We must do everything in our power to prevent future world wars. (*having* + past participle)

6. Editing

Each of the following sentences from a student's exam in a World Problems class contains an incorrect adverbial phrase. Correct each sentence.

1. Giving the options of doing nothing or of controlling population growth, we must choose the latter.

   Given the options of doing nothing or of controlling population growth, we must choose the latter.

   "Having plus past participle — actions or events that occured at diff. times

2. To observe that population and food supply grow at different rates, Malthus warned us of a problem.

   To prevent — infinitive: sense of purpose — involved in action

3. Preventing unrest, governments everywhere must ensure full employment.

4. Recognized that overpopulation was a problem, the Chinese government took action.

   present participle — events occured around same time
   Having + past participle

5. Established a policy of limiting births, Chinese government officials now have to enforce it.

   Having established

6. Leaders of governments throughout the world must do something comprehensive having prevented a major disaster.

   to prevent
   inf.

7. If carrying out right, the adoption of ZPG would cause the population to decrease.

   carried
   reduced adverb clauses

8. By we sponsor a needy child in the Third World, we make the world a little better.

   sponsoring
   clear sense of intention + purpose
   By + present participle

COMMUNICATION PRACTICE

7. Practice Listening

UNESCO expert Galina Malchevskaya is giving a talk to a class of college students. Listen to their conversation on the tape. Then listen again and circle the letter of the sentence that explains the meaning of certain of Ms. Malchevskaya's sentences.

1. a. Scientists will wipe out smallpox soon.

   (b.) Scientists wiped out smallpox.

2. a. A cure for AIDS has been discovered.

   b. A cure for AIDS hasn't been discovered.

3. a. We can prevent disaster if we ignore the need for population control.

   b. We can't prevent disaster if we ignore the need for population control.

4. a. Zero Population Growth has already been achieved.

   b. Zero Population Growth has not yet been achieved.

5. a. With ZPG, couples would not have more than two children.

   b. With ZPG, couples would reach childbearing age having had two children.

6. a. ZPG could work if it were carried out properly.

   b. If ZPG reduced the number of people properly, it would be carried out.

7. a. Someone would present proposals to us.

   b. We would present proposals to someone.

8. a. We have already arrived at a comprehensive solution for each country.

   b. We haven't yet arrived at a comprehensive solution for each country.

9. a. War and poverty have been prevented.

   b. War and poverty have not been prevented.

10. a. Higher-yield crops will be developed in the future.

    b. Higher-yield crops have already been developed.

8. Pair and Group Discussion

With a partner, write sentences expressing your opinions for or against the statements about the following topics. Then share your opinions with the class.

Topic 1. We need to solve the problem of overpopulation.
> **Example:** We *do* need to solve the problem of overpopulation. **To solve the problem of overpopulation,** we need to think about limiting births.

Topic 2. We need to persuade people to accept ZPG.
Topic 3. We can improve the lot of homeless people.

9. Debate

It is the year 2025. A colony on the asteroid Ceres has run out of space and resources. A law is being proposed making it illegal for a couple to have more than two children. Divide into two groups: those supporting the law and those opposing it. Within your group, prepare your argument. Then have a debate on the issue.

10. Essay

Choose one of the following topics and write a short essay of three or four paragraphs about it. Try to use at least four of the five types of adverbial phrases in your essay.

Topic 1. Having carefully thought about the problem of overpopulation, I believe . . .
Topic 2. To persuade people that overpopulation is an extremely serious problem, . . .
Topic 3. Given the choice between letting events follow their current course and making some serious changes, . . .

- MOST use all 5 adverbial modifying phrases in their total of SIX sentences

- must explain the construction of the phrase (inf., having + past participle) + why they used it

11. Picture Discussion

The addition of bovine growth hormone to cattle feed is one method of increasing milk production. Its use has caused considerable controversy. With a partner, prepare the script of an impartial news report about the recent availability of this product in your community.

I. *Read the conversations. Underline all adverb clauses.*

1. **A:** Honey, we're going to be late <u>if we don't leave right now</u>.
   B: OK. We can leave <u>as soon as you back the car out of the garage</u>.

2. **A:** Harry is a lot more responsible <u>than he used to be</u>.
   B: Yeah, I know. He never used to do his chores <u>unless I threatened him</u>. Now he does things without being told.

3. **A:** I'll call you <u>when the plane gets in</u>.
   B: OK, but you'd better take down Ida's number <u>in case I'm not home</u>.

4. **A:** Wasn't that a great dinner? I ate so much <u>that I can hardly move</u>.
   B: Yeah. Dad is such a fabulous cook <u>that I end up gaining a few pounds</u> <u>whenever I come home to visit</u>.

5. **A:** You know, there aren't as many good shows <u>as there used to be</u>.
   B: Oh, I don't know. You have access to some pretty impressive programming—<u>provided that you have cable</u>.

6. **A:** Joe, <u>since you didn't turn in your term paper</u>, you didn't pass the course—<u>even though you did well on the tests</u>.
   B: Yes, I know. I didn't do it <u>because I couldn't think of anything to write about</u>.

II. *Choose transitions from the box to complete the news item.*
Use each transition only once.

otherwise	however	thus
moreover	in fact	next

We focus _____next_____ on the mission of the Ares, the manned

space mission of WASA, the World Aeronautics and Space Association. The

Ares was launched seven months ago from Woomera Spaceport in

Australia. ____However____, contact had been lost with the Ares for the

past three weeks, and WASA officials had feared the worst. WASA officials

were ____thus____ elated when they received a radio message today

that the Ares has made a successful landing on Mars. Harald Svendorf,

chief of WASA, had this to say in today's news conference: "We needed a

victory; ____otherwise____, we might have lost our United Nations funding.

This successful landing should silence our critics, who have been calling

the Ares Project a boondoggle. The project will ____moreover____ be one

of the most cost-effective missions in the history of space exploration.

____In fact____, it will pave the way toward realization of other manned

missions to the Jovian moons and to Venus."

III. *Combine the two sentences into one sentence with a dependent clause and an independent clause. Use the indicated subordinating conjunction.*

1. Mel and Sarah Figueroa were in a difficult situation. They both had jobs and didn't have day care for their two children. (because)

    Mel and Sarah Figueroa were in a difficult situation because they both had

    jobs and didn't have day care for their two children.

2. They had been leaving the children with Sarah's mother. This wasn't a satisfactory situation. (though)

3. One of them was going to have to quit working. They could find a solution to the problem. (unless)

4. One of their neighbors proposed the creation of a day care co-op involving seven families. Their problem was solved. (when)

5. Each day, one of the parents in the co-op cares for all of the children. The other parents are working. (while)

IV. *Correct the eight mistakes in negative and focus adverbs in the letter.*

Dear Samantha,

I wanted to thank you again for your hospitality while we were in
Vancouver. Not only ~~did~~ you and Michael ~~showed~~ *show* us a wonderful time, but we
got to re-establish the close ties we used to have. The ~~even~~ kids enjoyed the
trip, and you know how kids can be on vacations. Only I hope that Dan and I
can reciprocate sometime.

The drive back to Edmonton was something else; ~~almost we~~ didn't make it
back in one piece. About four-thirty on the day we left, there was an ice
storm near Calgary which turned the highway into a sheet of ice. Little ~~we~~ *did*
knew that it would take us four hours to get through the city! Never I ~~have~~ *did*
been in such a colossal traffic jam. By the time we got off the freeway, it was
eleven-thirty at night, and the kids were crying. We stopped at a motel to try
to get a room. They were full up, but when we asked the proprietors if ~~just~~
we could *just* spend the night in their lobby, they took pity on us and made us up
a bed in their living room. People can be so kind sometimes. Never again I *will*
will think twice about helping people when they need it.

By the next morning, the roads had been cleared, and we made it safely
back to Edmonton.

So, that's all for now. Thanks again.

Love,
Barb

V. *Punctuate the following sentences, which form a narration, with commas or semicolons. Do not add periods or capital letters.*

1. Jeff and Jackie Donovan felt that their children were watching too much television **,** but they didn't know what to do about the problem.
2. They tried combinations of threats, punishments, and rewards however, nothing seemed to work.
3. Jeff and Jackie both got home about 5:30 P.M. and they needed to occupy the children's attention while they were fixing dinner.
4. Though they felt so much TV watching wasn't good they allowed it because they had no alternative.
5. Their children weren't getting enough exercise also, they weren't interacting with the neighborhood children.
6. Since a lot of their neighbors were having the same problem with their children someone came up with the idea of starting a neighborhood activities club.
7. The club met every afternoon from 5:00 until 6:30 and two parents from different families supervised activities.
8. The club has been a big success none of the children have watched very much television lately.

VI. *Each of the following sentences has four underlined words or phrases. The four underlined parts of each sentence are marked A, B, C, or D. Circle the letter of the one underlined word or phrase that is not correct.*

1. By pool the world's food supply, we might conceivably avert
   A B   C
   starvation—provided that the food were disbursed evenly.
              D
   A **Ⓑ** C D

2. To feel that pleas to sponsor orphans in Third World nations
   A
   were only rip-off schemes, I refused until recently even to consider
        B   C   D
   giving money.
   A B C D

3. Drivers should be extremely careful when give a ride to
                     A   B   C
   hitchhikers, even if they look completely respectable.
                D
   A B C D

4. Although his prose is dense, columnist James Makela, having written
   A   B
   in the *Carson City Courier,* forcefully makes the point that only rarely
                                C
   is capital punishment carried out in an evenhanded manner.
   D
   A B C D

5. Automobiles certainly cause many problems, however they
              A   B
   fortunately provide us with benefits also.
   C   D
   A B C D

6. Feeling that the subject was beneath me, I unfortunately learned
   A   B
   something at all when I took calculus last quarter.
   C   D
   A B C D

7. Happily, the leaders of almost all world nations seem to have
   A   B
   realized that something must quickly be done controlling
                                C   D
   the growth of population.
   A B C D

8. My having landed at Orly Airport, a taxi took me speedily to the
   A   B   C
   hotel where the conference was to be held.
         D
   A B C D

From Grammar to Writing

Sentences and Fragments

As you have learned, a sentence must have at least one independent, or main, clause. (See From Grammar to Writing after Part I, page 46, for a discussion of the sentence.) If a group of words does not have an independent clause, it is a fragment, not a sentence.

> We need to do something about violence. (sentence—independent clause)
> Because it's tearing apart the fabric of societies everywhere. (fragment—dependent clause)
> Sitting in my auto (fragment—no independent clause)

For correctness in writing, we normally avoid sentence fragments. To correct a fragment, we often attach it to an independent clause. We can do this with the fragment above.

> We need to do something about violence **because it's tearing apart the fabric of societies everywhere.**

If there is no independent clause nearby, we can correct a fragment by adding a subject and its verb.

> Interviewed by our news team. (fragment)
> **One commuter was interviewed** by our news team. (sentence)

A. *In the following sentences, underline dependent clauses once and independent clauses twice. Do not underline phrases. In the blank to the left of each item, write* S *for sentence or* F *for fragment.*

___S___ 1. Though you handled the car well, you ran a red light.

_____ 2. As soon as you learn the hand signals.

_____ 3. Although China is overpopulated, it is trying to correct the problem.

_____ 4. We don't solve the problem of violence until we control guns.

_____ 5. If a young basketball player from Nigeria can get a scholarship.

_____ 6. Because I was one of those students.

_____ 7. The economy is perhaps too dependent on the automobile.

_____ 8. Carried out right, this procedure would cause the population to stabilize.

_____ 9. By the time the train finally arrived in Santa Maria.

_____ 10. We need to make some personal sacrifices if we want to help.

B. *Read the following paragraph. Correct the fragments by joining them to the independent clauses to which they are logically connected. Where necessary, add commas and change capitalization, but do not add words.*

    The life of Dorothy and Patrick has improved immeasurably. Since they both got new jobs. Dorothy got a position as a proofreader and editor at a publishing company. That is pioneering new workplace methods. Patrick was hired as a full-time consultant for an engineering firm. The difference between their new jobs and their old ones can be summed up in one word:

flextime. Until they secured these new positions. Dorothy and Patrick had a very difficult time raising their two small children. Their life was extremely stressful. Because they were at the mercy of a nine-to-five schedule and had to pay a lot for day care. In order to get to work on time. They had to have the children at the day care center by 7:30 every morning. Both of their new companies, however, offer a flextime schedule. As long as Dorothy and Patrick put in their forty hours a week. They are free to work. When it is convenient for them. Now they can take turns staying home with the children, and day care is just a memory. Best of all, the children are much happier. Because they are getting the attention they need.

2.

If a sentence has only one clause, it is called a simple sentence.

> I bought a new car last month. (simple sentence: one independent clause)

If two independent clauses are connected by a coordinating conjunction (*and, but, or, nor, for, so, yet*), the larger sentence is called a <u>compound</u> sentence. We place a comma before the coordinating conjunction.

> The tea was virtually flavorless. The sandwich tasted like cardboard.
> The tea was virtually flavorless, **and** the sandwich tasted like cardboard.

We don't normally place a comma before a coordinating conjunction if it does not connect two independent clauses.* That is, there must be a subject and its verb in both clauses.

> We can go out to a film or stay home and watch television.
> (There is no subject in the second half of the sentence.)

Note, though, that if we join two very short independent clauses with a coordinating conjunction, we can eliminate the comma before the coordinating conjunction.*

> I love movies but I hate television.

If a sentence contains an independent clause and one or more dependent clauses, it is called a <u>complex</u> sentence. If the dependent clause comes first, we frequently put a comma after it. If it comes second, we usually don't put a comma before it unless the dependent clause establishes a contrast.

> **Because they provide activity,** school sports are worthwhile.
> School sports are worthwhile **because they provide activity.**
>
> **Though they aren't everything,** jobs are important.
> Jobs are important, **though they aren't everything.**
> (The subordinating conjunction **though** establishes a contrast, so we use a comma before it.)

*Remember that you can, however, use a comma before a coordinating conjunction when it is being used before the last item in a series: I don't like pie, cake**, or** ice cream.

C. *Place commas wherever possible in the following sentences. In the blank to the left of each item, write S for a simple sentence,* CPD *for a compound sentence, or* CX *for a complex sentence.*

<u>CPD</u> 1. Violence exists nearly everywhere in the world, and it is spreading.

<u>CX</u> 2. Since we usually watch TV at home in our living room, a TV show doesn't seem like a special event.

<u>CPD</u> 3. The population will continue to increase, but natural resources won't.

<u>CX</u> 4. We must make trains viable again if we expect people to use them.

<u>CX</u> 5. I listened politely for a while and then excused myself.

<u>CX</u> 6. The governor isn't in favor of higher taxes nor does she encourage the development of mass transit.

<u>CX</u> 7. We don't have to buy a lot of groceries at once, for we can always stop at the supermarket on the way home from work.

<u>CPD</u> 8. You passed your driving exam with flying colors, though you could use some practice in parallel parking.

<u>CX</u> 9. As I was entering the dining car, a violent lurch of the train threw me to the left.

3.

Coordinating conjunctions, subordinating conjunctions, and transitions often have similarities in meaning but are used with different sentence patterns and punctuation. Notice the use of *but*, *although*, and *however* in the following sentences:

> Cars provide many benefits, **but** they also do considerable harm.
> **Although** cars provide many benefits, they also do considerable harm.
> Cars provide many benefits; **however**, they also do considerable harm.

The meanings of these three examples are similar, but the emphasis is different. It is also correct to use a period and a capital letter in the third example:

> Cars provide many benefits. **H**owever, they also do considerable harm.

D. *For each of the following sentences, write two other sentences that express a similar meaning, using the connectors given.*

I tried to board the train and find a seat; however, there wasn't one available.

1. (but) _____ I tried to board the train and find a seat, but _____

_____ there wasn't one available. _____

2. (although) _____

_____

Heavy rail tracks are already there, so heavy rail has gotten the best press.

3. (because) _____

_____

4. (therefore) _____

_____

You ran a red light, in addition to the fact that you don't seem to know the hand signals.

5. (and) _____

_____

6. (also) _____

_____

VI

▼

Adjective
Clauses

INTRODUCTION

▣▣ *Read and listen to an excerpt from the script of a student's speech to a class.*

Questions to Consider

1. Are you an "extrovert" or an "introvert"?
2. Is it a good idea to classify people into personality types? Why or why not?

What Type Are You?

Are you a person **who acts on the world,** or are you someone **who lets the world act on you?** Today I'm going to tell you about various categories **that have been developed to classify people.** My hope is that you'll be able to learn something about yourself.

Let's start with the most familiar of the traditional types, the extrovert and the introvert. Many people think that an extrovert is a person **who is courageous, outgoing, and not at all shy.** They believe that an introvert is someone **who is shy, retiring, and fearful.** These are misconceptions. Actually, psychologists define an extrovert as a person **who needs the company of others to become energized,** while an introvert is the kind of person **who needs to be alone to become energized.** Let me illustrate with some examples.

Samantha is actually a shy person **whom others probably wouldn't consider extroverted.** However, Samantha opens up in situations **in which she starts to feel relaxed and appreciated.** At a large party **where she doesn't know many people,** she's shy at first, but when the number of guests thins down, Samantha comes alive. She likes to talk once she finds a group **she feels comfortable with,** and when she opens up she's the kind of person **others find interesting and stimulating.** By eleven o'clock in the evening, she's just getting warmed up. The later it gets, the more animated and activated she starts to feel. Samantha needs others to help energize her, **which is why she is to be considered an extrovert.**

Bill, on the other hand, is someone **whom everyone considers bold, outgoing, the antithesis of shy.** Bill goes to a party and has a good time for a while, but he usually stays only for a short time, for he's a person **whose energies need solitude for replenishment.** He often finds the conversation around him interesting, but he is just as likely to be remembering a time **when he was hiking alone in the mountains or strolling in solitude along the ocean shore.** He needs to be alone to reenergize, **which is why he is to be regarded as an introvert.** By 9:30, Bill is tired and has had enough of the party. He wants to go home and settle down with a good book.

There's a third category **many of us may fall into:** that of the ambivert. Mary, **who is energized sometimes by others and sometimes by being alone,** is a good example. There are times **when Mary is like Samantha.** She gets activated by the stimulation of others and becomes quite outgoing. But there are other times **when Mary is much more like Bill.** On certain Friday nights, for example, after a long, hard workweek, Mary likes nothing better than to spend a quiet evening at home, reading or working on her own projects. Many of us, perhaps even the majority, are probably ambiverts.

ADJECTIVE CLAUSES: REVIEW AND EXPANSION

IDENTIFYING ADJECTIVE CLAUSES

WHO

Are you a person **who acts on the world?**

THAT

I'm going to describe some categories **that have been developed to classify people.**

WHOM

Samantha is a person **whom others wouldn't consider extroverted.**

WHEN

There are times **when many of us feel extroverted** and other times **when we feel introverted.**

(continued on next page)

WHERE

> She feels shy at a party **where she doesn't know many people.**

WHICH

> A cocktail party is a setting **which can be threatening to a shy person.**

WHOSE

> Bill is a person **whose energies need solitude for replenishment.**

PREPOSITION + WHICH

> Harriet opens up in situations **in which she starts to feel relaxed and appreciated.**

PREPOSITION + WHOM

> The Grants are the couple **with whom we are negotiating.**

DELETED RELATIVE PRONOUN

> Harriet likes to talk once she finds a group **[that] she feels comfortable with.**

NONIDENTIFYING ADJECTIVE CLAUSES

WHO

> Meredith, **who is energized sometimes by others and sometimes by being alone,** is an ambivert.

WHOM

> The Ochoas, **whom you met at Jason's party,** are really very amiable people.

WHICH

> Introversion, **which is a common behavior pattern,** isn't necessarily accompanied by shyness.

WHOSE

> Luis, **whose brother is visiting from New York,** does not want to come to the party.

NONIDENTIFYING ADJECTIVE CLAUSE MODIFYING AN ENTIRE PRECEDING AREA

WHICH

> Samantha needs others to help energize her, **which is why she is to be considered an extrovert.**

Grammar Notes

1. Adjective clauses are dependent clauses that modify nouns and pronouns. They are introduced by the relative pronouns *who, whom, whose, that,* and *which,* or by *when* and *where.* Sentences with adjective clauses can be seen as a combination of two sentences.

> The man lives across the street from me. The man is the mayor.
> The man **who lives across the street from me** is the mayor.

2. Adjective clauses which are used to identify (distinguish one person or thing from another) are called <u>identifying</u> (or <u>restrictive</u>, <u>defining</u>, or <u>essential</u>).

> A person **who is energized by others** is an extrovert. (The clause, **who is energized by others,** identifies which kind of person is an extrovert.)

An adjective clause which is not used to identify something but simply adds extra information is called <u>nonidentifying</u> (or <u>nonrestrictive</u>, <u>nondefining</u>, or <u>nonessential</u>).

> Mary, **who sometimes likes to be with others and sometimes likes to be alone,** is an ambivert. (The adjective clause, **who sometimes likes to be with others and sometimes likes to be alone,** is not used to identify the person we are talking about; the name **Mary** identifies the person. The clause gives additional information about Mary.)

Punctuation note: Nonidentifying adjective clauses are enclosed by commas. Identifying adjective clauses have no commas around them.

See From Grammar to Writing after Part VI, pages 248 and 249, for more information about punctuation of adjective clauses.

Pronunciation note: In speech, identifying clauses have no pauses before or after them. Nonidentifying clauses do have a pause before and after them.

> identifying adjective clause
> My sister **who won the lottery** is an unemployed social worker. (I have more than one sister. One of them won the lottery.)

> nonidentifying adjective clause
> My sister, (PAUSE) **who won the lottery,** (PAUSE) is an unemployed social worker. (I have one sister. She won the lottery.)

3. Like all clauses, adjective clauses contain subjects and verbs. The relative pronouns *who, which,* and *that* are used as subjects.

> A person **who tells jokes** is an amusing person. (**Who** is the subject of the clause verb **tells.**)
> The house **that has been condemned** will be bulldozed. (**That** is the subject of the clause verb **has been condemned.**)
> The building **which was damaged by the earthquake** was later demolished by the wrecking crew. (**Which** is the subject of the clause verb **was damaged.**)

Be careful! Do not use a subject pronoun in an adjective clause in which the relative pronoun is the subject.

> The man **who lives down the street from me is a spelunker.** NOT ~~The man who he lives down the street from me is a spelunker.~~

4. The relative pronouns *whom, that,* and *which* are used as objects in adjective clauses.

> Bill, **whom** many regard as outgoing, is an introvert. (The relative pronoun **whom** is the direct object of the verb **regard.**)
> Samantha likes talking to people **that** she feels comfortable with. (The relative pronoun **that** is the object of the preposition **with.**)

(continued on next page)

The city **which** I find most interesting is Paris. (The relative pronoun **which** is the direct object of the verb **find.**)

Be careful! It is common in conversation to omit the relative pronoun *who, whom, which,* or *that.* This can only be done, however, if the relative pronoun is an object. You cannot omit the relative pronoun if it is the subject of a clause.

may be omitted
The woman **(that/who/whom)** I saw at the carnival is Bill's aunt. (The relative pronouns **that, who,** or **whom** can be omitted because they are objects.)

may not be omitted
A person **who** will help the needy is a caring person. NOT A person will help the needy is a caring person. (The relative pronoun **who** cannot be omitted because it is the subject of the clause.)

Also, you cannot omit a relative pronoun in a nonidentifying adjective clause.

Mary, **who sometimes likes to be alone,** also likes to go to parties. NOT Mary, sometimes likes to be alone, also likes to go to parties.

5. Note that *who* and *whom* are used to refer to persons, not things. *That* can be used to refer both to persons and things and is considered more informal than *who* and *whom. Which* is used to refer only to things.

The lady **who/that** stopped by is the president of the Women's Club. NOT The lady which stopped by is the president of the Women's Club.

Which and *that* are used interchangeably in identifying clauses.

The house **which/that** is on the corner is for sale.

In a nonidentifying clause, only *which* can be used.

Victoria, **which** is the capital of British Columbia, resembles an English city. NOT Victoria, that is the capital of British Columbia, resembles an English city.

6. *Whom* is considerably more formal than *who* and is appropriate for formal writing and careful speech. *Who* is appropriate

elsewhere. (Although *who* is used as a subject in adjective clauses, it is often used as an object in conversational speech.)

The people **whom we saw on our vacation** are from Manitoba. (very formal)
The people **who we saw on our vacation** are from Manitoba. (less formal, conversational—**who** used as object)

7. In conversation and informal writing, native speakers commonly place the preposition in an adjective clause at the end of the sentence, and they often omit the relative pronoun.

Samantha likes people she feels comfortable with.

Here are more formal equivalents of this sentence:

Samantha likes people **that she feels comfortable with.** (slightly more formal)
Samantha likes people **who she feels comfortable with.** (a bit more formal)
Samantha likes people **whom she feels comfortable with.** (even more formal)
Samantha likes people **with whom she feels comfortable.** (the most formal)

8. The relative pronoun *whose* is used to introduce an adjective clause in which a possessive is needed. *Whose* does not appear without a following noun in an adjective clause.

The family **whose dog escaped and bit the children** have to pay a fine.

9. Adjective clauses can be introduced with *when* and *where.* Adjective clauses with *when* describe a time; those with *where* describe a place.

Kelly is remembering a time **when life was hard for her.**
Owen feels nervous at parties **where he doesn't know anyone.**

10. The relative pronoun *which* can be used informally to introduce a clause that modifies an entire preceding idea. In these instances, *which* must be preceded by a comma.

I've discovered that Sam is actually quite a shy person, **which surprises me.**

The clause *which surprises me* modifies the entire preceding idea, that Sam is actually quite a shy person. Clauses of this type are common in conversation. They are not recommended for more formal speaking and writing, however. To construct the sentence above more formally, find a specific noun that *which* can modify or try to write the sentence in some other way.

I've discovered that Sam is actually quite a shy person, **a fact which** surprises me. (**Which** modifies the noun **fact.**)

I've been surprised to discover that Sam is actually quite a shy person. (recast sentence)

FOCUSED PRACTICE

1. Discover the Grammar

Read the next part of the student's speech on personality types. Underline all the adjective clauses.

Now here's another way of classifying people. In *The Presidential Character,* historian James Barber classifies presidents into four personality types: active-positive, active-negative, passive-positive, and passive-negative. However, Barber's categories might be applied to anyone, not just to presidents. Let's consider each of these.

First, the active-positive person is the type <u>who acts on the world and derives pleasure from doing so.</u> He or she is one whom others regard as a take-charge leader who gets things done. Active-positives are people who regard the world as their oyster. Daniela, who is president of her high school class, doesn't hesitate to use her power, for she is convinced that her actions will lead to developments that benefit everyone.

Second, the active-negative is a person whose behavior is similar to that of the active-positive in the sense of acting on the world. However, active-negatives feel negative about themselves and the world in certain ways. Martin, who is a good example of an active-negative, is like Daniela in that he gets out and does things, but unlike Daniela, he doesn't get much inner satisfaction from doing so, which is surprising, given that he puts a great amount of effort into his work.

Third, the passive-positive is the kind of individual others regard as a "nice person." Mark, who allows the world to act on him, is a good example of a passive-positive. He can't remember a time when he didn't have a lot of friends.

(continued on next page)

However, he's the kind of individual one can easily take advantage of. Partly because he doesn't have a very positive self-image, he's always agreeable, which is what people like about him.

Fourth, passive-negatives are similar to passive-positives in having a negative self-image and in allowing the world to act on them. However, they tend to view the world as a place where unfortunate things are likely to happen. Passive-negatives often try to compensate for the world's unpleasantness by getting involved in service to others and by stressing moral principles. Laura, who is always worried that disaster is just around the corner, is the perfect passive-negative. She's a member of her school's student review board, a disciplinary group that deals with infractions by students.

Are you an introvert, extrovert, or ambivert? Are you active-positive, active-negative, passive-positive, or passive-negative? Take a look in the mirror.

Reference: James David Barber, *The Presidential Character: Predicting Performance in the White House* (Englewood Cliffs: Prentice-Hall, 1972).

2. People in the Office

Dolores Atwood, a personnel officer for a publishing company, is writing an evaluation of the employees in her department who are being considered for promotion. Write adjective clauses with **which** *to modify entire preceding ideas.*

LOOK BOOKS
Personnel Evaluation
Confidential

Elaine Correa has only been with us for a year but is definitely ready for promotion,

_____which is not surprising_____, given the glowing recommendations she got from her last employer.
1. (not/be/surprising)

Burt Drysdale has proven himself to be a team player, _____, considering the fact
2. (I/find/somewhat amazing)

that he rubbed everyone the wrong way at first. I do recommend him for promotion.

Alice Anderdoff, on the other hand, is not performing up to expectations, _____
3. (bother/me)

because I was the one who recruited her. I don't believe she should be considered for promotion at this time.

Mel Tualapa is a very congenial employee, _____, but he can't be promoted
4. (be/what/everyone/like/about him)

yet because he's only been with us for six months.

Lately, Tom Curran has often been ill and consistently late to work, _____,
5. (be/mystifying)

because he was such a model employee at first. I don't recommend him at this time.

3. Formal and Informal

Read the following two descriptions. The first is a spoken report by a head attorney to her team of lawyers. The second contains the same information but is a formal written description. Complete the conversation with informal adjective clauses, omitting relative pronouns if possible and using contractions. Complete the written piece with formal adjective clauses. Do not omit relative pronouns, and place prepositions at the beginning of clauses in which they occur. Do not use contractions.

Spoken Report

Our client is a guy ___who's been in trouble___ for minor offenses, but I don't think he's a murderer,
        1. (have / be / in trouble)

_____ I feel comfortable defending him. He served time in the penitentiary from
    2. (which / be / why)

1992 to 1994, and according to all the reports he was a person _____. Since
            3. (the other prisoners / look up to)

he got out of jail in 1994, he's had a good employment record with Textrix, an electronics company

_____. The psychological reports on him show that when he was in prison he was
    4. (he / be / working / for)

a person _____ well balanced and even-tempered, _____
     5. (the psychiatrists / consider)   6. (which / be / why)

I don't think he's guilty.

Written Report

Our client is a man ___who has been in trouble___ for minor offenses, but I do not believe that he is a
        7. (have / be / in trouble)

murderer, _____ feel comfortable in defending him. He served time in the
    8. (a fact / which / make / me)

penitentiary from 1992 to 1994, and according to all the reports he was a person

_____. Since he was released from prison in 1994, he has had a good employment
    9. (whom / the other prisoners / respect)

record with Textrix, an electronics company _____. His psychological profile
          10. (for / which / he / be / working)

suggests that when he was in prison he was a person _____ well-balanced and
               11. (whom / the psychiatrists / consider)

even-tempered, _____ believe that he is not guilty.
    12. (evidence / which / make / me)

4. Editing

Read the letter from a college student to his parents. Find and correct the eight errors in relative pronouns in adjective clauses.

September 28

Dear Mom and Dad,

   Well, the first week of college has been hectic, but it's turned out OK. My advisor is a lady who ~~she~~ is also from Winnipeg, so we had something who we could talk about.

   Since I haven't decided on a major, she had me take one of those tests show you what you're most interested in. She also had me do one of those personality inventories that they tell you what kind of person you are. According to these tests, I'm a person whom is an extrovert. I also found out that I'm most interested in things involve being on the stage and performing in some way, who doesn't surprise me a bit. I always liked being in school plays, remember? I signed up for two drama courses.

   Classes start on Wednesday, and I'm getting to know the other guys which live in my dormitory. It's pretty exciting being here.

   Not much else. I'll call in a week or so.

Love,

Al

COMMUNICATION PRACTICE

5. Practice Listening 1

Listen to the conversation. Then listen again and circle the letter of the sentence which correctly describes what you hear on the tape.

1. a. Bob took the job because it pays well.

    b. Bob took the job because he likes the work.

2. a. Paperwork makes Bob angry.

    b. The fact that Bob has been assigned to do a lot of paperwork makes him angry.

3. a. Bob is irritated because his co-worker is a passive-aggressive type of person.

    b. Bob is irritated because he wasn't consulted before being assigned to his co-worker.

4. a. Jennifer is surprised that Bob is disgruntled.

    b. Jennifer is surprised that Bob took the job.

5. a. His feelings about his co-workers are making Bob wonder about himself.

    b. The fact that Bob didn't investigate the company is making him wonder about himself.

6. Tape Discussion

How can you get along better with a co-worker you don't like?

7. Practice Listening 2

Read and listen to the following excerpts from a telephone conversation that Al had with his parents. Then circle the letters of the sentences which correctly describe the meanings of certain sentences that you hear on the tape.

1. a. There is one supervisor.

    b. There is more than one supervisor.

2. a. All of Al's roommates are from Canada.

    b. Some of Al's roommates are from Canada.

3. a. Al has one English class.

    b. Al has more than one English class.

4. a. Al has one history class.

    b. Al has more than one history class.

5. a. There is one group of girls.

    b. There is more than one group of girls.

6. a. Al has one advisor.

    b. Al has more than one advisor.

8. Small Group Discussion

Do you think that astrology has any validity? Look at the chart and determine your astrological sign according to your date of birth. Divide into groups of four, in which each person has a different astrological sign. Begin by making sentences with adjective clauses about people born under a particular sign. Then discuss whether you think there is any validity to the characterizations.

Example:

1. A Gemini is a person **who was born between May 21 and June 20.**
   Geminis are supposed to be people **who are of two minds about everything.**
   They supposedly have trouble making decisions because they can easily see
   both sides to a question. To a certain degree, I think this is true because it fits
   me; I always agonize over decisions. In other ways, though, it doesn't. . . .

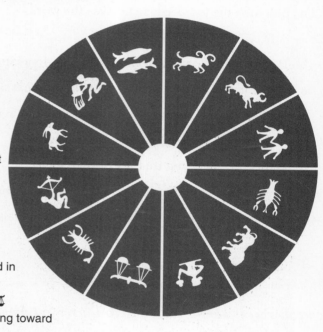

Aries the Ram 🐏 (March 21–April 20) 🐏
Strong-willed, daring, enthusiastic, good conversationalist

Taurus the Bull 🐂 (April 21–May 20) 🐂
Warm, stubborn, practical, good parent

Gemini the Twins 👥 (May 21–June 20) 👥
Quick, possessed of two personalities, energetic, impatient

Cancer the Crab 🦞 (June 21–July 22) 🦞
Emotional, patriotic, fond of change, needs to feel loved

Leo the Lion 🦁 (July 23–August 22) 🦁
Bright, proud, self-confident, frustrated with failure

Virgo the Virgin 🏃 (August 21–September 22) 🏃
Methodical, intellectual, tending toward perfectionism, good in
emergencies

Libra the Scales ⚖️ (September 23–October 22) ⚖️
Peaceloving, artistic, known for balance and fairness, tending toward
perfectionism

Scorpio the Scorpion 🦂 (October 23–November 22) 🦂
Powerful, intense, passionate, bullheaded

Sagittarius the Archer 🏹 (November 23–December 21) 🏹
Direct, highly honest, philosophical, impulsive

Capricorn the Goat 🐐 (December 22–January 22) 🐐
Steady, practical, conservative, stubborn

Aquarius the Water Bearer 🏺 (January 20–February 19) 🏺
Generous, creative, humanitarian, soft-spoken

Pisces the Fishes 🐟 (February 20–March 20) 🐟
Sympathetic, generous, dreamy, can be difficult to know

Adapted from Mary-Paige Royer, *Great Mysteries: Astrology* (San Diego: Greenhaven Press, Inc., 1991).

9. Essay

Consider again the personality categories which have been mentioned in this unit and choose the one that you believe fits you the best. Write an essay of from three to five paragraphs, showing why you fit the category. Include several examples from your own experience.

10. Picture Discussion

Look at this picture as a reflection of a time and a place. What was it like? How are the people dressed? How do they relate to each other?

Example:
The woman **who is standing in the center** of the picture is holding her daughter's hand very tightly.

Georges Seurat, French, 1859–1891, *A Sunday on La Grande Jatte—1884*
oil on canvas, 1884–86, 207.5 x 308 cm, Helen Birch Bartlett Memorial Collection, 1926.224.
Photograph ©1994, The Art Institute of Chicago, All Rights Reserved.

INTRODUCTION

▣ *Read and listen to the movie review.*

Questions to Consider

1. Do you like movies? What do you look for in a movie? Do you see movies primarily for entertainment, or do you want a film to be something more?
2. *Citizen Kane* is a search to unravel the mystery of a man's life. Can a movie do this better than a book?

☆ FLICK PICKS ☆ FLICK PICKS ☆ FLICK PICKS ☆

CITIZEN KANE:
NOW MORE THAN EVER

by Dartagnan Fletcher

With all the hoopla **surrounding the restoration and reissue of the Orson Welles classic movie** *Citizen Kane,* this reviewer thought it was time to put his two cents in. Approaching the writing of this review, I first jotted down twenty reasons why people should see this picture, **all of which I eventually threw away in favor of these four words:** Just go see it. Anyone **really serious about cinema** should know this film.

Citizen Kane, **said to be based loosely on** **the life and career of newspaper magnate William Randolph Hearst,** stars Orson Welles in the title role of a man who rises from rags to riches and dies in solitude and loneliness. Welles, **also the picture's director and script coauthor,** was only twenty-five when he made *Citizen Kane.* The film wasn't very popular when it was first released in 1941; rank-and-file moviegoers, **many of whom probably regarded its subject matter as too grim,** may have wanted something **happier and more upbeat.** The film won only one Oscar, **for** **best original screenplay.** In the years since, however, *CK*'s reputation has grown steadily, especially with critics, **most of whom regard it as one of the greatest films ever.** Why?

Citizen Kane opens in the bedroom of the dying millionaire businessman, Charles Foster Kane. As a nurse enters the room, we see the camera focus on the lips of Kane, who mutters his last word before dying: "Rosebud." The nurse's report creates a sensation in the press, **some members of which try frenetically to learn about the life of Kane,**

regarded as the quintessential man of mystery. The editor of one newspaper commissions a major investigation. Who or what was Rosebud? A lost love? Someone or something from Kane's childhood? In an attempt to find out, an investigative reporter interviews people **close to Kane during his life, including his business associates, his former best friend, and his second wife.** In a series of flashbacks **starting with Kane's boyhood in Colorado and ending with Kane's death in his lonely Florida mansion,** we learn about the key events of his life.

Citizen Kane has been criticized on the grounds that its plot hinges too much on a mere device, **the search for Rosebud.** I disagree with this criticism. *Citizen Kane* asks some important questions, **among which is this:** What is the measure of a person? Can a single icon, **Rosebud in this case,** symbolize one's life? Or are we all greater than the sum of our parts?

By the way, I must assure my readers that I will not be a member of that group **responsible for destroying the pleasure of many moviegoers by divulging the secret.** No, this reviewer will not reveal Rosebud's identity. The answer to that question is there to be seen by the careful observer, so if you want to know, find out for yourself by going and seeing the movie. Rumor has it, though, that the lines to get into *CK* are long, **in which case you might want to take along a sleeping bag and a picnic lunch.** The wait will be worth it.
Rating: ★ ★ ★ ★ ★ stars out of a possible ★ ★ ★ ★.

ADJECTIVE CLAUSES WITH QUANTIFIERS; ADJECTIVAL MODIFYING PHRASES

ADJECTIVE CLAUSES WITH QUANTIFIERS

Moviegoers, **many of whom love action-adventure,** are fond of the *Indiana Jones* trilogy.

Foreign films, **most of which are unfamiliar to mass audiences,** are getting more popular.

You may have to pay a lot to see a movie at night, **in which case you might try a matinee.**

ADJECTIVAL MODIFYING PHRASES

Filmmakers **responsible for such masterpieces as *2001* and *The Deer Hunter*** should be lionized.

The *Star Wars* trilogy, **directed by George Lucas,** is considered science fiction of high quality.

Akira Kurosawa has made many famous films, **including *Rashomon, Throne of Blood,* and *Ran.***

Grammar Notes

1. Certain nonidentifying adjective clauses have the following pattern: quantifier + preposition + relative pronoun *whom* or *which*. These relative pronouns refer to an earlier head noun.

> Moviegoers, **many of whom probably wanted something more upbeat,** didn't particularly care for *Citizen Kane* at first. (**Whom** refers to the head noun **moviegoers.**)

2. Another adjective clause with a preposition is made without a quantifier. Instead, the clause contains just a preposition and a relative pronoun.

> *Citizen Kane* asks some important questions, **among which is this:** . . .

Sentences containing nonidentifying clauses with *of whom* and *of which* are rather formal and more common in writing than in speech.

Sometimes a noun is used instead of a quantifier.

> Comedies, **examples of which** are *Beverly Hills Cop* and *Home Alone,* continue to be popular.

Be careful! Remember that we use *whom* to refer to people and *which* to refer to things.

3. The adjective phrase *in which case* is used to introduce a clause. Use this phrase when you could restate the phrase by saying *in that case, in that situation, if that is the case,* or *if that happens.* The relative pronoun *which* refers to an idea described earlier in the sentence.

> Rumor has it that lines to get into the movie are long, **in which case** you should take along a sleeping bag and a picnic lunch. (**In which case** can be restated as "If it is the case that the lines are long . . .")

4. Remember that a phrase is a group of words which doesn't have a subject and a verb. Adjective clauses, both identifying and nonidentifying, are often reduced to adjectival modifying phrases. Speakers and writers do this when they want to achieve an economy of language while maintaining clarity of meaning.

> Anyone **who is serious about cinema** should know this film.
> Anyone **serious about cinema** should know this film. (The relative pronoun **who** and the verb **is** are deleted, leaving an identifying phrase modifying **anyone.**)

> Welles, **who was also the picture's director and script coauthor,** was only twenty-five when he made *Citizen Kane.*
> Welles, **also the picture's director and script coauthor,** was only twenty-five when he made *Citizen Kane.* (The relative pronoun **who** and the verb **was** are deleted, leaving a nonidentifying phrase modifying **Welles.**)

5. There are two ways of reducing an adjective clause to an adjective phrase.

   a. If the adjective clause contains a form of the verb *be,* you can usually delete the relative pronoun, the form of *be,* and any accompanying auxiliaries.

   > *Citizen Kane,* ~~which is~~ **said to be based on the life of William Randolph Hearst,** was released in 1941.
   > Il will not be part of that group of critics ~~who have been~~ **responsible for revealing the identify of Rosebud.**

   b. If the adjective clause does not contain a form of the verb *be,* you can usually delete the relative pronoun and change the verb to its present participial form.

   > Charles Foster Kane had a career **that lasted forty years.**
   >
   > BECOMES
   >
   > Charles Foster Kane had a career **lasting forty years.** (The relative pronoun **that** is deleted, and the simple past tense verb **lasted** is changed to its present participial form.)

6. You can also combine two complete sentences by converting one of the sentences into an adjective phrase.

Ten movies were screened at the festival. They **included** *The Deer Hunter, Ran, 2001, La Dolce Vita,* and *Sweetie.*

Ten movies were screened at the festival, **including** *The Deer Hunter, Ran, 2001, La Dolce Vita,* and *Sweetie.*

OR

Ten movies, **including** *The Deer Hunter, Ran, 2001, La Dolce Vita,* and *Sweetie,* were screened at the festival.

FOCUSED PRACTICE

1. Discover the Grammar

Read the textbook discussion comparing the mediums of film and television. Underline adjective clauses with the form **quantifier + preposition + relative pronoun.** *Circle adjective phrases that could have been reduced from clauses.*

A recent survey asked one thousand people this question: Is a film seen in a movie theater basically the same as one seen on TV? The participants in the survey, most of whom answered yes to the question, were selected from a variety of ethnic and occupational groups in several countries, including the United States, Canada, Mexico, and Japan. Their responses illustrate the blurring of the perception of differences between the two mediums. Actually, however, film and television are quite dissimilar.

Canadian Marshall McLuhan, regarded as an expert in the field of mass media, is probably the person most responsible for redirecting our thinking about mediums of communication, especially television.

According to McLuhan, the images seen on a screen in a movie theater and on a TV set are fundamentally different. In a theater, projectors shine light through a series of transparent, moving celluloid frames, each of which contains a separate photograph. The image projected on the screen is essentially solid.

On a television screen, however, the image, composed of millions of dots, is not solid but representational. The human brain must perceive the pattern of dots and mentally convert it into pictures. Film, says McLuhan, is a "hot" medium, while television is a "cool" medium requiring more mental energy. Over the years, legions of people have railed against television, convinced that it leads to mental laziness. McLuhan would apparently disagree. His theory gives a plausible explanation for a frequent complaint by TV viewers, many of whom report an almost irresistible tendency to fall asleep while watching television. Their brains have to work harder to perceive the image.

2. Film Trivia

Complete the following statements about movies, writing adjective clauses in the
form **quantifier** + **preposition** + **relative pronoun**.

1. Jack Lemmon and Walter Matthau, __both of whom starred in <u>The Odd Couple</u>__ , also acted together in
   (both / star / in *The Odd Couple*)
   The Fortune Cookie, The Front Page, and *JFK*.

2. Sean Connery, Roger Moore, and Timothy Dalton, _____, come from Britain.
   (all / have / play / the role of James Bond)

3. *Star Wars, The Empire Strikes Back,* and *Return of the Jedi,* _____, are the
   (all / have / earn / over $100 million)
   middle three films in a projected nine-part series.

4. *Throne of Blood* and *Ran,* _____, are based on Shakespearean plays.
   (both / direct / by Akira Kurosawa)

5. Walt Disney's animated productions, _____, are known worldwide.
   (most / be / loved by children)

6. Lina Wertmüller and Wim Wenders, _____, are both highly regarded
   (neither / be / well known to American mass audiences)
   European film directors.

3. Popular Movies

Complete each sentence with a nonidentifying adjective phrase for each
film mentioned.

1. *E.T.,* __directed by Steven Spielberg__, was the top-earning film until it was toppled by Spielberg's own
   (direct / by / Steven Spielberg)
   dinosaur opera.

2. *Jurassic Park,* _____, is the biggest single moneymaking film of all time.
   (base / on / Michael Crichton's novel)

3. *Grease,* _____, is the top-grossing musical film with live actors.
   (star / John Travolta and Olivia Newton-John)

4. *Dances with Wolves,* _____, is the top-grossing western film.
   (direct and produce / by / Kevin Costner)

5. The *Star Wars* trilogy, _____, was conceived, written, and produced
   (feature / Harrison Ford, Carrie Fisher, and Mark Hamill)
   by George Lucas.

4. Movie Genres

*Combine each pair of sentences about types of movies into a single sentence with an
adjective clause or phrase.*

1. Many recent science fiction films have been huge financial successes. They include the *Star Wars* trilogy, *Close Encounters of the Third Kind*, and the *Terminator* movies.

   <u>Many recent science fiction films, including the *Star Wars* trilogy, *Close Encounters of the Third Kind*, and the</u>

   <u>*Terminator* movies, have been huge financial successes.</u>

   _____

2. Westerns have been making a comeback in recent years. Examples of them are *Dances with Wolves*, *Unforgiven*, and *Wyatt Earp*.

   _____

   _____

   _____

3. Musical animated films have also become very popular. They include *Aladdin*, *The Lion King*, and *Beauty and the Beast*.

   _____

   _____

   _____

4. It looks as though sequels to big movie hits may lose their appeal. In that case, moviemakers will be forced to become more creative.

   _____

   _____

   _____

5. Editing

Read the letter. Find and correct the ten errors involving adjective clauses and phrases. Delete verbs or change relative pronouns where necessary, but do not change punctuation or add relative pronouns.

Malibu Manor
Bed and Breakfast

July 15

Dear John,

Diana and I are having a great time in Los Angeles. We spent the first day at the beach in Venice and saw where <u>Harry and Tonto</u> was filmed—you know, that
starring
movie ~~starred~~ Art Carney and an orange cat? Yesterday we went to Universal
which
Studios and learned about all the cinematic tricks, most of them I wasn't aware of. Amazing! The funny thing is that, even though you know that an illusion is presented on the screen is just an illusion, you still believe it's real when you see the movie.

Then we took the tram tour around the premises and saw several actors
whom
working, some of them I recognized. I felt like jumping off the tram and shouting,
who
"Would everyone is famous please give me your autograph?" In the evening we
whom
went to a party at the home of one of Diana's friends, many of them are connected with the movie business. I had a really interesting conversation with a fellow
ing
works in the industry who claims that a lot of movies are made these days are modeled conceptually after amusement park rides. Just like the rides, they start slowly and easily, then they have a lot of twists and turns are calculated to scare you to death, and they end happily. Pretty fascinating, huh? What next?

Sorry to babble on so much about movies, but you know what an addict I am.
which
Anyway, I may be coming back a day early, in that case I'll call and let you know so that you can pick me up at the airport.

Love you lots,

Jean

COMMUNICATION PRACTICE

6. Practice Listening

Listen to the TV film reviewer give her weekly review. Then listen again to certain of the reviewer's sentences. For each numbered item, respond true (T) or false (F) to indicate if it correctly restates the sentence that you hear on the tape.

___T___ 1. The film festival can be seen this holiday weekend.

___F___ 2. None of these great movies have been seen in movie theaters in more than a decade.

___T___ 3. *My Life as a Dog* was created by Lasse Hallström, a Swedish director.

___F___ 4. In *My Life as a Dog,* a young boy sends his confused dog to his unhappy relatives in the country.

___F___ 5. In *The Discreet Charm of the Bourgeoisie,* hilarious, unsuccessful, middle-class French people try to get together for dinner.

___F___ 6. *The Deer Hunter* starred Michael Cimino.

___T___ 7. *The Deer Hunter* makes the reviewer cry.

___F___ 8. Jeff Bridges was responsible for launching *The Last Picture Show.*

___F___ 9. Black-and-white movies are not pretty.

___T___ 10. All who regard themselves as serious movie junkies must see *Casablanca.*

7. Group Discussion

Divide into groups of six to eight and discuss one of the following topics. Prepare carefully for the discussion by doing some research. Share the main points of your discussion with the class as a whole.

Topic 1. The rating system for films should be strengthened/should be left as it is.
Topic 2. Movies have/have not become too violent.
Topic 3. In general, "Hollywood" films are/are not inferior to European and Asian films.

8. Essay

Write your own movie review in an essay of three to five paragraphs. Choose a film that you liked or disliked, but try to be objective in your review.

9. Picture Discussion

Look at this picture for a few minutes. Take note of the details. Remember as best as you can the location and the description of the people in the scene. Then, with a partner and with books closed, discuss all the details you can remember. When you have finished, open your books and discuss how accurate you were.

Example:
The man **holding the paintbrush** might be the artist who painted this picture.

Diego Velázquez, *Las meninas.* Prado, Madrid, Spain. Giraudon/Art Resource, NY
(*The Maids of Honor*)

I. *Read the text and underline all of the adjective clauses.*

Recently at work I had an experience <u>that proved to me the truth of that old adage: Things may not be what they seem.</u> The experience involved two people I work with in my secretarial job. The first, whom I'll call "Jennifer," is one of those sunny types who always greet you in a friendly manner and never have an unkind word to say. The second, whom I'll call "Myrtle," is the type who rarely gives compliments and can sometimes be critical. Between the two of them, I thought Jennifer was the one who was my friend. Myrtle never seemed to care much for me, which is why I didn't seek out her friendship. I learned, though, that I had been reading them wrong.

About two months ago, some money was stolen from someone's purse in the office. It happened on an afternoon when all three of us, Jennifer, Myrtle, and I, were working together. Our boss, who tends to jump to conclusions, questioned the three of us and said that someone whose name he wouldn't reveal had implicated me in the theft. Jennifer, whom I expected to stand up for me, hemmed and hawed and said she didn't know where I'd been at the time of the theft, which was a lie. Myrtle, however, spoke up and said she knew I couldn't have been the one who had stolen the money because she and I had been working together all afternoon. The boss accepted her statement, and that ended the unpleasantness. It also ended my friendship with Jennifer. I found out later that she wanted my job. I don't know whether or not she was the one who took the money, but I do know that the old proverb that tells us not to judge a book by its cover has some truth in it. Myrtle and I have been friends ever since.

II. *Read the sentences, which form a narration. Circle the correct relative pronoun for each sentence.*

1. David and Rebecca Carter, that/(who) got married about a year ago, recently bought a new house.
2. The neighborhood in that/in which they have been living is a somewhat dangerous one.
3. The neighborhood that/who they are moving into is much safer.
4. Their new house, that/which they bought quite cheaply, does need some fixing up.
5. However, they will be receiving some help from their neighbors, most of who/most of whom they like.
6. The Rossis, who/whom live next door to them, have volunteered to lend their tools.
7. The Roybals, who/whom live across the street from David and Rebecca, have promised to help them put in a new lawn.
8. The Rossis, who/whose daughter is the same age as Mackenzie, David and Becky's daughter, are helping Mackenzie make new friends.
9. Rebecca, that/who works for a county hospital, will still have to commute to work.
10. David, whom/whose company is nearby, will be able to walk to work.

III. *Read the sentences, which form a narration. Put the relative pronoun in parentheses if it can be omitted. Do not omit relative pronouns if they are subjects.*

1. On our trip to Europe last summer, we met a lot of people (whom) we liked.
2. One of the most interesting was a young man from Spain who was named Jaime.
3. We were hitchhiking outside Madrid. Jaime, who was on his way home from Seville, stopped and picked us up.
4. The car that he was driving was a 1972 Volkswagen.
5. Jaime took us to his house, which was not far from downtown Madrid, and invited us to stay for a few days.
6. He also introduced us to a group of people that we felt very comfortable with.
7. We were scheduled to go to Portugal next, so Jaime gave us the address of a cousin of his who lived in Coimbra.
8. We had such a wonderful time in Spain and Portugal that we decided to go back next year, which will cost money but will be worth it.

IV. *Complete each sentence with a nonidentifying* **which** *clause that modifies the first clause. Add necessary pronouns and verbs.*

1. Frannie needs to stay home to reenergize herself, __which is why she can be termed an introvert__.
   (is / why / can be termed / an introvert)

2. Jonathan becomes energized when he is around other people,

   _____.
   (why / can be termed / an extrovert)

3. Passive-positive people appreciate the approval of others,

   _____.
   (why / often / have many friends)

4. Active-positive people like to make their mark upon the world,

   _____.
   (why / tend / to value accomplishment)

5. Active-negative people tend to have somewhat negative self-images,

   _____.
   (why / not always feel satisfied with their accomplishments)

V. *Each of the following sentences contains four underlined words or phrases, marked A, B, C, or D. Circle the letter of the one underlined word or phrase which is not correct.*

1. Federico Fellini, <u>whose</u> work <u>including</u> 8½, *La Dolce Vita*,
         A   B

   and *Satyricon* and <u>who</u> <u>is</u> one of the most famous film
                 C D

   directors in the world, died in 1993.

       A   Ⓑ   C   D

2. Marcello Mastroianni and Sophia Loren, <u>both</u> <u>of which</u>
                            A   B

   are well known internationally, appeared in certain films

   <u>directed</u> by Fellini, <u>including</u> *Blood Feud* and *Yesterday,*
    C   D

   Today, and Tomorrow.

       A   B   C   D

3. Police <u>in Charleston</u> are investigating a crime <u>that</u>
       A B

   <u>was committing</u> yesterday evening between 11:00 P.M.
   C

   and midnight at the city art museum, <u>which</u> is located
   D

   on Fifth Avenue.

   A   B   C   D

4. Detective Amanda Reynolds, <u>who</u> is the chief investigating
   A

   officer in the case, says <u>that</u> the police have no suspects
   B

   yet but are focusing on tips <u>suggest</u> <u>that</u> the theft may
   C D

   have been an inside job.

   A   B   C   D

5. Al, <u>whom</u> is a freshman at the university, is pleased with
   A

   his college living situation because he likes <u>the people</u>
   B

   <u>he</u> is rooming <u>with</u>.
   C D

   A   B   C   D

6. His courses, <u>none</u> <u>of which</u> are easy, are all classes <u>requiring</u>
   A B C

   a considerable amount of study, <u>that</u> is why he has joined
   D

   a study group.

   A   B   C   D

7. Textrix, <u>the company</u> <u>for that</u> Alex works, tends to employ
   A B

   people <u>who are</u> self-starters and <u>who have</u> at least ten years
   C D

   of experience in the field.

   A   B   C   D

8. Alicia, <u>an extrovert loves</u> working <u>with people</u> and can
   A B

   also work independently, had many accomplishments in her

   last job, <u>which is</u> why I think she's <u>the person we should hire</u>.
   C D

   A   B   C   D

9. The lines <u>to get into</u> *Sweetie*, <u>a film</u> <u>directed</u> by New Zealander
   A B C

   Jane Campion, may be long, <u>in that case</u> I would recommend
   D

   going to a matinee screening.

   A   B   C   D

10. Jaime, <u>who</u> has been employed for ten years at a company <u>that</u>
    A B

    stresses team-building and cooperative effort, is <u>a person who</u>
    C

    has learned to value <u>the people with he works</u>.
    D

    A   B   C   D

1.

Review the two types of adjective clauses: identifying and nonidentifying. Identifying adjective clauses identify or give essential information. Nonidentifying clauses give additional or nonessential information.

> I saw three movies last week. The movie **that I liked best** was *Jurassic Park*.

The adjective clause, *that I liked best*, is identifying because it says which movie I am talking about. If the clause were removed, the sentence would not express the same thought.

> The movie was *Jurassic Park*.

Therefore, the clause is essential for the sentence's meaning.

> Casablanca, **which contains the famous song "*As Time Goes By*,"** is considered a film classic.

The nonidentifying clause, *which contains the famous song "As Time Goes By,"* adds more information about *Casablanca*. This clause, however, is not used to identify. If it were removed, the sentence would still make sense.

> *Casablanca* is considered a film classic.

In speech, identifying clauses have no appreciable pauses before or after them. Therefore, they are not enclosed in commas when written. Nonidentifying clauses, on the other hand, do have pauses before and after them. In writing, they must be enclosed in commas.

> A person **who needs others to become energized** is an extrovert. (identifying; no commas)
> James, **who comes alive when he feels comfortable with the people around him,** is an extrovert. (nonidentifying; commas)

If you are unsure whether a clause is identifying or nonidentifying, try reading it aloud. The natural pauses made by your voice will help you to determine whether or not the clause needs to be enclosed in commas.

A. *Punctuate the following sentences that contain adjective clauses. They form a narration. Do not place commas around clauses that identify.*

1. Tom and Sandra, who have been married for more than twenty-five years, are both outgoing people.
2. Tom who is clearly an extrovert loves meeting new people.
3. Sandra who is very quick to make friends loves to have friends over for dinner.
4. Tom and Sandra have two married sons both of whom live abroad.
5. The son who is older lives with his family in Britain.
6. The son who is younger lives with his family in southern Italy.
7. Tom and Sandra own a house in the city and one in the country. The one that they spend most of their time in is in the city.
8. The house that they spend summers in is located in Vermont.

2.

Adjective phrases are also identifying or nonidentifying, depending on whether they add essential or extra information.

The postwar director **most responsible for putting Italian cinema on the map** is Federico Fellini.
   (identifying; no commas)
Federico Fellini, **the director of such classics as 8½**, died in 1993. (nonidentifying; commas)

B. *Punctuate the following sentences that contain adjective phrases.*

1. A film produced by George Lucas is almost guaranteed success. *no*
2. A film directed by Steven Spielberg is likely to be a blockbuster. *no*
3. *The Passenger,* directed by Michelangelo Antonioni and starring Jack Nicholson, is not well known in North America.
4. Many Canadians, including Donald Sutherland and Michael J. Fox, are major international film stars.
5. The Universal Studios resort located in California was built decades ago.
6. The Universal Studios resort located in Florida was built much more recently.

C. *The following letter from a first-year college student contains a number of identifying and nonidentifying adjective clauses and phrases. Punctuate the letter by adding commas where necessary.*

September 30
Dear Mom and Dad,
Thanks for bringing me down here to the university last Sunday. Classes didn't start until Wednesday, so I had a few days to get adjusted. I'm signed up for five classes: zoology, calculus, English, and two history sections. It's a heavy load, but they're all courses that will count for my degree. The zoology class which meets at 8:00 every morning is going to be my hardest subject. The history class that I have in the morning is on Western Civilization; the one in the afternoon is on early United States history. Calculus which I have at noon every day looks like it's going to be easy. Besides zoology, the other class that's going to be hard is English; we have to do a composition a week.

   I like all of my roommates but one. There are four of us in our suite including two girls from Texas and a girl from Manitoba. Sally who is from San Antonio is great; I feel like I've known her all my life. I also really like Anne who is the girl from Manitoba. Heather the other girl from Texas is kind of a pain, though; she's one of those types of people who never tell you what's bothering them and then get hostile. All in all, though, it looks like it's going to be a great year. I'll write again in a week or so.

                          Love,
                          Vicky

VII

Noun
Clauses

Noun Clauses: Subjects and Objects

INTRODUCTION

Read and listen to Jim Bresler's interview of Zeya Mason, one of the first participants in the recently expanded National Service Program.

Questions to Consider

1. Do you think that all citizens owe their country something?
2. Would you like to participate in some form of national service?

Jim: Zeya, I want to thank you for doing this interview. Do you mind **if I record your answers?**

Zeya: No, I don't mind at all. Go right ahead.

Jim: OK. Zeya, you're one of the very first participants in the program, so here's kind of an obvious first question: Tell me **what you think of National Service.**

Zeya: I think **it's a wonderful program.** It's given me something worthwhile to do, and it's helped me figure out **what my career is going to be.**

Jim: Do you believe **that citizens owe their country something?**

Zeya: I do, yes. The country has given all of us a lot. In return, we all need to do **whatever we can for the country.**

Jim: What are you doing in your National Service assignment?

Zeya: I'm working in a literacy program. I teach people who aren't completely literate how to read and write.

Jim: Are the people you work with immigrants?

Zeya: Some of them are, but others are people who were born in this country. Actually, I'm assigned to work with **whoever needs literacy training.**

Jim: Tell me **what made you decide to join the National Service Program.**

Zeya: Well, I graduated from high school a year ago, and I was going to go right on to college. But after thirteen years of school, I realized **I was tired. What became really clear to me** was the fact that I just wasn't ready for serious study. The National Service Program had just been approved, so I applied and was accepted.

Jim: What do you like about your job?

Zeya: Well, corny as it may sound, **the fact that I'm helping others** fulfills me. For instance, I've been working with a forty-seven-year-old lady from Laos; she and her husband came to this country five years ago. She never really learned to read and write, so I was assigned to do **whatever I could to help her**. She's a wonderful lady, and she's made great progress.

Jim: It's admirable that you're helping others, but there must be something else in it for you, some long-term benefits.

Zeya: Oh yes, definitely. By the time I finish my assignment in two years, I'll have earned $5,000 that I can apply to my college education.

Jim: So you do intend to go to college, then?

Zeya: Yes. I don't know **where I'm going,** but I do know **I'll be majoring in education.**

Jim: Great. Zeya, do you think **this program is for everyone?**

Zeya: Well, I don't know **if everyone would be interested,** but I do think **that just about anyone could benefit from it. Whoever isn't going right on to college from high schoo**l ought to give it serious consideration.

Jim: Well, Zeya, thank you again for doing this interview, and good luck in the future.

Zeya: My pleasure.

Noun Clauses: Subjects and Objects

SUBJECT
What became really clear to me was the fact that I wasn't ready for college.
Whoever isn't going right to college should consider National Service.
The fact that I'm helping others fulfills me.

OBJECT
Do you believe **that citizens owe their country something?**
I think **(that) it's a wonderful program.**
Tell me **what you think of National Service.**
We all need to do **whatever we can.**
Do you mind **if I record your answers?**
I don't know **where I'm going to be attending college.**
I'm assigned to work with **whoever needs literacy training.**

Grammar Notes

1. Noun clauses are dependent clauses that perform the same functions that regular nouns do: They can be subjects, direct objects, indirect objects, or objects of prepositions.

   SUBJECT
   What bothers me is his lack of initiative.
   DIRECT OBJECT
   We all need to do **whatever we can.**
   INDIRECT OBJECT
   The program should provide **whoever is unemployed** a two-year job.
   OBJECT OF
   I'm assigned to work with **whoever needs**
   PREPOSITION
   literacy training.

   See Unit 19 for a discussion of noun clauses as complements.

2. Noun clauses are often introduced by *what, that, who, whom, where, how, why, whether (or not),* and by the words *whatever, whichever (one), wherever, whoever, whomever, however.*

   What I need is a challenging job.
   Do **what you have to do.**
   Whatever you want to do tonight is all right by me.
   I know **that I'll enjoy National Service.**

   Be careful! Don't confuse *however* as a clause introducer with *however* as a transition word.

   However you finance your college education is up to you. (clause introducer)
   I want to go to college. **However,** I don't know how I'm going to finance it. (transition)

3. Remember the distinction between *who* and *whom*, *whoever* and *whomever*. *Who* and *whoever* are used as subjects, while *whom* and *whomever* are used as objects in formal English. Many native speakers don't use *whom* and *whomever*.

> SUBJECT   VERB
> Award the prize to **whoever** comes through the door first. (**Whoever** is the subject of the verb **comes** in the dependent clause.)
> OBJECT SUBJECT VERB
> Award the prize to **whomever** you like. (**Whomever** is the direct object of the verb **like.**)

Be careful! If you are unsure whether to use *whoever* or *whomever*, be aware that the noun clause (like all clauses) must have both a subject and a verb.

> SUBJECT   VERB
> I'm assigned to work with **whoever** needs literacy training.

In this sentence, the noun clause *whoever needs literacy training* is the object of the preposition *with*. This would seem to require the object form *whomever*. However, the verb in the noun clause *must* have a subject, so *whoever* is the correct choice.

Usage note: Although native speakers often replace *whom* and *whomever* with *who* and *whoever* in conversation or informal writing, in careful speech and formal writing the use of *whom* and *whomever* is recommended.

> Appoint **whomever** you like. (formal)
> Appoint **whoever** you like. (informal)

4. When a noun clause beginning with *that* functions as a direct object, the word *that* may be omitted.

> Do you think **(that) National Service is for everyone?**

5. Noun clauses are sometimes embedded questions with *if* or *whether (or not)*.

> Do you mind **if I record your answers?**
> Do you know **whether or not she has left?**

6. Indirect speech is expressed in noun clauses. Remember to follow the sequence of tenses in changing direct speech to indirect speech.

> "Mary, what are you going to be when you grow up?" John asked.
> John asked Mary **what she was going to be when she grew up.**

7. Note that a noun clause sometimes includes the phrase *the fact that*.

> **The fact that I'm helping others** fulfills me. (The clause **the fact that I'm helping others** is the subject of the entire sentence.)
> I'm bothered by **the fact that I'm not doing anything socially useful.** (The clause **the fact that I'm not doing anything useful** is the object of the preposition **by.**)

FOCUSED PRACTICE

1. Discover the Grammar

Read the editorial, which recently appeared in The Pleasantville Herald.
Underline all noun clauses used as subjects or objects.

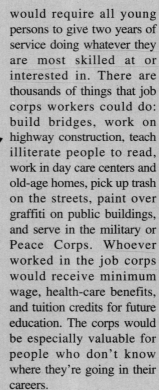

Make National Service Mandatory

Congress recently approved a bill to fund a National Service program, and the president signed it. We think <u>this is a small step in the right direction</u>, but we also believe it doesn't go nearly far enough.

In our view, whoever gets something from the nation should be required to give the nation something in return. Think for a minute about what we receive. We all have access to free education through high school, police protection, national security, roads and highways, national parks—the list goes on and on. We suggest that it is time to reinvoke John F. Kennedy's famous call to action: "Ask not what your country can do for you; ask what you can do for your country."

We propose that Congress pass new legislation creating a job corps and requiring all youths to serve in it. It would require all young persons to give two years of service doing whatever they are most skilled at or interested in. There are thousands of things that job corps workers could do: build bridges, work on highway construction, teach illiterate people to read, work in day care centers and old-age homes, pick up trash on the streets, paint over graffiti on public buildings, and serve in the military or Peace Corps. Whoever worked in the job corps would receive minimum wage, health-care benefits, and tuition credits for future education. The corps would be especially valuable for people who don't know where they're going in their careers.

What this country needs is a sense of community and togetherness. Mandatory national service is the way to achieve it.

2. Is There Life After High School?

Two high school seniors are having a conversation about life after graduation.
Fill in the blanks in their conversation with clauses from the box.

whoever hires me	if you might have a point
what you're going to do	what I have to do
the army will help me decide	whatever I'm told
I'm going into the army	what I want as a career
I'll get a job	whatever your boss tells you

Colleen: We graduate next month. Do you know _____what you're going to do_____?
1.

Amanda: I don't have a clue. I guess _____I'll get a job_____.
2.

Colleen: Doing what?

Amanda: Doing _____whatever I'm told_____.
3.

Colleen: By whom?

Amanda: By _____whoever hires me_____. What about you?
4.

Colleen: I think _____I'm going into the army_____.
5.

Amanda: The army? Why?

Colleen: Well, I don't know yet _____what I want as a career_____. I figure _____the army will help me decide_____.
6. 7.
Why don't you join along with me?

Amanda: What? And be told _____what I have to do_____ every minute of the day?
8.

Colleen: You just said you're willing to do _____whatever your boss tells you_____. Anyway, it's not like that. You
9.
can learn a lot of new things and get away from home to boot. Think it over.

Amanda: Hmm . . . I wonder _____.
10.

3. Reach Out and Help Someone

Two friends in their late twenties, Brady and Pablo, are talking. Fill in the blanks in their conversation with **whatever, whichever, whoever,** *or* **however** *and correct forms of the indicated verbs. You will use some of these words more than once.*

Pablo: What's the matter with you lately? You seem really down in the dumps.

Brady: I don't know. I'm just not very happy. Take girls, for example.

_____Whoever I meet_____ bores me. I'd like to meet some new and interesting people.
1. (I / meet)

Pablo: What about work? Doesn't that satisfy you?

Brady: Nah, I've been there so long that I can do _____whatever I want_____, but there's no challenge
2. (I / want)

anymore. Right now there are five major projects the company is doing. My boss tells me to work

on _____whichever one interests me_____ the most. The trouble is, none of them interest me.
3. (one / interest me)

Pablo: Why don't you try doing some volunteer work? That's what I do—I go down to the community

center and work with _____whoever needs help_____ on that day. You get your mind off yourself
4. (need / help)

when you're volunteering.

Brady: What kind of things do you do?

Pablo: Sometimes I just sit and talk to old people. Sometimes I umpire a baseball game. Sometimes I

help a kid with his homework. I do _____whatever I can_____ .
5. (I / can)

Brady: How much time do you have to put in, say, every week?

Pablo: You can put in _____however much_____ . There are no rules on that.
6. (much / time / you / want)

Brady: OK, so what do I do?

Pablo: Just go down to the community center some evening. Talk to _____whoever is_____ at
7. (be)

the main desk. Say you're there to help. You'll do _____whatever needs_____ .
8. (need / to be done)

Brady: OK, I'll give it a try. Helping others might cheer me up. What's the address?

4. Editing

Read and edit the letter, correcting the seven errors in noun clauses.

September 22

Dear Colleen,

　　Well, old pal, here I am at Fort Jackson. I have to say you were right about
joining the army. I just wish we could have been stationed together. I'll admit ~~what~~ *that*
basic training was tough, but now that it's over with, I'm having a great time.
Whomever says that you're treated like a slave is wrong. There are rules to follow,
but they're not unreasonable. That I like best about my situation is what I get to
study whatever I want. I chose telecommunications. I assume that things are the
same for you. Is that right?

　　The other thing what I like about the army, believe it or not, is the social life. In
the evenings and on some weekends we're free to spend our time with whomever
we want. I've met some interesting women, and there are dances and get-togethers
attended by guys from off the base. I met a nice one at the dance last weekend.

　　I just wonder that I would be doing if I hadn't gone in the army. I hope what
things are going as well for you as they are for me. Write soon.

Best,

Amanda

COMMUNICATION PRACTICE

5. Practice Listening

*Listen to the conversation between a returned Peace Corps volunteer and a local newspaper reporter who is
interviewing her. Then listen again to certain of the sentences in the interview. For each item, circle the letter of
the sentence which correctly restates the sentence that you hear.*

1. (a.) Describe your Peace Corps experience.

　 b. Tell us if you liked the Peace Corps.

2. (a.) It was the most important experience I've ever had.

　 b. I'd have to say that life is an experience. It was the most difficult experience I've ever had.

(continued on next page)

3. a. Describe what the experience did for you.

   b. Describe your job experience.

4. a. We gave medical attention to all people asking for it.

   b. We needed to give medical attention to everyone.

5. a. I especially liked the villagers.

   b. I especially liked the villagers' attitude. *grateful*

6. a. However, many people would show up at the town hall.

   b. I taught English as a second language to all the people who showed up for it at the town hall.

7. a. What was the most difficult thing about being in the Peace Corps?

   b. What does being in the Peace Corps tell us?

8. a. Loneliness bothered me more than anything else.

   b. Whatever bothered me made me lonely.

9. a. We were allowed a room.

   b. We were allowed to choose a roommate.

10. a. I adjusted to another culture.

    b. I learned about the difficulties of adjusting to another culture.

11. a. Volunteers can use any of the skills they have.

    b. Whatever you can volunteer is a skill.

6. Small Group Discussion

Divide into small groups. Discuss one or more the of the following topics. Share your findings with the other groups.

1. What I want out of life is . . .
   Example:
   A: **What I want out of life** is a challenging job and a fulfilling relationship with someone.
   B: Tell us **what you would consider a challenging job.**

2. What I find hardest about being an adult is . . .
3. What I find most interesting about being an adult is . . .
4. What this country needs is . . .

7. Debate

Divide into two groups and have a debate on this topic:

The government should (OR shouldn't) require some sort of national service from every citizen.

National Service could be interpreted narrowly to refer to military service only, or it could be interpreted broadly, allowing many options, such as medical service, working with youths, park or conservation service. Whichever side you choose, do some research on the issue and try to include information you might have about national service in other countries.

8. Essay

After you have participated in the debate in exercise 7 on page 260, write an essay in which you clarify your own position. Did the debate change your ideas at all, or is your position basically the same as it was originally?

9. Picture Discussion

Study this picture individually for a few minutes. Jot down your ideas about what happened before this situation and what might happen next.

Example:
What might have happened is . . .
I think . . .

Edward Hopper, *Cape Cod Evening.* (1939)
Oil on canvas, 30 ¹/₄ x 40 ¹/₄". National Gallery of Art, Washington. John Hay Whitney Collection

INTRODUCTION

Read and listen to the radio interview of Dr. Sandra Stalley, an expert on educational problems, about issues in U.S. education.

Questions to Consider

1. What makes a good educational system?
2. Do you know about the educational systems of more than one country? How are they different? How are they the same?

WVIV: Dr. Stalley, recently there's been a lot said and written about the crisis in American education. Is it true **that we're in a crisis?**

Stalley: Yes, it's quite apparent **that education is in a crisis situation in this country.** In fact, it's absolutely astounding **that the system has degenerated so much so quickly.**

WVIV: What would you say are examples of this?

Stalley: Well, for one thing, it's a fact **that more students are dropping out of high school than fifteen or twenty years ago.** For another, it's obvious **that violence has gotten more and more commonplace in schools.** But the most important indicator is **the fact that test scores have dropped and continue to stay low.**

WVIV: But isn't it true **that test scores don't necessarily measure students' knowledge all that well?**

Stalley: There's some truth in that, yes. However, there's no doubt **that American students compare rather poorly with students from other industrialized nations in subjects like science, mathematics, and geography.**

WVIV: What do you think is wrong with our educational system?

Stalley: Well, the fact that many schools are large and impersonal is one thing that's wrong. And it's frequently the case **that there are too many students in individual classes.** Teachers can't do a very effective job if they can't give students individual attention. That kind of job assignment is hard enough on teachers, but it's the students who suffer the most. Another example is **that schools often don't teach students the things they really need to know.** However, the main problem in education is the belief **that the school system is the place to solve most of society's ills.**

WVIV: What do you mean, exactly?

Stalley: Well, it seems pretty clear **that society expects the schools to do just about everything.** Some parents insist **that schools be open early in the morning and late in the afternoon for babysitting purposes.** Teachers are even expected to call parents if their children aren't coming to school. It's my belief, however, **that the business of schools should simply be teaching.** We need to leave the socializing and babysitting of students to the parents.

WVIV: Dr. Stalley, we're about out of time. Maybe we can talk about this issue in more detail in a future broadcast.

COMPLEMENTATION

ADJECTIVE COMPLEMENTS

It	Linking Verb	Adjective	Noun Clause
It	seems	clear	**that society expects the schools to do everything.**

It	Linking Verb	Adjective of Urgency	Noun Clause with Base (Subjunctive) Form
It	is	essential	**that schools be smaller and that more teachers be hired.**

SUBJECT COMPLEMENTS

A main problem in education is **that the schools don't have a uniform curriculum.**

Grammar Notes

1. One type of noun clause functions as an adjective complement. It follows the pattern *It* + linking verb + adjective. (Some linking verbs are *be, seem, feel, smell, look, taste,* etc.). The clause further identifies or explains the adjective.

noun clause as adjective complement
It seems clear **that society expects the schools to do everything.**

This kind of sentence can be restated so that the noun clause becomes the subject of the sentence.

subject
That society expects the schools to do just about everything seems clear.

A sentence rearranged in this way is rarely heard in conversation.

2. When noun clauses in this pattern follow adjectives of urgency, the noun clause must contain the base (or subjunctive) form of the verb, since it is not known whether the action in the noun clause will ever take place. Expressions of urgency include *it is essential, it is necessary, it is important, it is advisable,* and *it is desirable.*

base form
It is essential that schools **be** smaller and
base form
that more teachers **be** hired. NOT ~~It is essential that schools are smaller and that more teachers are hired.~~

Sentences of this type can be restated, with the noun clause becoming the

subject and occurring at the beginning of the sentence. Note that *it* is not needed in this restated sentence.

That more teachers be hired is essential.

A sentence arranged in this way is rarely heard in conversation.

3. Note that, as with sentences containing noun clauses after adjectives of urgency, certain verbs of urgency also require the base (or subjunctive) form of the verb in the noun clause. These verbs include *insist, demand, suggest,* and *recommend.*

The judge **insists** that Robert **be** at the hearing.

See Appendix 23 on page A26 for a list of verbs and expressions that require the base (or subjunctive) form of the verb in a following noun clause. See Unit 21 for more practice of this structure.

4. Another type of sentence contains a noun clause functioning as a subject complement.

The main problem in education is
noun clause functioning as subject complement
that the schools don't have a uniform curriculum.

In formal and academic writing this type of sentence often includes the words *the fact that* or *the belief that.*

The main problem in education is
the fact that the schools don't have a uniform curriculum.

FOCUSED PRACTICE

1. Discover the Grammar

WVIV TV is covering a teachers' strike. Listen to the broadcast. Then listen again and underline the five noun clauses that function as adjective complements.

Reporter: We're stationed in front of the Board of Education building, where striking teachers are picketing and carrying signs, and it's obvious to even the most casual viewer <u>that there are a lot of angry people here</u>. Frances Baldwin, the spokesperson for the teachers' union, has agreed to talk with us. Ms. Baldwin, why are you all on strike?

Baldwin: Well, after three months of fruitless negotiations, it's clear that the Board of Education isn't taking our concerns seriously. It's important that the board do something positive if they want to break this impasse. Something has to change.

Reporter: What do you think has to happen?

Baldwin: It's absolutely essential that the board sincerely negotiate with us on our request for higher salaries, smaller classes, better discipline, and a real commitment to education.

Reporter: According to the president of the Board of Education, it's the students who are really going to come out the losers in this strike. What's your comment on that?

Baldwin: We sympathize with the students, and we want to get back to teaching them. However, we can't teach effectively now. The fact that there hasn't been a raise in teachers' salaries for six years shows the board's true colors. It's appalling <u>that the board has refused even to talk with us</u>. The students have just become pawns in this situation.

Reporter: All right, Ms. Baldwin. Thank you for your comments. Back to you in the studio, Ron.

2. What Do the Students Think?

*KMBR went to a local high school and asked some students their opinion of their education. The results were mixed. Fill in the blanks in the conversation, using the indicated verbs and structures. Be sure to follow the sequence of tenses. Include the words **that** and **to** in the appropriate places.*

Reporter: Thank you all for agreeing to talk with us. It's obvious ___that you are all concerned students___.
1. (you / be / all / concerned students)

Rachel, let me start with you. How would you evaluate your education?

Rachel: It's lousy. I'd give it a poor grade.

Reporter: Why? What do you think is wrong with it?

Rachel: Well, it's pretty apparent _____. Most of them are just
2. (a lot of the teachers / not / want / teach)

putting in their time and drawing a paycheck.

Reporter: Carlos, what do you think? Do you agree with Rachel?

Carlos: Not completely. It depends on the teacher. I've had some do-nothing types. But every once in

a while you get a teacher who makes it clear _____ and
3. (we / be / there / learn)

_____.
4. (he or she / be / there / teach)

(continued on next page)

Reporter: OK. Monique, what about you? What's been your experience?

Monique: I've had mostly good teachers.

Reporter: That's nice to hear. Who do you feel makes a good teacher?

Monique: For me it's someone who wants you to succeed. I had a fabulous math instructor last year

who made it obvious from day one _____ but

5. (she / would / not tolerate / any nonsense)

_____ .

6. (she / be / there / help us / as much as / she / can)

Reporter: Uh-huh. OK, good. Andrew, where do you stand in this?

Andrew: I mostly agree with Rachel about the teachers. But it's also pretty clear

_____ .

7. (the whole system / need / be / change)

Reporter: What do you think needs to be done?

Andrew: Right now we study a lot of useless things. The Board of Education says everybody has to

study English literature, but that's not important for me. I want to study automotive

technology. Lots of times it's the students like me who lose out.

Reporter: Well, very interesting. I want to thank all of you for your excellent comments.

3. Demands

*The Teachers' Union has written a list of demands that it wants to negotiate with
the Board of Education. Write the union's demands in noun clauses in the form **it is**
+ adjective + clause.*

1. _____ It's necessary that class sizes be limited to twenty students. _____

(necessary / class sizes / be / limit / to twenty students)

2. _____

(essential / salaries / be / raise / at least 5 percent per year)

3. _____

(desirable / teachers / be / give / release time to complete special projects)

4. _____

(important / no instructor / be / ask / teach / more than five classes per day)

5. _____

(essential / strict discipline / be / maintain in the classroom)

4. Editing

For an English class assignment, a student has written a composition comparing two high school classes. Read the composition, and find and correct the nine errors.

Night and Day

Last year I took two classes, a history class and a Spanish class, that were as different as night and day. The history class was taught by Mr. Mattair, the basketball coach. From the start of the semester, it was obvious ~~what~~ *that* the class was going to be a total waste of time. Mr. Mattair made it clear right away that the basketball players *were* going to be his special pets. Just about all we ever did was watch him diagram basketball plays on the chalkboard and listen to him tell stupid jokes. To pass the course, there were only two things that were necessary. One was that you were there every day to laugh at his jokes. The other was that you turned in a take-home midterm and final exam that you mostly copied out of the textbook. I didn't learn a bit of history the whole year. There was a TV interview with some students the other day, and a reporter asked this question: "What do you think needs to be changed to improve the educational system?" I'd say we need to get rid of teachers who can't and don't want to teach.

Mrs. Ochoa's Spanish class was 180 degrees away from Mr. Mattair's class. Starting on the first day, Mrs. Ochoa made it clear that we *were* be there to learn Spanish. I can still remember what she told us: "If a student is going to learn Spanish, or any language, it's absolutely essential that he or she learns to speak it. We're going to be doing a lot of speaking in this class." Well, speak we did. We also read, wrote, listened to Spanish music, learned the geography of Spanish-speaking countries, and even taught our own mini-lessons. The class was hard, and at first some of the students didn't like the fact what Mrs. Ochoa kept us active for the whole fifty minutes every day. But by the end of the year, most of us could carry on a decent conversation in Spanish.

People say what the educational system is falling apart. The topic for this essay was "What do you think is necessary to improve the educational system?" The answer is "It needs more teachers like Mrs. Ochoa." The fact that teachers like Mrs. Ochoa *are* be out there in the school system is evidence that our educational system isn't all bad.

COMMUNICATION PRACTICE

5. Practice Listening

Jim, a junior in high school, wants to drop out of school and get a job. He is talking with his cousin Frank, eight years older. Listen to the conversation. Then listen again and mark the following statements true (T) *or false* (F), *based on what you hear on the tape.*

____T____ 1. Jim believes that he doesn't belong in school.

____F____ 2. Jim believes that he has learned something in school this year.

____T____ 3. Jim believes that quitting school will make his life better.

____T____ 4. Frank quit high school.

____F____ 5. Frank's friends wanted to continue their friendship with him.   *minimum wage*

____F____ 6. According to Jim, Frank's owning a house and a car is unimportant.

____T____ 7. Frank thinks Jim should stick it out in school.

____T____ 8. According to Frank, each individual has the chance to control the quality of his or her life.

____F____ 9. Frank believes that the school system is definitely good.   *Look before you leap*

____T____ 10. According to Frank, each individual has the chance to control the quality of his or her education.

6. Role Play in Pairs

Work with a partner. Choose one of the following topics and role-play the situation. Then reverse the roles and play it again.

1. A student wants to get a better grade in a course and is talking with the teacher.

   Example:
   Student: I'm not doing as well in this course as I'd like to. What do you think would help me do better?
   Teacher: Well, it seems pretty apparent **that you're only interested in the grade you get.** I think it's important **that a student concentrate on learning the material.** The grades will follow naturally. That's what I'd suggest.

2. A student has been expelled from school for disciplinary reasons. The parents are discussing the problem with the school principal.

3. A principal has observed a teacher's class and has given the teacher a poor evaluation. The teacher disagrees. They are discussing the evaluation.

4. A student wants to drop out of school, but the parents don't agree. They are discussing the issue.

7. Debate

Choose one of the following topics to debate. Then divide into groups of six to eight. Three to four people should be on each side of the issue. Take time to prepare your argument.

should use the words: insist demand suggest recommend

Topic 1. Teachers should (OR should not) be paid on the basis of evaluations by their students.
Topic 2. Letter or numerical grades should (OR should not) be abolished as a means of evaluating students.
Topic 3. Starting with high school, a country's educational system should (OR should not) be structured so that students would choose between studying an academic or a vocational program.
Topic 4. School should (OR should not) be compulsory after the eighth year.

it is essential " " necessary important advisable desirable

8. Letter

Write a letter to a politician (governor, premier, legislator, representative, etc.) about an educational reform that you think needs to be made. You may choose from the topics mentioned in the preceding debate or develop another topic. In your letter, state the problem that needs to be addressed, explain why you think it is a problem, offer possible solutions to the problem, and ask the politician to support your proposal legislatively.

9. Picture Discussion

This is an advertisement for life insurance. Why do you think the life insurance company presented this picture in its advertisement? Talk about the picture and speculate about the advertiser's intent.

Example:
It's obvious **that the father loves his child.**

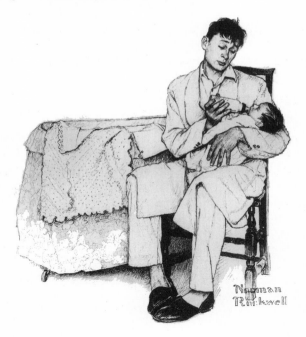

Norman Rockwell: (detail) Massachusetts Mutual
"Father Feeding Infant." Photo courtesy of
The Norman Rockwell Museum at Stockbridge.

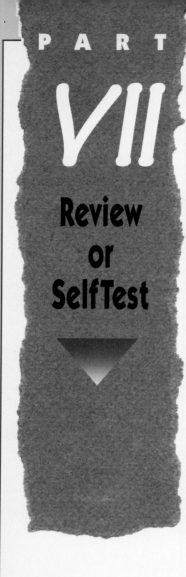
I. *Read the conversations and underline each noun clause.*

1. **A:** I don't know <u>what we should do tonight</u>.

   B: Whatever you want to do is fine with me.

2. **A:** We haven't decided where we want to go on vacation.

   B: Don't you think that Hawaii would be nice?

3. **A:** How do we decide who wins the prize?

   B: Give the prize to whoever gets the most points.

4. **A:** Do you think she is guilty?

   B: Well, the fact that she waited so long to contact the police doesn't
   help her case.

5. **A:** I can't believe what I'm seeing. The Broncos might even win this
   game.

   B: Yeah, I know. I'm amazed that they've been able to do this well.

6. **A:** Mr. Jones, I'm sorry to say that I need more time to complete the
   assignment.

   B: That's all right. Take however long you need to do the job well.

7. **A:** In your view, what is the answer to the problem of violence in
   schools?

   B: I think that we need to ban weapons of all kinds.

8. **A:** What is Marilyn's problem?

   B: Well, it's clear that she's very unhappy.

II. *Read the letter, and find and correct the eight errors in pronouns that introduce noun clauses.*

November 28

Dear Manny,

Well, my first month as a literacy volunteer is over, and I feel

exhilarated! ~~That~~ *What* I like best is the chance to work with real people. In

the mornings I report to that's called "Open Classroom." I'm assigned

to tutor whatever comes in and asks for help. Most of the students are

wonderful; sometimes I'm amazed what they're so motivated to learn.

In the afternoons I tutor my regular students. I usually work with a

lady from Vietnam named Mrs. Tranh. When I started working with

her, she could hardly read at all, but I'm really impressed by who she's

learned. At first I chose the assignments, but now we work on whoever

Mrs. Tranh chooses. If she wants to practice reading aloud, that's that

we do. If she wants to work on comprehension, we do that for

whatever long she wants to do it. Sometimes we spend all afternoon

on one thing, but it's very rewarding.

Well, that's all for now. Write soon, and I'll do the same.

Best,

Zeya

III. *Complete the conversations with noun clauses, using the words given. Be sure to include the word* **that** *if it is correct to do so.*

1. **A:** How long do you want to spend in San Francisco?

   B: ___However long you want to spend___ is fine with me.

a. (However / long / you / want / spend)

2. **A:** Where's Hattie?

   B: I don't know _____. Maybe she's out in the back yard.

b. (where / she / be)

3. **A:** Do you think _____?

c. (Bill / be / an asset / to our firm)
   B: Well, _____ says something, I think.

d. (the fact / he / ill / a great deal)

4. **A:** What do you think we need to do about Bill's excessive absences?

   B: I think _____ _____.

e. (we / need / do)   f. (whatever / be / necessary)

5. **A:** Who do you think is behind this rumor?

   B: I don't know, but _____ needs a talking to. It's obvious

g. (whoever / it / be)
   _____. He has too much to lose.

h. (it / not / be / Ron)

IV. *Read the sentences about education. Circle the letter of the correct answer to complete each sentence.*

1. _____ student test scores have not improved   **A**   **Ⓑ**   **C**   **D**
   in the last decade suggests that the American educational system
   is in need of a major overhaul.
   - A. The fact which
   - B. The fact that
   - C. Which
   - D. What

2. Many educators seem convinced _____ students   **A**   **B**   **C**   **D**
   would respond favorably to a change in the system.
   - A. what
   - B. the fact
   - C. that
   - D. whatever

3. _____ America needs now is a two-track   **A**   **B**   **C**   **D**
   program in high schools.
   - A. Whatever
   - B. What
   - C. That
   - D. Whoever

4. In the majority of high schools at present, many students   A   B   C   D
are allowed to take _____ courses they want.
   A. whoever
   B. however
   C. whatever
   D. whenever

5. In a two-track system, students would choose after the eighth grade   A   B   C   D
_____ educational track they wanted to study:
academic or vocational.
   A. which
   B. who
   C. whom
   D. when

6. _____ was interested in a college education would   A   B   C   D
study in the academic track.
   A. Whatever
   B. Whoever
   C. Whomever
   D. Whichever

7. _____ wanted to go right into the workplace after   A   B   C   D
graduation would choose the vocational track.
   A. Whoever
   B. However
   C. Whatever
   D. Whomever

8. _____ America is one of only two industrialized   A   B   C   D
nations without a two-track choice is a telling statistic.
   A. The fact which
   B. Which
   C. What
   D. The fact that

9. It is obvious _____ the country needs this   A   B   C   D
educational reform.
   A. what
   B. who
   C. which
   D. that

1.

Direct speech quotes the exact words (or thoughts) of a speaker. Indirect speech (or reported speech) reports the words or thoughts of a speaker and contains most but not all of that speaker's exact words or thoughts.

Both direct and indirect speech usually occur in noun clauses, normally as direct objects.

> direct speech
> Jack asked Margo, **"Do you think James should go to a private school?"** (The quotation is the direct object of the verb, answering the question "What did Jack ask?")

> indirect speech
> Jack asked Margo **if she thought James should go to a private school.** (The noun clause **if she thought James should go to a private school** is the direct object, answering the question "What did Jack ask?")

2.

In direct speech, quotation marks surround the quotation. The reporting verb, such as *said, asked, told,* or *responded,* is followed by a comma if it introduces the quotation. Quotation marks come after a final period, question mark, or exclamation point.

> James said**,** "Mom, I want to keep going to public school**."** (statement)
> Margo asked Jack**,** "Can we afford to send James to a private school**?"** (question)
> James said to Jack and Margo**,** "I won't go**!"** (exclamation)

If the reporting statement comes after the quotation, a comma follows the last word of the quotation, and the second set of quotation marks comes after the comma. A period ends the sentence.

> "I don't want to go to a private school**,"** James said**.**

If the quotation is a question or an exclamation, that question or exclamation ends with a question mark or exclamation point.

> "James, do you like school**?"** asked Aunt Colleen**.**
> "I won't go to a private school**!"** James yelled.

If the reporting statement comes within the quotation, each part of the quotation is enclosed in quotation marks. The part of the quotation after the reporting statement does not begin with a capital letter if the remainder of the quotation is not part of a new sentence. Look at the quotation marks, the commas, and the capitalization in this example:

> "Ms. Baldwin," **the reporter asked, "w**hy are you all on strike?"

3.

In indirect speech there are no quotation marks. The first word of the indirect speech is not capitalized. The reporting statement is not followed by a comma. An indirect question does not have a question mark at the end of the sentence. Note that indirect speech is presented as a noun clause and can be introduced by the word *that.*

> James said **(that) he wanted to keep going to public school.**
> James told his mom **(that) he wanted to keep going to public school.**
> Margo asked Jack **if they could afford to send James to a private school.**

A. *Punctuate the following sentences in direct speech. Add capital letters if necessary.*

1. **"**Dad, I want to quit school and go to work**,"** Jim murmured**.**
2. Sally, how would you evaluate your education the reporter queried
3. I absolutely despise going to school Sally responded (exclamation)
4. Jim, Frank said, you're crazy if you think it's going to be easy to get a job
5. Frank, said Jim, don't be a fool (exclamation)
6. The Teachers' Union spokesperson asked the superintendent when are you going to start taking our concerns seriously

B. *Correct the capitalization and punctuation in the following examples of indirect speech.*

1. Spokesperson Frances Baldwin said, that the Board of Education had even refused to talk to them.
2. Board President Bates responded that "There was simply no money for salary raises."
3. TV reporter Joan Matthews asked Fumiko if, she agreed with Sally that most teachers don't want to teach.
4. Frank asked Jim, What he would do if he couldn't find a job after he quit school?
5. Reporter Jim Bresler asked Zeya if she intended to go to college when her term was over

4.

In conversation and informal writing, the most common reporting verbs in both direct and indirect speech are *say, tell,* and *ask.* In more formal writing, the following reporting verbs are often used: *report, respond, query, wonder, confess, claim, maintain, add,* and *comment.*

> Chairman Bates **maintained** that the school district had no money to raise teachers' salaries. (argued)
> The teachers' union **claimed** that the chairman hadn't considered the union's demands. (expressed the opinion)

C. *In the following paragraph, change each instance of* **said** *to another reporting verb from the box.*

responded	maintained
claimed	added
commented	

Reporter Jennifer Goodenough asked Heidi Dennison what had been the single most enjoyable experience in her Peace Corps service. Heidi ~~said~~ responded that it had been the vacation she had taken
1.
to Kenya, Tanzania, and Uganda at the end of her first year. Jennifer ~~said~~ that she was surprised at Heidi's
2.
answer because she had expected her to mention one of her accomplishments in Nigeria.
Many people ~~said~~ the purpose of the Peace Corps was to give Americans the chance to take vacations
3.
in exotic places. But Heidi ~~said~~ that the chance to learn about other countries was a valuable learning
4.
experience. She ~~said~~ that she thought it would contribute to international understanding in the long run.
5.

VIII

Unreal
Conditions

INTRODUCTION

Read and listen to the story and think about the questions.

Questions to Consider

1. Do you believe in intuition (knowing something without proof)?
2. Have you had any experiences in which your intuition or someone else's proved correct?

Intuition

It was a sweltering day. Thain and Aurora were driving down Maple Street, looking for a yard sale, when they spotted the old man. Waving at them with a halfhearted gesture, he looked **as if he hadn't eaten** for days.

"Honey, pull over. Let's give that old man a ride. He's going to faint if he doesn't get out of this sun."

"Thain, **I wish you'd stop** taking pity on every weirdo you see. He's probably an ax murderer. I bet he'll kill us and steal the car if we pick him up."

"I don't think so. He looks harmless to me—just a poor old guy. He's acting as if he's sick."

"But Sweetie, we have to get to that yard sale. There won't be anything worth buying if we don't get there soon."

"My male intuition is telling me we ought to stop."

"If I had a nickel for all the times we've done things because of your male intuition, I'd be a rich woman. Aren't females supposed to have the intuition, anyway? OK. I just hope we don't end up in the newspaper headlines. I can see it all now: YOUNG MARRIED COUPLE MUTILATED BY SERIAL KILLER!"

They pulled up to the curb in front of the old man. "Need some help, sir?" Thain asked.

The old man smiled. "Yes, thank you. Could you take me to a pharmacy? I'm diabetic and I've run out of medicine. I'm on a trip around the country, but I keep forgetting to buy enough insulin. If I don't take my medicine regularly, I go into shock. . . . **If only I weren't so forgetful.**"

They found a pharmacy and got the insulin. Back in the car, the old man said, "Now, if you can just take me to the bus station, I'll be on my way." Aurora frowned. Thain said, "Sure. We can do that." At the bus station, they helped the old man out of the car. "Can you tell me your names and your address? When I get back home, I'll send you a token of my appreciation." They gave him their names and address, said good-bye, and proceeded to the yard sale.

As Aurora had predicted, all of the good merchandise had been sold. **"I wish we'd been able to get here in time to buy that chest of drawers,"** she said, "but I'm glad we stopped for the old guy. He did need our help. I'll be surprised if we ever hear from him, though. You don't really believe all that about his taking a trip around the country, do you?"

In a few days they had forgotten about the incident. Three months later they returned from a short vacation, and Aurora was going through the pile of mail that had accumulated in their absence. She opened a long envelope with no return address.

"What in the world? Thain, come here and look at this!" There was a letter inside, neatly typed.

Dear Thain and Aurora,

I finished my trip around the country and had a marvelous time. I'm now back at home and shan't be traveling anymore, I don't think. I met some wonderful people in my travels, the two of you among them.

Thank you for your kindness to a forgetful old man. **If you hadn't come along when you did and taken me to the pharmacy, I might have died.** At the very least, **I would have become very ill. I wish that there had been time for us to get to know one another. If I had been fortunate to have any children of my own, I couldn't have had any nicer ones than you two.** At any rate, I am enclosing a token of my gratitude. My warmest regards,

Quentin Wilkerson

Something fluttered out of a second sheet of folded paper. It was a check for $50,000.

UNREAL CONDITIONALS AND OTHER WAYS TO EXPRESS UNREALITY

UNREAL CONDITIONALS

If I **had** a nickel for all the times we've done things because of your male intuition, I**'d be** a rich woman.
If you **hadn't helped** me, I **might have died.**
If my daughter **hadn't been given** poor advice, she would have taken the right courses.

OTHER WAYS TO EXPRESS UNREALITY

I **wish** (that) I **could** save money.
I **wish** (that) we**'d been able to get** to know one another better.
If only Barbara **would apply** herself.
If only I **hadn't done** that.
He acts **as though** he **were** president.
He acted **as if** he **hadn't eaten** for days.

Grammar Notes

1. Unreal Conditionals:

Conditional sentences consist of two clauses, a dependent *if*-clause and an independent result clause.

> *if*-clause   result clause
> If I had a car, I would drive to work.

Note the descriptions of unreality in the following examples.

a. In conditional sentences that express unreal ideas in the present time, use the simple past tense form of the verb in the *if*-clause and *would, could,* or *might* plus the base form of the verb in the result clause.

> If I **were** you, I **would buy** a house. (Unreal: I'm not you.)
> If we **had** enough money for a down payment, we **might buy** ten acres of land. (Unreal: We don't have enough money.)

If she **knew** Japanese well, she **could get** a job as an interpreter. (Unreal: She doesn't know Japanese very well.)

Be careful! Remember to use *were* for all persons with the verb *be*.

b. A variant form of the present unreal conditional is to use *were* plus an infinitive in the *if*-clause. The effect of this is to make the condition seem more tentative or hypothetical.

> If I **were to offer** you a job, would you take it?

c. To express unreal ideas in the past time, use *had* plus a past participle in the *if*-clause, and use *would, could,* or *might* + *have* + past participle in the result clause.

> If you **hadn't come along, I might have died.** (Unreal: You did come along.)

Usage note: You will hear some speakers use *would have* in the *if*-clause. However, this usage is not acceptable in formal speaking or writing.

If I **had known** he needed financial help, I would have lent him the money. NOT ~~If I would have known he needed financial help, I would have lent him the money.~~

2. Other Ways to Express Unreality:

a. Notice the difference between *wish* and *hope. Hope* is used to express a desire or an expectation about something that may be real or possible.

I **hope** he **comes** to the party. (And maybe he will.)

I **hope** he **wasn't** angry. (And maybe he wasn't.)

Wish is used to express a desire or a regret about something unreal and therefore not possible or probable. When talking about the present, use *wish* with a simple past tense verb or *would* or *could* plus a base form. Remember to use *were* for all persons of *be*.

I **wish** she **were** here now. (Unreal: She is not here now, and I regret that.)

I **wish** she **would work** faster. (Unreal: She is not willing to work faster.)

In past time, use *wish* with *had* + past participle.

I **wish** we **had been able to get** to know one another last year. (Unreal: We weren't able to get to know one another last year.)

b. The phrase *if only* has meanings somewhat similar to those of *wish* and *hope.* Use the simple past tense form after *if only* if you are wishing for something that is unreal at present.

If only she **loved** me. (Unreal: She doesn't love me.)

Use *had* plus a past participle after *if only* if you are wishing that something had happened differently in the past.

If only he **had buckled** his seat belt. (Unreal: He didn't buckle his seat belt.)

Use a simple present tense after *if only* if you are hoping for something that may become real in the present or future.

If only she **gets** the news on time!

c. Note the use of the phrases *as if* and *as though.* These forms are followed by simple present tense or *will* + base form to express situations that are probably real.

You are talking **as though** you **know** something about the crime. (Could be real)

d. *As if* and *as though* are often followed by past verb forms to express situations that are unreal or probably unreal. (Remember that in contrary-to-fact situations, *were* is used for all persons of *be.*) Note the sequence of tenses in the following examples:

He's acting **as if he were** the president. (Unreal: He's not the president.)

The old man looked **as though** he **hadn't eaten** for days. (Probably unreal)

Remember that when these are followed by simple present tense or *will* + base form, they express situations that could be real.

He's talking **as if** he**'ll be** president some day.

FOCUSED PRACTICE

1. Discover the Grammar

Read the following excerpt from a student's classroom speech on intuition.
Underline clauses with real conditionals once and those with unreal conditionals
twice.

How many of you believe in intuition? Is it just some sort of acting without thinking? <u>If you act on the basis of intuition, will the results be disastrous?</u> Today I'm going to try to convince you that intuition is more than some sort of mystical mumbo jumbo and that, if we all paid more attention to our intuitive feelings, we would do better.

Intuition is defined as a way of knowing something more or less immediately without having to go through a conscious process of figuring out the answer. In other words, if a new situation presents itself, you don't have to weigh the evidence on both sides of the question. You just know the answer.

Here's an example. You've been out of work for several months, so you apply for a job that will involve doing something you don't like. You get a call saying you've been selected for the job. Your intuition tells you that if you accept the job, you'll soon be bored and will hate it. Unfortunately, however, you suppress that idea and persuade yourself rationally that, if you just approach the job with the right attitude, things will turn out well. Besides, you're desperate for employment, so you take the job and hope you end up liking it.

For a while you manage to act as if you liked the work, but you're only fooling yourself. Three months later you wish you hadn't been so hasty. You're miserable and hate going to work every day. "If only I'd waited a little longer," you say to yourself. If you'd listened to your intuition, you wouldn't be in this situation. By now you probably would have found a job more to your liking.

Where did you go wrong? You knew the answer to the question, but you ignored it. You didn't follow your intuition.

2.   An Educational Trip

On the spur of the moment, Lee decided to visit the zoo. Later he wrote about the visit in his journal. Complete Lee's journal entry by writing unreal conditional forms after **as if** *or* **as though,** *using the verbs provided. Also complete the sentences containing* **I wish** *and* **I hope.**

August 28

Journal

Today I had the afternoon off. On the spur of the moment, I decided to visit the zoo. I hadn't been there in years, and I guess it might have been an angry letter-to-the-editor about zoo conditions that planted the idea in my head. My eyes were really opened.

The first thing I saw was the graffiti covering all the buildings near the entrance. The area almost looked as though it __had been abandoned__ . I wish
1. (be/abandon)

people _____ more respect for public buildings. After all, we
2. (have)

taxpayers are the ones who pay for them, ultimately. The next thing I noticed was that there was trash everywhere; the place looked as if it

_____ for at least a month. I wish there _____
3. (not/be/clean)   4. (be)

more money to clean up the whole city, the zoo included.

Anyway, I kept walking and looked at all the animal exhibits, or should I say animal prisons. Aren't zoos supposed to be enlightened places these days? Not our zoo! Take the hippopotamus pond, for example. I could smell it from a hundred yards away. It's no wonder the pond stank; it appeared as though the

water _____ for months. Then I saw the monkeys in their
5. (not/be/change)

cages. Poor creatures! They acted as if they _____ hope.
6. (give up)

Their cages were small and mostly filthy, and they just sat there in a dispirited manner.

I pushed on and saw the other animals in their exhibits, and their situations were all pretty much the same—especially the large animals like bears and cats. This sort of thing is so unfair to the animals. I hope someone _____
7. (do)

something about this. At any rate, today was really a day of learning. I just wish I

_____ about this sooner. I'm going to write my senators.
8. (know)

3. Tragedy

Part 1 *Read and think about the poem. Then write past-time conditional sentences based on the verbs given. Use* **would** *unless another auxiliary, such as* **might** *or* **could,** *is given.*

> ### 'Out, Out—'
> #### Robert Frost
> The buzz saw snarled and rattled in the yard
> And made dust and dropped stove-length sticks of wood,
> Sweet-scented stuff when the breeze drew across it.
> And from there those that lifted eyes could count
> Five mountain ranges one behind the other
> Under the sunset far into Vermont.
> And the saw snarled and rattled, snarled and rattled,
> As it ran light, or had to bear a load.
> And nothing happened: day was all but done.
> Call it a day, I wish they might have said
> To please the boy by giving him the half hour
> That a boy counts so much when saved from work.
> His sister stood beside them in her apron
> To tell them 'Supper.' At the word, the saw,
> As if to prove saws knew what supper meant,
> Leaped out at the boy's hand, or seemed to leap—
> He must have given the hand. However it was,
> Neither refused the meeting. But the hand!
> The boy's first outcry was a rueful laugh,
> As he swung toward them holding up the hand
> Half in appeal, but half as if to keep
> The life from spilling. Then the boy saw all—
> Since he was old enough to know, big boy
> Doing a man's work, though a child at heart—
> He saw all spoiled. 'Don't let him cut my hand off—
> The doctor, when he comes. Don't let him, sister!'
> So. But the hand was gone already.
> The doctor put him in the dark of ether.
> He lay and puffed his lips out with his breath.
> And then—the watcher at his pulse took fright.
> No one believed. They listened at his heart.
> Little—less—nothing!—and that ended it.
> No more to build on there. And they, since they
> Were not the one dead, turned to their affairs.

1. If the boy had been in school, he wouldn't have died.
   (the boy / be / in school / he / not / die)

2. _____
   (the doctor / arrive / sooner / he / might / be / able / save / the boy)

3. _____
   (the boy / not / doing / a man's job / he / probably / not / be killed)

4. _____
   (the saw / cut / the boy's finger instead of his hand / the boy / could probably / survive)

5. _____
   (the boy / might / not / be cut by the saw / the sister / not say "supper" / at a crucial moment)

6. _____
   (the work boss / say / "Call it a day" / the boy / escape / his fate)

Part 2 *Now assume that the time is the present and that the accident has just happened. Write sentences about what certain people probably wish or hope.*

7. The sister probably wishes (that) everyone had decided to quit work early.
   (The sister / probably / wish / everyone / decide / quit work early)

8. _____
   (The doctor / probably wish / he / arrive sooner)

9. _____
   (The boy's parents / probably wish / they / not allow / the boy / work at a man's job)

10. _____
    (Other parents / probably hope / this kind of accident / not happen / to their children)

4. Editing

Read the following diary entry. Find and correct the ten errors in conditionals.

July 4

Dear Diary,

   This has been one of those days when I wish I ~~would have~~ _{had}
stayed in bed. It started at 7:30 this morning when Trudy called
me up and asked me for "a little favor." She's always asking me to
do things for her and never wants to take any responsibility for
herself. She acts as if the world owe her a living. I wish she won't
do that! Today she wanted me to take her to the mall because
she had to get her mother a birthday present. I told her I had to
be downtown at 10:00 A.M. for a job interview, and she said it
wouldn't take long to drive to the mall and that I'd have plenty of
time to get downtown. I gave in and agreed to take her, but
something told me I shouldn't. If I would have listened to my inner
voice, I might had a job today.

   When we were on the freeway, there was a major accident, and
traffic was tied up for over an hour. By the time we got to the
mall, it was ten-thirty, so I missed my job interview. I think I
probably would get the job if I would have managed to make it to
the interview, because my qualifications are good. If only I
wouldn't have listened to Trudy! I just hope she never asked me to
do something like this again, and if she does, I hope I didn't agree.

COMMUNICATION PRACTICE

5. Practice Listening

Listen to the conversation between two women who are members of Warm Hearts, a matchmaking service. Then listen again. For each item given, circle the letter of the sentence that explains the meaning of certain of the sentences you hear.

1. (a.) Rosa has met some interesting people.
   b. Rosa hasn't met any interesting people.

2. a. Phyllis followed her intuition.
   b. Phyllis didn't follow her intuition.

3. a. Phyllis went out with Les.
   b. Phyllis went out with Wayne.

4. a. Phyllis didn't pay attention to her feelings.
   b. Phyllis did pay attention to her feelings.

5. a. Phyllis is in a good relationship now.
   b. Phyllis isn't in a good relationship now.

6. a. Wayne seemed to think he was Phyllis's boss.
   b. Wayne didn't seem to think he was Phyllis's boss.

7. a. Phyllis thinks it's possible or likely that Wayne is gone for good.
   b. Phyllis thinks it's unlikely or improbable that Wayne is gone for good.

8. a. Phyllis doesn't regard herself as a coward.
   b. Phyllis regards herself as a coward.

9. a. Rosa thinks Phyllis puts herself down too much.
   b. Rosa doesn't think Phyllis puts herself down too much.

10. a. Phyllis thinks it's possible that Les hasn't found someone else.
    b. Phyllis thinks that Les has probably found someone else.

6. Discussion in Pairs

Work with a partner. Interview your partner about something in the past he or she wishes had turned out differently. Then reverse the roles.

7. Essay

Write an essay of three to five paragraphs about a time when you ignored your intuition and inner "gut" feelings and opted instead for a rational decision which turned out unsuccessfully. Describe your original intuitive feeling, explain why you ignored it, and speculate on what would or might have happened if you had acted intuitively.

8. Picture Discussion

Look at this picture. Discuss the events that may have led to this situation. Then divide into two groups. One group will explore the woman's point of view while the other group will speculate on Brad's point of view. Finally, talk as a class about what Brad and the woman might wish.

Roy Lichtenstein, *Drowning Girl.* (1963)
Oil and synthetic polymer paint on canvas, 67 ⁵/₈ x 66 ³/₄".
The Museum of Modern Art, New York. Philip Johnson Fund and
gift of Mr. and Mrs. Bagley Wright.
Photograph ©1995 The Museum of Modern Art, New York.

INTRODUCTION

Inverted and Implied Conditionals; Subjunctive in Noun Clauses

▣◉ *Read and listen to the letter to the advice columnist and the columnist's response.*

Questions to Consider

1. In your opinion, what is the difference between being assertive and being aggressive?
2. Do you agree with the saying "Don't say yes when you mean no"?

Dear Pamela,

I've always been considered a "nice guy," but I guess you could also call me "a soft touch." A year ago my wife's brother, Stan, was in a desperate situation and needed a thousand dollars immediately to pay off a loan he had defaulted on. He **asked that we lend him the money.** At first I **suggested that he go through the usual channels and get a bank loan.** He said he'd tried that and had been turned down. He pressured my wife for a loan, and she pressured me. He assured us that if we lent him the money, he would pay it back with interest. I gave in and advanced him a thousand dollars from my own account, but I shouldn't have. In fact, **had I known what was going to happen, I never would have said yes.** We didn't put anything in writing, and Stan hasn't paid us a cent. I am extremely angry about this, but whenever I mention it to Carol, my wife, she says that Stan is going through a rough time right now, and **it's important that we keep peace in the family.** Pamela, what should I do?

Furious in Frankfort

Dear Furious,

Sweetie, it's one thing to be a nice guy, but it's another to be a doormat. It sounds like you let people take advantage of you. **If so,** I'd say it's time you got some assertiveness training; **without it,** you'll just keep letting people tell you what to do.

In my view you should have **insisted that Stan sign** a notarized agreement spelling out the terms of repayment. It's too late for that now, though, so I **recommend that you arrange** a meeting between yourself and Stan. Leave Carol out of it. Perhaps you can call and ask Stan to meet you for lunch at a restaurant. At the lunch meeting, tell him calmly but in no uncertain terms that you're angry and that this thing has gone far enough. **Insist that he start** making immediate repayments. **Should he balk** at what you're saying or mention Carol, simply tell him that this is between you and him, that you don't want family squabbles, and that there won't be any as long as he makes the payments. Make it clear that he *must* make the payments; **if not,** you'll take him to small claims court. **It's essential that Stan understand** that you're serious; **otherwise,** he'll simply go on taking advantage of you.

Tell Carol what you've done after you've met with Stan. You don't need to get angry; just say that it was your money that was lent, that this is the way things are going to be from now on, and that you'd rather you and she not get into a fight about it.

Then look around for a course in assertiveness. **With a little work,** you can learn not to let people walk all over you. Good luck, and be calm but courageous!

Pamela

INVERTED AND IMPLIED CONDITIONALS; SUBJUNCTIVE IN NOUN CLAUSES

INVERSION

Had I known what would happen, I wouldn't have advanced him the money.
Were she to apologize now, I would forgive her.
Should you return before I do, please pick up the mail.

IMPLIED CONDITIONALS

I don't believe you want to get a divorce. **If so,** you would have already left.
Without your help, I would never have been able to get there on time.
What if I offered you this job?

SUBJUNCTIVE IN NOUN CLAUSES FOLLOWING CERTAIN VERBS AND ADJECTIVES

I insist (that) she **be** here by the time the session begins.
It is important that you **be** aware of certain facts.
It is essential that he **start** accepting responsibility.

Grammar Notes

1. You can express an unreal condition by deleting *if* and inverting the auxiliaries *had, were,* or *should* and the subject in an *if-*clause.

> **Had I known** that would happen, I wouldn't have advanced him the money. (= If I had known . . .)
>
> **Were I to offer** you a job, I'd need a strong recommendation from your former employer. (= If I were to offer you a job . . .)
>
> **Should that happen,** I'd be ready for it. (= If that should happen . . .)

2. Unreal and real conditionals are sometimes implied rather than stated directly with an *if-*clause and a result clause. Implied conditionals often use the following phrases and words: *if so, if not, otherwise, with,* and *without.*

> **Without** a clear policy, you would continue to be manipulated by others. (**Without** = If you didn't have . . .)
>
> **With** some training, you could learn not to be a doormat. (**With** = If you got . . .)
>
> It sounds like you let people take advantage of you. **If so,** you need to learn to be more assertive. (**If so** = if you do let people take advantage of you . . .)

> **If not,** maybe you're just unlucky. (**If not** = If you don't let people take advantage of you . . .)
>
> Stan needs to understand that you're serious. **Otherwise,** he'll continue taking advantage. (**Otherwise** = If he doesn't understand . . .)
>
> **What if** I told you the truth? (= What would happen if I told you the truth?)

3. The subjunctive form of the verb is used in a noun clause following adjectives and verbs of urgency. The subjunctive form is used to convey a sense of unreality of the outcome at the moment the statement is made. It is impossible to know whether the action in the noun clause will ever occur.

> It is essential that he **understand** clearly what you want. (It may be essential, but we don't know if he will or he won't.)
>
> I suggest that she **go** to the doctor first thing in the morning. (I may suggest it, but I can't know if she will actually go.)

4. Two commonly used expressions, *it's time* and *would rather,* are followed by the base form (subjunctive) or the simple past tense form of the verb.

> **They'd rather** we **didn't smoke** here.
> **I'd rather** she **use** only English in class.
> **It's time** you **grew** up!

FOCUSED PRACTICE

1. Discover the Grammar

🔲 *Read and listen to the following radio advertisement on assertiveness training. Then underline all subjunctive verb forms and circle all implied conditionals.*

A few minutes ago your friend Mary called and asked that you <u>babysit</u> her children for the fifth time in the last three weeks. Had you known she was going to call, you wouldn't have answered the phone. The last time this happened, it was ten o'clock at night and Mary still hadn't picked up her kids. You finally had to call and insist that she come and get them. You politely suggested that Mary look into day care, but she said she wouldn't be able to afford it until she got a job. After that you swore you wouldn't be manipulated again, but when Mary called up and said, "Just this once," you gave in and said yes. Now you're boiling inside, though, because you feel Mary treats you like her slave.

Does this sound like you? If so, we can help. We're Lionhearts, and we specialize in assertiveness training. With a little bit of practice, you can learn how to say what you think and not feel guilty about it. Call 232-9195 now for an appointment. Money back if you're not completely satisfied.

2. Growing Up

Complete the sentences with past forms of the indicated verbs after **what if, would rather, as if,** *and* **it's time.**

Dad: Liz, the swim meet starts in an hour. It's time we _____were leaving_____.
1. (be leaving)

Liz: Dad, can't I just go by myself? I'd rather you and Mom _____ me drive. I do have my
2. (let)
license, you know.

Dad: Liz, it's a dangerous world out there. What if you _____ into an accident?
3. (get)

Liz: Dad, I'm sixteen years old. It's time you and Mom _____ treating me like an adult.
4. (start)

Dad: You're not an adult yet, Liz.

Liz: OK, maybe not, but you guys treat me as if I _____ a baby. It's embarrassing, always
5. (be)
getting dropped off.

Dad: Hmm. All right. Do you really think you can handle it?

Liz: Of course, Dad.

3. Aggressiveness vs. Assertiveness

Complete the following page from The Assertive Individual's Handbook. *Use subjunctive forms of the indicated verbs in the noun clauses. Read the page from left to right, following the numbered items in order.*

The Agressive Person

1. The aggressive person insists that

___she be allowed___
(she/be/allow)

to have her own way.

3. For an aggressive person, it is essential that

_____ .
(an argument/be/win)

5. The aggressive person demands that

_____
(you/adopt)

his viewpoint.

7. An aggressive person is likely to order that

_____ .
(something/be/do)

The Assertive Person

2. The assertive person requests that

_____ .
(her way/be/consider)

4. For an assertive person, it is important that

_____
(an argument/be)

fair.

6. The assertive person asks that

_____
(you/give)

consideration to his viewpoint.

8. An assertive person is likely to suggest that

_____ .
(a course of action/be/follow)

4. Job Hunting

Fill in the blanks in the story with items from the box.

if so	if not	with	otherwise	had she stayed	had she known

Linda had recently moved to Atlanta from Ponders, the small town where she had grown up.

_____Had she known_____ how difficult it would be to find employment, she might have stayed in her home
　　　　　1.

town. She loved the big city, though, and she felt that, _____ in Ponders, she would
　　　　　　　　　　　　　　　　　　　　　　　　　　　　　　2.

have fallen into a rut that she would never escape from. The only problem was that Linda needed to find a

job soon; _____, she wouldn't be able to pay next month's rent, and she'd have to go
　　　　　　3.

back to Ponders. The trouble was, she was shy about asking for work.

One day Linda was wandering around downtown, feeling that _____ a bit of luck, she
　　　　　　　　　　　　　　　　　　　　　　　　　　　　　　　　4.

might find something. She saw a pleasant-looking florist's shop. Maybe they were hiring.

_____, she might get a job. _____, she wouldn't lose anything by
　　　　5.　　　　　　　　　　　　　　　　　　　　6.

going in and asking. Without even thinking further, she walked in.

"I'm Linda Hilliard, and I was wondering whether you were doing any hiring. I have a lot of experience
with flowers and gardening."

The manager said, "Actually, we do need someone to work part time. I was just going to put up a sign in
the window. Tell me more about your experience."

Linda got the job.

*Now rewrite the phrase in each blank above with an **if**-clause that restates the meaning.*

7. _____If she had known_____
　　　　　　　　　　　　　　　　　　　(she / know)

8. _____
　　　　　　　　　　　　　　　　　　　(she / stay)

9. _____
　　　　　　　　　　　　　　　　　　　(she / not / find / work)

10. _____
　　　　　　　　　　　　　　　　　　　(she / have)

11. _____
　　　　　　　　　　　　　　　　　　　(they / be / hiring)

12. _____
　　　　　　　　　　　　　　　　　　　(they / not / be / hiring)

5. Editing

Read the letter. Find and correct the eight verb errors.

December 10

Dear April,

    I wanted to write and fill you in on what's been happening since I left Ponders.

    I finally got a job! Remember when you suggested I just ~~went~~ go walking around, getting a sense of what Atlanta was like? A few weeks ago I was really getting worried, and I had spent almost all the money I had saved up to tide me over until I found work. I had gotten to the point where it was absolutely essential that I found something or just came home. So I decided to try your advice. Had I know how easy this would be, I would have tried it the first week I was here. I started walking around in the downtown area, and before I knew it I saw a beautiful little florist's shop. I walked right in as if I have courage and experience and asked whether they had a job. Can you believe that they did?

    I was really happy in my job until my boss hired a new assistant manager who has been making my life miserable. He treats me as if I be his personal slave. I took this job to work with plants, not to serve him coffee. I think it's time I'm telling him where I stand.

    I have a few days off for the holidays. What if I had come home as a surprise to Mom and Dad? Could we plan some kind of party? Write and let me know, OK?

Love,

Linda

COMMUNICATION PRACTICE

6. Practice Listening

●● *Listen to a segment of the radio talk show "Wimp No More."*

Comprehension

Now listen again and mark the following statements true (T) *or false* (F), *based on what you hear.*

___T___ 1. Callers are supposed to turn down their radios when they're on the air.

_____ 2. Mildred's mother-in-law takes Buddy shopping every day.

_____ 3. Mildred's mother-in-law owns the house Mildred and Buddy live in.

_____ 4. Buddy's mother treats Mildred like an intruder.

_____ 5. Buddy doesn't want his mother to set foot in the house.

_____ 6. Buddy doesn't want Mildred to excite his mother.

_____ 7. Forrest thinks Mildred needs to do something about the situation soon.

_____ 8. Forrest will sit down with Buddy and tell him the situation can't continue.

_____ 9. Forrest thinks Buddy should find his mother a new place to live.

_____10. Buddy got mad and chose his mother over Mildred.

_____11. Forrest suggests that Buddy take a chance and get married.

Optional Dictation

Now listen once more, filling in the blanks in certain of the sentences.

1. We _____ask_____ only _____that you turn down_____ your radio when you're on the air

2. and _____ your language clean.

3. She _____ her shopping every day

4. and _____ dinner with her.

5. She makes it seem _____ the place

6. and I _____ some sort of intruder.

7. I _____ set foot in the house.

8. He says it's really _____ her too much.

9. _____ some action here.

10. If _____ with Buddy and tell him this can't go on.

11. I _____ her a new place to live.

12. _____ get mad and choose her over me?

13. I _____ Buddy a chance to show who he's married to.

7. Role Play in Pairs

Work with a partner. Choose one of the following situations and role-play it.
Then reverse the roles and play it again.

1. A spouse who feels under the control of an in-law has decided to confront the in-law about the problem.
2. A parent and a strong-willed child are having an argument. The parent is having difficulty with the child, who is refusing to do chores.
3. Two spouses are having a discussion. One spouse feels constantly belittled and put down by the other but has decided to confront the other spouse about the problem.

8. Essay

Choose one of the following topics and write a narrative essay of three or four paragraphs about it.

Topic 1.   A time when being assertive was a mistake for you. What happened? What should you have done instead? What might have happened had you behaved differently?

Topic 2.   A time when you weren't assertive and should have been. What did you do? What could you have done?

Topic 3.   A time when you were successfully assertive. What action did you take? Why was it successful?

9. Picture Discussion

In groups of four or five, discuss this picture. Talk about what you think the artist might have wanted to show. What do you think the title means? Then discuss your group's ideas and opinions with those of the other groups.

Example:
The artist seems to treat time **as if it were** . . .

Salvador Dalí, *Persistence of Memory*. (1931)
Oil on canvas, 9 ½ x 13".
The Museum of Modern Art. Given anonymously.
Photograph ©1995 The Museum of Modern Art, New York.

I. *Read the paragraph about Brandon's car problem. Then complete the sentences with conditional forms.*

Recently I had an experience that taught me a lesson. I'd been meaning to get the oil in my car changed, but I kept putting it off. Last Tuesday on the Appleton Expressway I was on my way to a job interview when the car just quit. The engine seized because it was out of oil. Before I could make it to the side of the road, another car rear-ended me. That did about a thousand dollars worth of damage to the car, and I had to have the car's engine completely replaced. I had to pay a towing bill of $150, and I didn't make it to the job interview, either. Hopefully, I've learned my lesson.

1. _Brandon wishes he hadn't put off changing the oil in the car._
(Brandon / wish / not put off / changing the oil in the car)
_____

2. _____
(If / he / change / the oil / the engine / not seize)
_____

3. _____
(If / the engine / not seize / the other car / not rear-end him)
_____

4. _____
(He / not / have to / pay a towing bill)
_____

5. _____
(He / not / have to / replace the engine)
_____

6. _____
(He / could / make it to the job interview / if / all this / not happen)
_____

7. _____
(If / he / make it to the job interview / he might / get the job)
_____

8. _____
(Brandon / hope / that / he / learn his lesson)
_____

II. *Complete the conversations with **as if/as though** and the correct form of the verb.*

1. **A:** Harriet is really arrogant, don't you think?

   B: Yes. She's always acting _____as if she were_____ the boss.
   (as if / she / be)

2. **A:** How's the weather there?

   B: Well, an hour ago it looked _____ pour.
   (as though / it / going to)
   The sun is shining now, though.

3. **A:** Chief, Mr. Bransford is acting _____ guilty.
(as if / he / be)

   B: Just remember, Officer, that he's innocent until proven guilty.

4. **A:** Where did you get this dog? He's really cute.

   B: We found him on the street. He looked _____ in some sort of accident.
(as though / he / be)

   He's OK now, though.

5. **A:** What do you think of our new boss?

   B: She needs to be more decisive. She's acting _____ one of the
(as if / she / be)

   employees.

6. **A:** What are you so mad about?

   B: You're behaving _____ this whole thing was my fault. I didn't have
(as though / you / think)

   anything to do with it, remember?

III. *Read the answer from an advice columnist. Then complete five subjunctive sentences that restate the columnist's suggestions.*

To Mary in Montreal:

No one should have to put up with a dog that barks all night. First, it's essential for you to talk with your next-door neighbor. At the same time, though, it's important not to lose your temper while you're explaining your side of the issue. Ask your neighbor to bring the dog in at night. Stay calm. If she refuses to, insist on her getting rid of the animal. If all else fails, I'd recommend calling the animal control bureau.

1. It is essential that Mary

   _____talk with her next-door neighbor_____.

2. It is important that Mary

   _____

   while she is explaining her side of the issue.

3. Mary should ask that her neighbor

   _____.

4. If she refuses to, Mary should insist that she

   _____.

5. The columnist recommends that Mary

   _____

   if all else fails.

IV. *Complete the conversation by writing verb phrases with* **wish, hope,** *and* **if only.**

Aurora: I can't believe Mr. Wilkerson sent us a check for $50,000. I wish

_____*we'd been able to*_____ get better acquainted with him the day he was here.
1. (we / be able to)

Thain: Yeah. If only _____ what was happening.
2. (we / realize)

Aurora: I just hope _____ taking his insulin, and I hope
3. (he / keep)

_____ someone around to remind him in case he forgets.
4. (there / be)

Thain: You know, I really wish _____ him in some way. The trouble is,
5. (we can / contact)

there's no return address on the envelope. Hey! What about the postmark? Where is that

envelope, anyway?

Aurora: Here it is. Oh, no. Look at this! If only the postmark _____ so
6. (not / be)

blurred. You can't see the city name.

Thain: I wish _____ a magnifying glass. . . . Hey, wait; I can make out the
7. (we / have)

zip code. It's 93302. Honey, get the almanac, will you?

Aurora: Here it is. Zip codes that start with nine are on the West Coast, aren't they? I hope

_____ like finding a needle in a haystack. Try California.
8. (this / not / be)

Thain: OK. . . . Here it is! 93302—that's Bakersfield. I wish _____ someone
9. (we / know)

in Bakersfield.

Aurora: I know! Let's go to the library and look in the Bakersfield telephone directory. Maybe his

name will be listed. Let's hope _____.
10. (it / be)

V. *Circle the letter of the correct answer to complete each sentence.*

1. You need to get some job retraining. _____ it,   **A**   **B**   **C**   **Ⓓ**
   you risk being laid off.
   A. If so
   B. If not
   C. With
   D. Without

2. I recommend that Miriam _____ a boarding   **A**   **B**   **C**   **D**
   school. She'd be much more challenged academically.
   A. attends
   B. attend
   C. is attending
   D. were attending

3. Ambrose had to take a job at a fast-food restaurant;   **A**   **B**   **C**   **D**
   _____, he wouldn't have been able
   to make his car payment.
   A. otherwise
   B. if so
   C. had he done so
   D. were that the case

4. I hope you _____ make it to the
   family reunion on the fifteenth. Everyone will be there.
   A. could
   B. were
   C. can
   D. should

   A   B   C   D

5. I hope Anna passed her exams. _____,
   she'll have to repeat her senior year.
   A. If not
   B. Without
   C. With
   D. If so

   A   B   C   D

6. At this point, Shannon wishes she _____
   mechanical drawing. She hates the course.
   A. didn't take
   B. wouldn't take
   C. hadn't taken
   D. were to take

   A   B   C   D

7. You were right when you suggested I _____
   my intuition in this business deal. I did, and it worked.
   A. follow
   B. followed
   C. were to follow
   D. had followed

   A   B   C   D

8. I wish we _____ to get to know one
   another better in the time we had.
   A. will be able
   B. were able
   C. would have been able
   D. had been able

   A   B   C   D

9. I'll be home by 7:00 P.M. on the eighteenth.
   _____ before me, please pick up the mail.
   A. Should arrive
   B. Should you arrive
   C. You should arrive
   D. Should you have arrived

   A   B   C   D

10. It sounds like something is wrong with the car's
    engine. _____, we'd better take it to the garage
    immediately.
    A. Otherwise
    B. Without it
    C. If not
    D. If so

    A   B   C   D

1.

A sentence is made up of at least one independent clause. A sentence containing more than one independent clause must be punctuated properly to avoid two kinds of errors: the run-on sentence and the comma splice.

A run-on sentence is a group of words containing at least two independent clauses without any punctuation separating them; the sentences are "run together."

independent clause   independent clause

Thain and Aurora were on their way to a yard sale an old man waved feebly to them.

The following are four ways to correct a run-on sentence.

a. Separate the two independent clauses with a period. Capitalize the first word of the second clause.

Thain and Aurora were on their way to a yard sale. **A**n old man waved feebly to them.

b. Separate the two independent clauses with a semicolon. Do not capitalize the first word of the second clause.

Thain and Aurora were on their way to a yard sale**; a**n old man waved feebly to them.

c. Join the two independent clauses with a comma and a coordinating conjunction.

Thain and Aurora were on their way to a yard sale**, and** an old man waved feebly to them.

d. Make one of the independent clauses dependent by adding a subordinating conjunction, and separate the two clauses with a comma if the dependent clause comes first.

When Thain and Aurora were on their way to a yard sale**,** an old man waved feebly to them.

A. *Correct the following run-on sentences by using the method suggested.*

1. The old man had forgotten to buy medicine ● he went into diabetic shock. (period)
2. Thain asked Aurora to pull over his intuition told him the old man needed their help. (semicolon)
3. Kate knew she had to change her relationship with her boss she didn't know how to do it. (coordinating conjunction and comma)
4. Aurora wished they had gotten to the yard sale on time she was glad they had stopped to help the old man. (subordinating conjunction at beginning of sentence and comma)

2.

A <u>comma splice</u> is the joining of two independent clauses with only a comma. A comma, however, does not provide adequate separation.

independent clause   independent clause

Marsha read *The Assertive Individual's Handbook,* she learned a lot about expressing herself in the process.

A comma splice can be corrected by the same four methods used to correct a run-on sentence.

a. Use a period.

Marsha read *The Assertive Individual's Handbook.* **S**he learned a lot about expressing herself in the process.

b. Use a semicolon.

Marsha read *The Assertive Individual's Handbook***;** **s**he learned a lot about expressing herself in the process.

c. Use a comma and a coordinating conjunction.

Marsha read *The Assertive Individual's Handbook***, and** she learned a lot about expressing herself in the process.

d. Make one of the clauses dependent by adding a subordinating conjunction.

When Marsha read *The Assertive Individual's Handbook***,** she learned a lot about expressing herself in the process.

A fifth way of correcting a comma splice is to convert one of the clauses into an adverbial *-ing* phrase if the subjects of the two clauses are the same.

Marsha read *The Assertive Individual's Handbook,* **learning a lot about herself in the process.**

The period and semicolon are similar punctuation marks in that they are both used between independent clauses. The period can be thought of as separating two clauses and the semicolon as joining two clauses.

Do not capitalize the first word after a semicolon (unless it is *I* or a proper noun).

The teachers considered the Board of Education's offer**; t**hen they went on strike.

Use a semicolon instead of a period to join independent clauses if you feel that the two clauses have a close connection in meaning.

Kate's job situation deteriorated a great deal**; s**he had to speak to her boss.

Be careful! Do not use a semicolon to connect an independent clause and a dependent clause.

While I was learning to be assertive**, I** learned many things about myself.

NOT

~~While I was learning to be assertive; I learned many things about myself~~.

B. *Correct each of the following comma splices by using the suggested method in each case.*

1. The old man looked ill, he needed to get out of the sun quickly. (semicolon)
2. Thain and Aurora drove to a pharmacy, they got the old man his insulin. (period)
3. Aurora wanted to get to the yard sale, there was a chest of drawers for sale. (semicolon)
4. Aurora didn't want to stop for the old man, Thain persuaded her it was necessary. (comma and coordinating conjunction)
5. Harold says he will seek professional help to overcome his anger, there is no assurance that he will carry out his promise. (subordinating conjunction at beginning of sentence, dependent clause and comma)
6. Nancy felt dominated by her mother-in-law, she needed to take assertive action. (Convert the first clause to an adverbial *-ing* phrase and place the noun subject in the second clause.)

3.

Notice the specific types of punctuation in sentences containing transitions.

> You are three months behind in paying your electric bill; therefore, we are
>   terminating your service.
> You need to take some positive action. Also, you need to respect yourself.

If a transition begins a clause, place a period or a semicolon before it. Remember to use a semicolon if you feel that the clauses connected are closely related in meaning; otherwise, use a period.

C. *Correct the following run-on sentences, using the suggested punctuation mark in each case. Capitalize where necessary.*

1. A tiny voice inside Arthur told him he would hate the job; therefore, he turned it down. (semicolon)
2. Nancy says she wants to do something worthwhile if so, she should join the Peace Corps. (period)
3. I need to get a bank loan otherwise, I'll have to file for bankruptcy. (semicolon)
4. Jack and Margo would like to send James to a private school however, the school is expensive, and James doesn't want to go. (period)
5. Becky and David love their new neighborhood in fact, they're going to buy a house there. (semicolon)

D. *Carefully read and study the following passage, which contains thirteen independent clauses. Correct the errors in run-on sentences and comma splices by adding periods or semicolons and capitalizing correctly.*

Call it either intuition or good vibrations. Whatever you want to call it, it works last summer, I was one of four members of a committee to hire a new head nurse at the nursing home where I work we interviewed two candidates as finalists, a man named Bob and a woman named Sarah on paper, Bob was better qualified he had had extensive experience in a similar position, while Sarah had only had one administrative job however, Sarah was the one who really impressed us she answered all of the questions straightforwardly and simply Bob, on the other hand, evaded some of our questions while simultaneously trying to make us think he knew everything and could do everything all of us on the committee simply liked Sarah better in fact, she got the job because she was the person we all felt we wanted to work with. Our intuition wasn't wrong she's turned out to be a wonderful head nurse.

Appendices

1. VERB TENSE CHARTS

SIMPLE PRESENT

USES
For habitual actions: She **eats** cereal for breakfast.
For general truths or general present: Water **boils** at 100°C.
For a definite and close future: The course **starts** tomorrow afternoon.

FORM	
AFFIRMATIVE	
Base form	They **eat** cereal for breakfast.
Third-person singular form	She **eats** cereal for breakfast.
NEGATIVE	
Do + *not* + base form	They **don't eat** cereal for breakfast.
Does + *not* + base form	She **does not eat** cereal for breakfast.

SIMPLE PAST

USES
For completed past actions: We **saw** *Citizen Kane* last night.
For habitual past actions: We **saw** a movie every Saturday.

FORMS	
AFFIRMATIVE	
Regular verb: base form + *-ed*	We **liked** *Citizen Kane*.
Irregular verb: see Appendix 2	We **ate** dinner before the show.
NEGATIVE	
Did + *not* + base form	We **didn't like** the movie theater.
	We **didn't eat** afterwards.

FUTURE

USES
For future actions or plans: They **will call** next Monday.
For promises (with *will*): I **will** always **be** there for you.

FORMS	
AFFIRMATIVE	
Will + base form	He **will call** tomorrow.
Am/is/are going to + base form	He**'s going to call** tomorrow.
NEGATIVE	
Will + *not* + base form	He **will not call** today.
Won't + base form	He **won't call** tonight.
Am/is/are + *not going to* + base form	He **is not going to call** on Tuesday.

PRESENT PROGRESSIVE

USES
For present actions: They **are talking** on the phone.
For a close future: We **are going** in five minutes.

FORMS	
AFFIRMATIVE	
Am + progressive form	I **am writing** a letter.
Is + progressive form	She **is sleeping**.
Are + progressive form	They **are listening** to music.
NEGATIVE	
Am + *not* + progressive form	I **am not writing** a letter.
Is + *not* + progressive form	She **is not sleeping**.
Are + *not* + progressive form	They **are not listening** to music.

PAST PROGRESSIVE

USES
For actions in progress in the past: Matthew **was skiing** when he broke his ankle.

FORMS	
AFFIRMATIVE	
Was/were + progressive form	I **was talking** to Isao.
	They **were playing** the guitar last night.
NEGATIVE	
Was/were + *not* + progressive form	I **wasn't talking** to Isao.
	They **were not playing** the guitar last night.

FUTURE PROGRESSIVE

USES
For an action in progress in the future: She **will be traveling** in Spain next fall.

FORMS	
AFFIRMATIVE	
Will + *be* + progressive form	We **will be talking** to Dr. Tanaka tomorrow.
NEGATIVE	
Will + *not* + *be* + progressive form	We **will not be talking** to Dr. Tanaka tomorrow.
Won't + *be* + progressive form	We **won't be talking** to Dr. Tanaka tomorrow.

PRESENT PERFECT

USES
For an action that began in the past and continues: I **have wanted** that bike for months.
For something that has been experienced: I **have taken** the train many times.

FORMS	
AFFIRMATIVE	
Have + past participle	I **have studied** marine biology for two years.
Has + past participle	She **has studied** marine biology for two years.
NEGATIVE	
Have + *not* + past participle	I **have not worked** here for very long.
Has + *not* + past participle	He **has not worked** here for very long.

PAST PERFECT

USES
For an action that was completed in the past before another past action: I **had seen** that movie many times before I began to understand it.

FORMS	
AFFIRMATIVE	
Had + past participle	She was tired because she **had run** in the race.
NEGATIVE	
Had + *not* + past participle	She **had not competed** before.

FUTURE PERFECT

USES
For an action that will be completed before another future action: By the year 2000, scientists **will have made** many new discoveries.

FORMS	
AFFIRMATIVE	
Will + *have* + past participle	We **will have found** new sources of energy.
NEGATIVE	
Will + *not* + *have* + past participle	By 11:00, we **will not have finished** the exam.
Won't + *have* + past participle	By 11:00, we **won't have finished** the exam.

PRESENT PERFECT PROGRESSIVE

USES
For an action that began in the past and continues: I **have been waiting** for hours.

FORMS	
AFFIRMATIVE	
Have + *been* + progressive form	Environmentalists **have been trying** to save the spotted owl.
Has + *been* + progressive form	Sally Trezona **has been trying** to save the spotted owl.
NEGATIVE	
Have + *not* + *been* + progressive form	I **have not been working** very hard.
Has + *not* + *been* + progressive form	He **has not been working** very hard.

PAST PERFECT PROGRESSIVE

USES
For a past action in progress before another past action: I **had been talking** on the telephone when you interrupted me.

FORMS	
AFFIRMATIVE	
Had + been + progressive form	We **had been planning** our vacation for months.
NEGATIVE	
Had + not + been + progressive form	He **had not been feeling** well.

FUTURE PERFECT PROGRESSIVE

USES
For an action in progress in the future before another future action: She **will have been training** for ten years when she skates in the Olympics.

FORMS	
AFFIRMATIVE	
Will + have + been + progressive form	We **will have been driving** for two hours when we reach Kennewick.
NEGATIVE	
Will + not + have + been + progressive form	We **will not have been driving** for very long when we reach Boise.
Won't + have + been + progressive form	We **won't have been driving** for very long when we reach Boise.

2. Irregular Verbs

Base Form	Simple Past	Past Participle
arise	arose	arisen
awake	awoke	awoken
be	was, were	been
bear	bore	borne
beat	beat	beaten/beat
become	became	become
begin	began	begun
bend	bent	bent
bet	bet	bet
bite	bit	bitten
bleed	bled	bled
blow	blew	blown
break	broke	broken
bring	brought	brought
build	built	built
burn	burned/burnt	burned/burnt
burst	burst	burst
buy	bought	bought
catch	caught	caught
choose	chose	chosen
cling	clung	clung
come	came	come
cost	cost	cost
creep	crept	crept
cut	cut	cut
deal	dealt	dealt
dig	dug	dug
dive	dived/dove	dived
do	did	done
draw	drew	drawn
dream	dreamed/dreamt	dreamed/dreamt
drink	drank	drunk
drive	drove	driven
eat	ate	eaten
fall	fell	fallen
feed	fed	fed
feel	felt	felt
fight	fought	fought
find	found	found
fit	fit, fitted	fit, fitted
flee	fled	fled
fling	flung	flung
fly	flew	flown
forbid	forbade/forbad	forbidden/forbade/forbad
forget	forgot	forgotten
forgive	forgave	forgiven

Base Form	Simple Past	Past Participle
forgo	forwent	forgone
freeze	froze	frozen
get	got	gotten/got
give	gave	given
go	went	gone
grind	ground	ground
grow	grew	grown
hang	hung/hanged	hung/hanged
have	had	had
hear	heard	heard
hide	hid	hidden
hit	hit	hit
hold	held	held
hurt	hurt	hurt
keep	kept	kept
kneel	knelt/kneeled	knelt/kneeled
knit	knitted/knit	knitted/knit
know	knew	known
lay	laid	laid
lead	led	led
leap	leapt/leaped	leapt/leaped
leave	left	left
lend	lent	lent
let	let	let
lie (down)	lay	lain
light	lit/lighted	lit/lighted
lose	lost	lost
make	made	made
mean	meant	meant
meet	met	met
pay	paid	paid
prove	proved	proved/proven
put	put	put
quit	quit	quit
read /riʸd/	read /rɛd/	read /rɛd/
ride	rode	ridden
ring	rang	rung
rise	rose	risen
run	ran	run
saw	sawed	sawed/sawn
say	said	said
see	saw	seen
seek	sought	sought
sell	sold	sold
send	sent	sent
set	set	set
sew	sewed	sewn/sewed
shake	shook	shaken
shave	shaved	shaved/shaven
shear	sheared	sheared/shorn
shine	shone/shined	shone/shined

(continued on next page)

Base Form	Simple Past	Past Participle
shoot	shot	shot
show	showed	shown/showed
shrink	shrank/shrunk	shrunk/shrunken
shut	shut	shut
sing	sang	sung
sink	sank	sunk
sit	sat	sat
slay	slew	slain
sleep	slept	slept
slide	slid	slid
sneak	sneaked/snuck	sneaked/snuck
speak	spoke	spoken
speed	sped	sped
spend	spent	spent
spill	spilled/spilt	spilled/spilt
spin	spun	spun
spit	spat/spit	spat/spit
split	split	split
spread	spread	spread
spring	sprang	sprung
stand	stood	stood
steal	stole	stolen
stick	stuck	stuck
sting	stung	stung
stink	stank/stunk	stunk
strew	strewed	strewn
strike	struck	struck/stricken
strive	strove/strived	striven/strived
swear	swore	sworn
sweep	swept	swept
swim	swam	swum
swing	swung	swung
take	took	taken
teach	taught	taught
tear	tore	torn
tell	told	told
think	thought	thought
thrive	thrived/throve	thrived/thriven
throw	threw	thrown
undergo	underwent	undergone
understand	understood	understood
upset	upset	upset
wake	woke/waked	woken/waked
wear	wore	worn
weave	wove	woven
weep	wept	wept
win	won	won
wind	wound	wound
withdraw	withdrew	withdrawn
wring	wrung	wrung
write	wrote	written

3. Common Verbs Usually Used Statively

Appearance
appear
be
concern
indicate
look
mean (= signify)
parallel
represent
resemble
seem
signify (= mean)
sound

Emotions
abhor
admire
adore
appreciate
care
desire
detest
dislike
doubt
empathize
envy
fear
hate
hope
like

love
regret
respect
sympathize
trust

Mental States
agree
amaze
amuse
annoy
assume
astonish
believe
bore
care
consider
deem
deny
disagree
disbelieve
entertain (= amuse)
estimate
expect
fancy
favor
feel (= believe)
figure (= assume)
find
guess

hesitate
hope
imagine
imply
impress
infer
know
mean
mind
presume
realize
recognize
recollect
remember
revere
see (= understand)
suit
suppose
suspect
think (= believe)
tire
understand
wonder

Perception and the Senses
ache
feel
hear
hurt
notice

observe
perceive
see
sense
smart
smell
taste

Possession
belong
contain
have
own
pertain
possess

Wants and Preferences
desire
need
prefer
want
wish

Other
cost
include
lack
matter
owe
refuse
suffice

4. Common Uses of Modals and Modal-like Expressions

A. Ability

can	I can speak French.
could	She could talk when she was a year old.
was/were able to	Henry was able to get a scholarship.
will be able to	Sarah will be able to buy a new house.

B. Advice

should	You should study harder.
ought to	You ought to sing in the choir.
should have	You should have acted sooner.
ought to have	We ought not to have said that.
had better	You'd better do something fast.
shall	Shall I continue?[1]

[1]The use of *shall* in a question to ask another's opinion or direction is the only common use of *shall* in American English.

(continued on next page)

C. Certainty: Present and Past

must	He's not here. He must be on his way.
must have	I must have forgotten to pay the bill.

D. Certainty: Future

should	They should be here by nine.
ought to	That ought to help the situation.

E. Expectation: Present and Past

be to	You are to report to the traffic court on April 1.
	He was to be here by nine.
be supposed to	A person accused of a crime is supposed to have a speedy trial.
	The boys were supposed to feed the pets.

F. Futurity

will	He will do it.
shall	I shall never travel again.[2]
be going to	They are going to visit us.
be about to	The bell is about to ring.

G. Habitual Action: Past

used to	I used to procrastinate, but I don't anymore.
would	When I was a child, we would spend every summer at our beach cabin.

H. Habitual Action: Present and Future

will	Many people will gossip if given the chance.

I. Impossibility: Present and Past

can't	This can't be happening.
couldn't	She couldn't be here. I heard she was ill.
can't have	They can't have arrived yet. It's a two-hour trip.
couldn't have	They couldn't have bought a car. They didn't have any money.

J. Lack of Necessity

don't have to	We don't have to leave for work yet.
needn't	You needn't rewrite your essay.

K. Necessity

must	Everyone must pay taxes.
have to	She has to have surgery.
have got to	We've got to do something about the situation.
had to	John had to fly to New York for a meeting.

L. Necessity Not to

mustn't	You mustn't neglect to pay your car insurance.

[2]*Shall* used to express futurity is rare in American English.

M. Opportunity

| could | We could go to the park this afternoon. |
| could have | You could have done better in this course. |

N. Possibility

may	He may be sick.
may have	Zelda may have saved enough money.
might	I might go to the play; I'm not sure.
might have	The money might have been stolen.
could	Frank could be on his way.
could have	They could have taken the wrong road.

O. Preference

| would rather | Martha would rather stay home tonight than go to the play. |

P. Willingness (Volition)

| will | I'll help you with your homework. |

5. Irregular Noun Plurals

Singular Form	Plural Form
alumna	alumnae
alumnus	alumni
amoeba	amoebas, amoebae
analysis	analyses
antenna	antennas/antennae
appendix	appendices, appendixes
axis	axes
basis	bases
businessman	businessmen
businesswoman	businesswomen
calf	calves
	cattle
child	children
crisis	crises
criterion	criteria
datum	data
deer	deer
dwarf	dwarfs, dwarves
elf	elves
fireman[1]	firemen[1]
fish	fish, fishes[2]
foot	feet
genus	genera

[1]also: firefighter, firefighters

[2]fishes = different species of fish

(continued on next page)

goose	geese
half	halves
index	indexes, indices
knife	knives
leaf	leaves
life	lives
loaf	loaves
louse	lice
mailman[3]	mailmen[3]
man	men
millennium	millenniums, millennia
money	moneys, monies
moose	moose
mouse	mice
octopus	octopuses, octopi
ox	oxen
paramecium	paramecia
	people[4]
phenomenon	phenomena, phenomenons
police officer	police, police officers
policeman	policemen
policewoman	policewomen
postman	postmen[3]
protozoan	protozoa, protozoans
radius	radii, radiuses
series	series
sheaf	sheaves
sheep	sheep
shelf	shelves
species	species
thesis	theses
tooth	teeth
vertebra	vertebrae, vertebras
wharf	wharves, wharfs
wife	wives
woman	women

[3]also: letter carrier, letter carriers

[4]also: person, persons; a people = an ethnic group

6. Some Common Non-Count Nouns

Abstractions

advice
anarchy
behavior
chance
choice
decay
democracy
energy
entertainment
entropy
evil
freedom
fun
good
happiness
hate
hatred
honesty
inertia
integrity
love
luck
momentum
oppression
peace
responsibility
slavery
socialism
spontaneity
stupidity
time
totalitarianism
truth
violence

Activities

badminton
baseball
basketball
billiards
bowling
boxing
canoeing
cards
conversation
cycling
dancing
football
golf
hiking
reading
sailing
singing
soccer
surfing
talk
tennis
volleyball
wrestling

Ailments

AIDS
appendicitis
cancer
chicken pox
cholera
diabetes
flu (influenza)
heart disease
malaria
measles
mumps
polio
smallpox
strep throat

Solid Elements

calcium
carbon
copper
gold
iron
lead
magnesium
platinum
plutonium
radium
silver
tin
titanium
uranium

Gases

air
carbon dioxide
fog
helium
hydrogen
nitrogen
oxygen

Foods

barley
beef
bread
broccoli
cake
candy
chicken
fish
meat
oats
pie
rice
wheat

Liquids

coffee
gasoline
juice
milk
oil
soda
tea
water

Natural Phenomena

aurora australis
aurora borealis
cold
electricity
hail
heat
ice
lightning
mist
rain
sleet
smog
smoke
snow
steam
thunder
warmth

Occupations

banking
computer technology
construction
dentistry
engineering
farming
fishing
law
manufacturing
medicine
nursing
retail
sales
teaching
writing
work

Particles

dust
gravel
pepper
salt
sand
spice
sugar

Subjects

accounting
art
astronomy
biology
business
chemistry
civics
economics
geography
history
Latin
linguistics
literature
mathematics
music
physics
psychology
science
sociology
speech
writing

7. Some Common Ways of Making Non-Count Nouns Countable

Abstractions

a matter of choice
a piece of advice
a piece *or* bit of luck
a type *or* form of entertainment
a unit of energy

Activities

a game of badminton, baseball, basketball, cards, football, golf, soccer, tennis, volleyball
a badminton game, a baseball game, etc.

Foods

a grain of barley
a grain of rice
a loaf of bread
a piece of cake, bread
a piece *or* wedge of pie
a portion *or* serving of—
a slice of bread

Liquids

a can of oil
a can *or* glass of soda
a cup of coffee, tea
a gallon *or* liter of gasoline
a glass of milk, water, juice

Natural Phenomena

a bolt *or* flash of lightning
a clap *or* bolt of thunder
a drop of rain

Particles

a grain of pepper, salt, sand, sugar
a speck of dust

Subjects

a branch of accounting, art, astronomy, biology, business,
chemistry, civics, economics, geography, linguistics, literature,
mathematics, music, physics, psychology, science, sociology

Miscellaneous

an article of clothing
an article of furniture
an item of news *or* a news item *or* a piece of news
a period of time
a piece of equipment

8. Some Countries Whose Names Contain the Definite Article

The Bahamas
The Cayman Islands*
The Central African Republic
The Channel Islands
The Comoros
The Czech Republic
The Dominican Republic
The Falkland Islands
The Gambia
The Isle of Man
The Leeward Islands
The Maldives
The Marshall Islands
The Netherlands
The Netherlands Antilles
The Philippines
The Solomon Islands
The Turks and Caicos Islands
The United Arab Emirates
The United Kingdom (of Great Britain and Northern Ireland)
The United States (of America)
The Virgin Islands
The Wallis and Futuna Islands

*Some countries are referred to in more than one way—for example, The Cayman Islands *or* The Caymans.

9. Selected Geographical Features and Regions Whose Names Contain the Definite Article

Bodies of Water

The Adriatic Sea
The Aegean Sea
The Antarctic (Ocean)
The Arabian Sea
The Arctic (Ocean)
The Atlantic (Ocean)
The Baltic Sea
The Black Sea
The Caribbean (Sea)
The Caspian Sea
The Gulf of Aden
The Gulf of Mexico
The Gulf of Oman
The Indian (Ocean)
The Ionian Sea
The Mediterranean (Sea)
The North Sea
The Norwegian Sea
The Pacific (Ocean)
The Panama Canal
The Persian Gulf
The Philippine Sea
The Red Sea
The Sea of Japan
The South China Sea
The Strait of Gibraltar
The Strait of Magellan
The Suez Canal
The Yellow Sea

Mountain Ranges

The Alps
The Andes
The Appalachian Mountains
The Atlas Mountains
The Caucasus Mountains
The Himalayas (The Himalayan Mountains)
The Pyrenees
The Rockies
The Urals

Rivers

The Amazon*
The Congo
The Danube
The Ganges
The Hudson
The Mackenzie
The Mississippi
The Niger
The Nile
The Rhine
The Rio Grande
The St. Lawrence
The Seine
The Thames
The Volga
The Yangtze
The Zambezi

*The names of all rivers include the word "river": the Amazon *or* the Amazon River.

Other

The Equator
The Far East
The Middle East (The Near East)
The North Pole
The Occident
The Orient
The Sahara
The South Pole
The Tropic of Cancer
The Tropic of Capricorn

10. Common Verbs Followed by the Gerund (Base Form of Verb + -*ing*)

abhor
acknowledge
admit
advise
allow
appreciate
attempt
avoid
be worth
began
can't bear
can't help
can't stand
celebrate
confess
consider
continue
defend
delay
deny
detest
discontinue
discuss
dislike
dispute
dread
endure
enjoy
escape
evade
explain
fancy
feel like
feign
finish
forgive
give up (= stop)
hate

imagine
justify
keep (= continue)
like
love
mention
mind (= object to)
miss
necessitate
omit
permit
picture
postpone
practice
prefer
prevent
prohibit
propose
quit
recall
recollect
recommend
regret
report
resent
resist
resume
risk
shirk
shun
start
suggest
support
tolerate
understand
urge

11. Common Verbs Followed by the Infinitive (*To* + Base Form of Verb)

afford	learn
agree	like
appear	long
arrange	love
ask	manage
attempt	mean
begin	need
can't afford	offer
can't bear	pay
can't stand	plan
can't wait	prefer
care	prepare
chance	pretend
choose	profess
claim	promise
come	prove
consent	refuse
continue	request
dare	resolve
decide	say
deserve	seek
determine	seem
elect	shudder
endeavor	start
expect	strive
fail	swear
get	tend
grow (up)	threaten
guarantee	turn out
hate	venture
hesitate	volunteer
hope	want
hurry	wish
incline	would like
intend	yearn

12. Verbs Followed by the Gerund or Infinitive with a Considerable Change in Meaning

forget
quit
remember
stop
try

forget
I've almost **forgotten meeting** him. (= At present, I can hardly remember.)
I almost **forgot to meet** him. (= I almost didn't remember to meet him.)

quit
Ella **quit working** at Sloan's. (= She isn't working there any more.)
Ella **quit to work** at Sloan's. (= She quit another job to work at Sloan's.)

remember
Velma **remembered writing** to Bill. (= Velma remembered the activity of writing to Bill.)
Velma **remembered to write** to Bill. (= Velma wrote to Bill. She didn't forget to do it.)

stop
Hank **stopped eating**. (= He stopped the activity of eating.)
Hank **stopped to eat**. (= He stopped doing something else in order to eat.)

try
Martin **tried skiing**. (= Martin sampled the activity of skiing.)
Martin **tried to ski**. (= Martin tried to ski but didn't succeed.)

13. Verbs Followed by Object + Infinitive

advise	force	remind
allow	hire	require
ask*	invite	teach
cause	need*	tell
choose*	order	urge
convince	pay*	want*
encourage	permit	warn
expect*	persuade	would like*
forbid	prepare*	

*These verbs can also be followed by the infinitive without an object (example: *want to go* or *want someone to go*).

14. Common Adjectives Followed by the Infinitive

Example:
I was glad to hear about that.

afraid	frightened
alarmed	furious
amazed	glad
angry	happy
anxious	hesitant
ashamed	interested
astonished	intrigued
careful	lucky
curious	pleased
delighted	prepared
depressed	proud
determined	ready
disappointed	relieved
distressed	reluctant
disturbed	sad
eager	scared
ecstatic	shocked
embarrassed	sorry
encouraged	surprised
excited	touched
fascinated	upset
fortunate	willing

15. Common Adjective + Preposition Expressions

Example:
Amanda is fed up with you.

accustomed to	excited about	ready for
afraid of	famous for	responsible for
amazed at/by	fascinated with/by	sad about
angry at	fed up with	safe from
ashamed of	fond of	satisfied with
astonished at/by	furious with	shocked at/by
aware of	glad about	sick of
awful at	good at	slow at
bad at	happy about	sorry for/about
bored with/by	interested in	surprised at/about/by
capable of	intrigued by/at	terrible at
careful of/about	mad at (= angry at/with)	tired of
concerned with/about	nervous about	used to
content with	obsessed with/about	weary of
curious about	opposed to	worried about
different from	pleased about	
excellent at	poor at	

16. Common Verb + Preposition (or Particle) Combinations

advise against
apologize for
approve of
believe in
choose between/among
come across
complain about
deal with
dream about/of
feel like
figure out
find out
get rid of
insist on

look forward to
object to
plan on
rely on
resort to
run across
run into
stick to
succeed in
talk about
think about
think over
wonder about
write about

17. Spelling Rules for the Progressive and the Gerund

1. Add -*ing* to the base form of the verb.

   read   read*ing*
   stand   stand*ing*

2. If a verb ends in a silent -*e*, drop the final -*e* and add -*ing*.

   leave   leav*ing*
   take   tak*ing*

3. In a one-syllable word, if the last three letters are a consonant-vowel-consonant combination (CVC), double the last consonant before adding -*ing*.

   CVC
   ↓↓↓
   s i t   sit*ting*

   CVC
   ↓↓↓
   r u n   run*ning*

   However, do not double the last consonant in words that end in *w, x,* or *y*.

   sew   sew*ing*
   fix   fix*ing*
   enjoy   enjoy*ing*

4. In words of two or more syllables that end in a consonant-vowel-consonant combination, double the last consonant only if the last syllable is stressed.

   admít   admit*ting*   (The last syllable is stressed.)
   whísper   whisper*ing*   (The last syllable is not stressed, so don't double the *r*.)

5. If a verb ends in -*ie*, change the *ie* to *y* before adding -*ing*.

   die   d*ying*

18. Spelling Rules for Nouns and for the Simple Present Tense: Third-Person Singular (*he, she, it*)

1. Add *-s* for most verbs.

work	work*s*
buy	buy*s*
ride	ride*s*
return	return*s*

2. Add *-es* for words that end in *-ch, -s, -sh, -x,* or *-z.*

watch	watch*es*
pass	pass*es*
rush	rush*es*
relax	relax*es*
buzz	buzz*es*

3. Change the *y* to *i* and add *-es* when the base form ends in a consonant + *y.*

study	stud*ies*
hurry	hurr*ies*
dry	dr*ies*

Do not change the *y* when the base form ends in a vowel + *y.* Add *-s.*

play	play*s*
enjoy	enjoy*s*

4. A few verbs have irregular forms.

be	is
do	does
go	goes
have	has

Answer Key

Note: In this answer key, where the full form is given, the contracted form is also acceptable. Where the contracted form is given, the full form is also acceptable.

PART I The Verb Phrase: Selected Topics

UNIT 1 Tense and Time

1.

2. First: I've bought presents for everyone.
  Second: I don't have time to go to the post office.
  Third: I'm going to send them after the New Year.
3. First: I'd failed the first exam.
  Second: I was sure.
  Third: I was going to fail anthropology.
4. First: We'll have gotten to know each other really well.
  Second: When I get to Spain . . .
  Third: I'm going to be rooming with two other guys.

2.

2. I'm making 3. I bring 4. is everybody getting 5. I love
6. Do you want 7. She's being 8. come 9. knocked
10. yelled 11. was working 12. was hearing 13. cries
14. keeps 15. were seeing 16. broke 17. she's 18. gotten
19. needs 20. We're going to be dancing and singing
21. I run

3.

2. 'd been studying *or* 'd studied 3. do you think 4. have changed 5. 've been 6. would speak or spoke 7. 've discovered 8. would take *or* took 9. does 10. have changed
11. had 12. became 13. 've always felt 14. was 15. 've met 16. aren't 17. ends 18. 'll have become 19. 'll have been working

4.

2. would go 3. would rent 4. would teach 5. would take
6. didn't you use to live 7. used to have 8. would spend
9. wouldn't have to

5.

2. I thought I'd *or* I would make a lot of new friends
3. I was sure I wouldn't *or* would not have to study very much
4. I was sure I wasn't *or* was not going to have any difficulty with my courses
5. I thought I was going to be doing a lot of serenading of señoritas on their balconies
6. I expected that I'd *or* I would love Spanish food and would learn to prepare it
7. I was sure that the Spanish people would turn out to be fun-loving and carefree
8. I hoped that I was going to write in my diary every day

6.

2. Isao thought people in Spain wore large Mexican sombreros.
3. He has discovered *or* is discovering, however, that large sombreros are relatively uncommon in Spain.
4. Luis assumed that everyone in Spain could speak Portuguese.
5. Until she met Mark, Alicia believed a lot of Americans were arrogant.
6. She has learned *or* is learning that this is not necessarily true.
7. Mark and Alicia thought all Italians expressed their emotions freely.
8. They have found out *or* are finding out that not all Italians are outwardly emotional.
9. Elena thought Japanese and American people always had plenty of money until she met Isao and Mark.
10. Now she expects *or* is expecting that she'll *or* she will have to lend them money.
11. When Luis told Isao he was going to introduce him to a young woman from Egypt, Isao expected *or* was expecting that the woman would be wearing a veil.
12. He has learned *or* learned from Jihan that many Muslim women do not wear veils.

7.

I have been → I am
when I will get → when I get
Would I make → Will I make
Am I happy? → Will I be happy?
These had been → These were
I used to be timid → I was timid
I have heard → I had heard
so I am very scared → so I was very scared
Americans will be rude → Americans would be rude
would carry → carried
he can do → he could do
I had been arriving → I arrived
and are going → and go

I had not been mugged → I have not been mugged
ideas I would have → ideas I had
people are thinking → people think
family is meaning → family means
I will have been going → I will go
I will have understood → I will understand

8.

2. F 3. F 4. T 5. F 6. F 7. T 8. T 9. F 10. T

UNIT 2 Certainty and Necessity (Modals)

1.

2. must have told: near certainty 3. she'd better mind: strong advice 4. shouldn't go: advice
5. had to pay: obligation 6. Could your son be: possibility
7. may not have thought: possibility
8. he's got to act: strong advice

2.

(When more than one choice is given, the first is preferable.)
2. had to 3. didn't have to 4. don't have to
5. should *or* ought to 6. needn't 7. has to *or* must
8. shouldn't have 9. should have 10. have to *or* must
11. should *or* ought to *or* had better 12. Shall *or* Should

3.

2. Parents shouldn't allow their children to drink alcohol.
3. Physical abuse in families mustn't be tolerated.
4. Parents ought to help their children with their homework.
5. Spouses shouldn't consider divorce except as a last resort.
6. Parents should give their children an allowance.
7. Parents needn't pay their children for doing household chores.
8. When they are wrong, parents should apologize to their children.
9. Spouses shouldn't take separate vacations.
10. Parents mustn't use corporal punishment on their children.
11. Spouses must work at a marriage to make it succeed.
12. Families ought to hold regular family councils to air problems.

4.

2. could have had 3. might not have finished
4. may not have seen 5. are *or* were supposed to meet
6. must have forgotten 7. may be doing 8. must be feeling
9. may not be taking 10. is not to miss

5.

(Where a second choice is given, it is less preferable.)
2. can't have 3. must have *or* could have
4. could have *or* must have 5. is *or* must be 6. can't be
7. must not have

6.

2. ought to 3. might 4. couldn't have been 5. may
6. could

7.

must be spend → must be spending
I supposed to → I was supposed to
I had to wear → I have to wear
must have forgetting → must have forgotten
haven't to dress up → don't have to dress up
may had raised → may have raised
must have gone → had to go
Why can Pat → Why can't Pat
ought go → ought to go
should have going → should have been going
It can hurt → It can't hurt
might growing → might be growing
we hadn't better → we had better

8.

2. a 3. a 4. b 5. a 6. a 7. b 8. a 9. b 10. a 11. b 12. a
13. a

UNIT 3 Contrast and Emphasis (Auxiliaries)

1.

I (am) a little bit angry

What (do) you want

You (do) want to pass

And I (have) been studying

I (do) pay attention

she (does) know how to teach

I (will) call every week

You (can) read a library book

That (is) the truth

2.

2. does seem 3. did score 4. does have 5. is
6. did submit 7. do appreciate 8. does have

3.

4. pardoned 5. cost 6. did help 7. signed 8. caused
9. did promote 10. freed 11. does have 12. founded
13. led 14. influenced 15. do have

4.

2. were you 3. You weren't 4. that's 5. I was 6. do sleep
7. I wasn't 8. haven't you 9. We have 10. you'd
11. you were going to be 12. I'd 13. I am 14. I did go
15. was 16. it was 17. That's 18. I don't 19. do you
20. you do have 21. you did serve 22. I wouldn't 23. I am
24. That was 25. I was 26. I did 27. don't you
28. I do have 29. it's 30. do look 31. I still don't
32. it was 33. She did get 34. That is 35. it's
36. She could have 37. does look 38. it's not 39. That's
40. I'm not 41. you're giving 42. I am going to give
43. Can you 44. you were 45. I can 46. You can go
47. We'll be 48. It may take 49. we will get

PART I Review or SelfTest

I.

2. was going to 3. 're going to 4. he was going to
5. we'll eat 6. Weren't you going to turn over 7. we'd try
8. he'll take

II.

b. used to c. used to d. 'd e. would take f. 'd go
g. used to own h. 'd spend i. used to be

III.

2. were supposed to move out 3. may not get out
4. might consider 5. needn't try 6. was to register
7. must have forgotten 8. I'd better shut up
9. Shall I have it out 10. must be 11. should have it out
12. may be 13. ought to suggest 14. can get
15. should get 16. had better learn

IV.

b. He could be feeling c. She may have turned him down
d. mustn't miss e. he may not pass f. won't have to repeat
g. He might have to h. Could he have been angry
i. He may have been feeling sick
j. he can't have been feeling k. he must have had to go

V.

b. 'm c. 'm not d. am e. didn't earn f. did earn
g. haven't lived h. have traveled i. isn't j. is
k. does offer l. would like

VI.

2. A 3. A 4. C 5. C 6. C 7. A 8. D 9. D 10. B

PART I From Grammar to Writing: The Sentence

A.

2. not a sentence: no subject and no verb
3. sentence
4. not a sentence: no subject
5. not a sentence: no subject and no verb
6. sentence
7. not a sentence: dependent clause
8. sentence

B.

2. They stayed in a youth hostel for a very reasonable price.
3. They visited the Sagrada Familia, Gaudí's famous cathedral.
4. All three boys were impressed by the cathedral's beauty.
5. Nearing the top, Isao began to feel vertigo and had to start down again.
6. Mark and Luis continued climbing.
7. Both he and Luis agreed that the view was magnificent.
8. The three decided to return to Barcelona.

C.

If they . . . together.
Fortunately, . . . counseling.
The process . . . change.
The challenge . . . mother.
For Bruce . . . done.
Though there were . . . succeeding.
Often feeling . . . other.
In the process . . . granted.
In the past year . . . bright.

PART II The Noun Phrase: Selected Topics

UNIT 4 Non-Count Nouns: Count and Non-Count Use

1.

Non-count nouns: aurora borealis, nonproliferation, progress, structure, DNA, capability, intelligence, astronomy, data, pasadenium, oil, protection, news
Count nouns: earthquake, quake, scale, location, quake, scientists, observatory, phenomena, skies, researcher, cross, UFO, officials, accord, nations, geneticists, children, telescope, desert, astronomers, frontiers, amount, physicists, discovery, element, engineers, issues, hour, developments

2.

2. Heredity is   3. Metaphysics is, investigates
4. DNA, is, controls   5. Intelligence is
6. Genetics is, involves   7. Cloning is
8. Artificial intelligence is

3.

2. A flash of lightning   3. a herd of cattle   4. a piece of jewelry *or* an article of jewelry   5. A clap of thunder
6. a current of electricity   7. an article of furniture *or* a piece of furniture   8. a grain of rice   9. a speck of dust
10. a branch of astronomy   11. a game of soccer
12. a grain of sand

4.

2. rains   3. a reading   4. a work   5. progress   6. a history
7. a talk   8. space   9. a time   10. time   11. Work   12. Soda
13. milk   14. wine   15. a red wine   16. an indigenous people
17. a film   18. peoples

5.

with the nature ➔ with nature
balance of the nature ➔ balance of nature
carries a malaria ➔ carries malaria
end a malaria ➔ end malaria
balance of the nature ➔ balance of nature
take away a people's ➔ take away people's
eliminate a violence ➔ eliminate violence
reduce a responsibility ➔ reduce responsibility
a genetic engineering ➔ genetic engineering
remove a chance ➔ remove chance
the unpredictability ➔ unpredictability
a genetic engineering ➔ genetic engineering

UNIT 5 — Definite and Indefinite Articles

1.

2. a 3. b 4. a 5. a 6. a 7. b 8. a

2.

2. the northern spotted owl 3. the spotted owl
4. an endangered species 5. the timber industry
6. The administration 7. the middle

3.

2. the 3. an 4. The 5. the 6. The 7. 0 8. the 9. the
10. The 11. the 12. 0 13. the 14. 0 15. an 16. the
17. the 18. the 19. 0 20. the 21. 0 22. The 23. The
24. the 25. 0 26. 0 27. 0 28. 0 29. The 30. the 31. the
32. the 33. the 34. the 35. the 36. the 37. the 38. the
39. the

4.

2. a member
3. a member
4. a pouch
5. The ozone layer
6. fluorine and carbon
7. The stratosphere
8. a distinctive odor
9. the eucalyptus tree
10. a member

6.

Preparation
2. light 3. life 4. an atmosphere 5. life 6. people 7. spirit
8. atmosphere 9. culture 10. peoples 11. cultures
12. an interesting life 13. food 14. foods 15. talk
Comprehension
2. b 3. a 4. b 5. b 6. a 7. a 8. a 9. b 10. b 11. a 12. a
13. b 14. a 15. b

5.

2. . . . not birds
3. An orangutan is an anthropoid ape . . .
4. The Mesozoic Era was the third . . .
5. The Jurassic Period . . .
6. The Milky Way galaxy is the galaxy . . .
7. A meltdown is . . .
8. . . . hypothesizing the meltdown of a nuclear reactor . . .
9. . . . raising cows.
10. Acid rain is . . .

6.

Comprehension
2. a 3. b 4. a 5. b 6. b
Optional Dictation
2. 0 3. 0 4. The 5. 0 6. the 7. 0 8. 0 9. The 10. 0
11. 0 12. the 13. the 14. the 15. a 16. 0 17. An
18. the 19. the 20. 0

UNIT 6 Modification of Nouns

1.

2. Your <u>two</u> <u>best</u> <u>film-buff</u> (friends) have seen the <u>reissued</u> *Citizen Kane*.

3. They rave about its <u>superb</u> <u>black-and-white</u> (photography) and applaud its <u>profound</u>, <u>sensitive</u>, <u>serious</u> (treatment) of the <u>lonely</u> (life) of an <u>anxiety-ridden</u> <u>business</u> (tycoon).

4. Children often do not meet their <u>parents'</u> <u>career</u> (expectations) of them.

5. I asked Robert Stevens whether there is an <u>actual</u> <u>scientific</u> (basis) for the negativity of expectations.

6. There is a <u>documented</u> <u>medical</u> (phenomenon) called <u>focal</u> (dystonia), which is an <u>abnormal</u> <u>muscle</u> (function) caused by <u>extreme</u> (concentration).

7. Can we generalize this phenomenon beyond the <u>sports</u> (arena) into <u>common</u>, <u>everyday</u> (occurrences)?

8. I stand at the top of a <u>steep</u>, <u>icy</u> (slope), plotting my <u>every</u> (move) down the course.

9. This <u>skiing</u> (example) illustrates the <u>basic</u> (problem) of expectations.

10. Right now we're really in the <u>elementary</u> (stages) of <u>biological</u> and <u>psychiatric</u> <u>brain</u> (research).

2.

2. a one-paragraph *or* paragraph-long assignment
3. a 300-page *or* page-long book
4. a six-year ordeal
5. a stress-related problem
6. an eyesight-related problem
7. a ten-gallon hat
8. performance-induced anxiety
9. a two-month program

3.

2. A phobia is an irrational fear of a particular thing.
3. Repression is a psychological process in which bothersome things are kept from conscious awareness.
4. Multiple personality is a mental disorder in which several different personalities exist in a single mind.
5. A neurosis is a nervous disorder having no apparent physical cause.

4.

2. my new silk tie   3. that ugly pink denim shirt   4. an uneducated lower-middle-class hippie   5. a lot of important business people   6. a good, well-rounded impression
7. a brash, uncultured husband   8. my round blue sapphire earrings   9. the oval green emerald ones   10. our first two guests   11. some excellent miniature ham and cheese pastries   12. an elegant, dress-up party   13. that beautiful purple denim shirt

5.

school medical → medical school
right the → the right
psychiatry child clinical → clinical child psychiatry
child class our psychology → our child psychology class
local a → a local
children disturbed many → many disturbed children
personal some → some personal
class medical our surgery → our medical surgery class
teacher student → student teacher
male young a → a young male
usual our → our usual
viewpoint a student → a student viewpoint
only The → The only
food the cafeteria tasteless! → the tasteless cafeteria food!
lunch own brown-bag my → my own brown-bag lunch
program this computer new → this new computer program

6.

Comprehension
2. false 3. true 4. false 5. true 6. true
7. I don't know 8. I don't know 9. true

Optional Dictation
2. a brain breaker 3. a total, complete idiot 4. an ugly, high-pitched, squeaky voice 5. an adolescent growth spurt
6. a lot of twelve-year-old boys 7. fear-of-oral-reading problem 8. a short, easy-to-remember phrase 9. an icy, dark, stormy evening 10. those legendary three-dog nights
11. a three-dog night 12. three large, warm, furry dogs

UNIT 7 Quantifiers

1.

(several) months
(all) the points
(a few) new ones
(a little of) it
(Many of) us
(plenty of) money
(Most of) us
(a great deal of) money
(lots of) cash

(Many of) the books
(None of) us
(little) justification
(few of) us
(each) month
(a little) more
(a great many) years
(a lot of) money
(much) good luck

2.

2. less 3. Neither one of 4. the amount of 5. either one of
6. both of 7. fewer 8. much 9. the number of 10. many
11. most of 12. both 13. plenty of 14. every 15. some

3.

2. many 3. a little 4. a great deal 5. several 6. few
7. the number of 8. most of 9. less 10. a few 11. a little
12. many 13. some 14. any 15. all 16. no 17. little
18. a great many 19. the amount of

4.

(Other answers are possible.)
any foreign countries ➜ some foreign countries
a great deal of years ➜ a great many years
all person ➜ every person
number of debt ➜ amount of debt
a few less ➜ a little less
some man ➜ every man
too many ➜ too much
less and less programs ➜ fewer and fewer programs
every purchases ➜ all purchases

5.

Comprehension
2. F 3. T 4. T 5. T 6. F 7. F 8. F

Optional Dictation
2. no payments 3. few of your payments
4. any more extensions 5. much more money
6. certain policies 7. little 8. a little 9. a few more days
10. some money 11. a bit more time
12. How much more time 13. much

PART II Review or SelfTest

I.

2. no article 3. no article 4. the 5. the 6. no article
7. no article 8. no article 9. no article 10. no article
11. no article 12. no article 13. the 14. A 15. a
16. no article 17. no article 18. an 19. A 20. the 21. an
22. a 23. no article 24. no article 25. no article 26. the
27. no article 28. no article 29. no article 30. the 31. the
32. no article

II.

2. The last thing I remember hearing before I was knocked
out was a clap of thunder.
3. I want this room so clean that I don't see a speck of
dust anywhere!
4. We bought several beautiful and inexpensive articles of
furniture *or* pieces of furniture at the yard sale.
5. Astrophysics is a branch of astronomy dealing with the
properties of stars and planets.
6. I love having a cup of tea every afternoon about five
o'clock. It's such a civilized custom.
7. We saw several flashes of lightning above the forest
before the fire started.
8. I heard an interesting piece of news yesterday
afternoon.

III.

b. a chilly late winter day c. my new pink satin tie
d. a handsome upper-class European businessman
e. our own new brick house f. a dirty little old hovel

IV.

b. number c. many d. any e. some f. many g. amount
h. less i. fewer j. a little k. a lot l. a few m. much n. a
great many of o. anything p. a great deal of
q. little r. Few

V.

2. C 3. A 4. D 5. B 6. D 7. B 8. C 9. B 10. C

From Grammar to Writing: Subject-Verb Agreement

A.

2. Far too many individuals
3. The Siberian tiger and the spotted owl
4. That man who is sitting at the mahogany desk
5. Relatively few adults or teenagers
6. The expectation that we will like well-known works of art, literature, or music

B.

2. A ⟨list⟩ of available jobs was posted on the office bulletin board.
3. ⟨Much⟩ of what you were told was inaccurate.
4. ⟨Neither⟩ of those two environmentalists is in favor of the clear-cutting of forests.
5. The ⟨number⟩ of species on the Endangered Species List is increasing.
6. ⟨None⟩ of the work has been completed satisfactorily.
7. Very ⟨little⟩ of this work can be done by a single person working alone.
8. That clever little Canadian fox ⟨terrier⟩ is near and dear to my heart.
9. The ⟨singing⟩ of that famous Australian opera star is uplifting.
10. More and more old-growth ⟨forest⟩ is being cut down.

C.

2. are 3. isn't 4. have 5. were 6. are 7. weren't 8. are

D.

2. are 3. was 4. is 5. qualify 6. is

E.

2. are 3. has 4. is 5. have

F.

legislation . . . were passed → legislation . . . was passed
politicians encourages → politicians encourage
there is no bins → there are no bins
nor the owners . . . has → nor the owners . . . have
trash cans . . . is overflowing → trash cans . . . are overflowing
lots . . . is littered → lots . . . are littered
Trash . . . are rarely cleaned → Trash . . . is rarely cleaned
The owner and publisher . . . have → The owner and publisher . . . has

PART III Passive Voice

The Passive: Review and Expansion

1.

⟨be committed⟩ ⟨are getting pelted⟩ ⟨is⟩ dimly ⟨lit⟩
⟨get bludgeoned⟩ ⟨is⟩ slowly ⟨getting stained⟩
⟨has been committed⟩ ⟨get paid⟩ ⟨was killed⟩
⟨haven't been noticed⟩ ⟨can be saved⟩

2.

2. have never been cracked 3. who was named
4. was befriended 5. was shot and killed 6. were pursued
7. was elected 8. was gunned down 9. was buried
10. was interred 11. was seen 12. was later sighted
13. was found 14. was determined
15. had been abandoned 16. had apparently been set
17. was threatened 18. was caused
19. has never been proved *or* proven 20. was accompanied
21. were received 22. were located
23. Were . . . simply killed
24. was . . . forced down and murdered

3.

2. gotten rousted   3. getting harassed   4. gets bothered
5. get robbed   6. get the locks changed   7. get disturbed

4.

2. He was hit by a blue Toyota Corolla.   3. The boy sustained massive injuries.   4. He was taken to Harborview Medical Center by paramedics.   5. He is being cared for in the intensive-care ward.   6. Anyone with information about the accident is asked to contact the sheriff's office at 444-6968.   7. A reward is being offered.

5.

2. b   3. a   4. b   5. b   6. b   7. a   8. a   9. b

UNIT 9 Reporting Ideas and Facts with Passives

1.

information is considered

epicenter. was located

sections. are reported

number. is not known

it is estimated

flooding is believed

Looting is alleged

martial law is expected

It is assumed

It is hoped

2.

2. is not known   3. are thought   4. are known   5. is assumed
6. Can...be regarded   7. is said   8. was supposedly located
9. was called   10. was believed by Plato   11. were reputed
12. were also said   13. was thought   14. has been claimed *or* is claimed   15. is thought   16. is not yet known

3.

it thought → it was thought
was allege → was alleged
perpetual youth regarded → perpetual youth was regarded
they popularly called → they were popularly called
they were locate → they were located
what known → what is known
streets said → streets were said
that...thought → that . . . was thought
people call → people called
It was claim → It was claimed
Lemurians were report → Lemurians were reported
They were say → They were said

4.

Comprehension
2. b   3. d   4. a   5. c

Optional Dictation
2. is considered   3. is thought to have been
4. is not known   5. was said to hear   6. was found to be
7. is regarded   8. was known   9. are presumed to have been
10. was thought to have been murdered
11. has been...rumored

P A R T III Review or SelfTest

I.

b. was discovered   c. get beaten   d. got hit   e. we've been getting overcharged   f. have the company investigated
g. Aren't they cleaned   h. didn't get done   i. are fed
j. getting fed   k. They'll be fed

II.

2. He parked his motorcycle in a handicapped-parking space.
3. When Mason came out of the interview, he discovered that his motorcycle had been removed from the handicapped spot.
4. It had been placed upside down in the pool of the adjacent fountain.
5. No one had been noticed in the area.
6. After recovering his motorcycle, Mason said, "I'll never do that again. . . .

III.

2. was located   3. were found   4. are assumed
5. is believed   6. should not be considered

IV.

2. A   3. B   4. C   5. A   6. A   7. C   8. D   9. C

 P A R T III From Grammar to Writing: Parallelism

A.

writer of detective fiction → a writer of detective fiction
koala → a koala
Picasso → a Picasso
Gauguin → a Gauguin

B.

2. and buried *or* was killed in a gunfight
3. driven away by drought *or* . . . might have been decimated by crop failures, or might have been driven away by drought
4. but found no trace of Earhart and Noonan
5. and swallowed up by the ocean

C.

the secretary was asked → asked the secretary
a girlfriend could have murdered him → murdered by a girlfriend

PART IV Gerunds and Infinitives

U N I T 10 Gerunds

1.

slowing	speeding
driving	charging
coursing	being
churning	enjoying
tightening	barreling

2.

2. collapsing   3. vegetating   4. worrying
5. my never having   6. punching   7. working   8. making
9. socializing   10. meeting   11. paying off   12. killing
13. working   14. playing   15. joining   16. doing
17. your trying   18. her joining   19. dancing
20. playing cards   21. going   22. becoming   23. saying

3.

2. e. Taking
3. h. Being, pursuing
4. d. Acting
5. g. pursuing
6. c. Assuming
7. a. Being
8. f. Spending

4.

2. Seward's having perceived
3. Court's having outlawed
4. Parks's having decided
5. her having carried out
6. John F. Kennedy's having agreed
7. his having been warned
8. Their having misjudged
9. protestors' having seized the moment and demanded *or* having demanded

UNIT 11 Infinitives

1.

to handle
(had expected it) to (increase)
to be . . . reinforced and repaired
to approve
to finance
to be closed
for . . . to be done
to have been completed
to be delayed
To ask for
to let
not to travel
To get
to bring

2.

2. f   3. a   4. e   5. d   6. b
a. to die, to live   b. to light, to curse   d. to seek, to find
e. To err, to forgive   f. to have loved and lost, never to have loved

3.

2. to be   3. them to procrastinate   4. to put off   5. to fail
6. to make   7. to be rejected   8. (to be) told   9. to invite
10. to be turned down   11. to turn out   12. to change
13. to do   14. to adhere   15. never to put off
16. to be done   17. not to resist   18. to avoid   19. to do
20. to take   21. them not to put off

5.

He not let ➔ His not letting
hear ➔ hearing
get used to ➔ getting used to
rush ➔ rushing
write ➔ writing
Get out ➔ Getting out
ride ➔ riding
raft ➔ rafting
hike ➔ hiking
get taken care of ➔ getting taken care of
be chauffeured ➔ being chauffeured
country western dance ➔ country western dancing
I have taken ➔ my having taken
kick ➔ kicking
weave ➔ weaving
Native American dance ➔ Native American dancing
learn ➔ learning
see ➔ seeing

6.

2. true   3. I don't know   4. false   5. true   6. false
7. I don't know   8. true   9. I don't know   10. false

4.

2. are thought to have been smuggled
3. are believed to have been aided
4. to have been installed
5. are thought to be armed
6. are believed to be
7. are also warned not to approach
8. are asked to contact

5.

wanted keep ➔ wanted to keep
managed get ➔ managed to get
get it done ➔ to get it done
done for to stop ➔ done to stop
supposed turned ➔ supposed to be turned
call ➔ to call
talk ➔ to talk
not see ➔ not to see
to loved ➔ to have loved
to never have loved ➔ never to have loved
started feel ➔ started to feel
swear keep ➔ swear to keep

6.

1. b   2. a   3. b   4. a   5. a   6. b

PART IV Review or SelfTest

I.

b. going   c. to tell   d. lying   e. to defend   f. defending
g. majoring   h. being

II.

2. your saying   3. Everybody's having
4. a family's getting together   5. our trying
6. your insisting on   7. the family's sitting down together
8. your assigning

III.

2. slowing   3. were expected to have been completed
4. having caused   5. to be finished   6. to be cleared
7. taking

IV.

b. was supposed to   c. plan to   d. ought to
e. didn't have time to   f. don't want to

V.

2. C   3. A   4. A   5. B   6. D   7. B   8. C

 PART IV From Grammar to Writing: Parallelism of Gerunds and Infinitives

A.

2. scheduling   3. slowing   4. Ms. Bono's renting
5. my having stopped working . . . having joined *or* my
having stopped working . . . joined a singles group, and
found some interesting new hobbies

B.

2. to seek   3. not to take out a loan   4. to be taken seriously . . .
or and remembered fondly   5. to have worked

C.

to face an audience ➔ facing an audience
to deliver a speech ➔ delivering a speech
to be scorned ➔ scorned
to think about ➔ thinking about
to attend the class ➔ attending the class
to force themselves ➔ forcing themselves
making fools ➔ to make fools
speaking comfortably ➔ speak comfortably
expressing themselves ➔ express themselves

PART V Adverbials and Discourse Connectors

UNIT 12 Adverb Clauses

1.

2. <u>We won't be able to correct the problem of violence unless we treat its underlying causes</u>.
3. <u>Some cartoons contain as much violence as R-rated movies do</u>.
4. <u>Though the drug problem has worsened, there are some positive signs</u>.
5. <u>Some parents curtail their children's TV watching because they think it encourages passivity</u>.
6. <u>There are so few programs of quality on television that some people have gotten rid of their TV sets</u>.
7. <u>Whenever there is an economic downturn, there is a corresponding increase in crime</u>.

2.

because they give students opportunities to be involved in something (why)
on account of the fact that they don't have enough to do to keep themselves busy (why)
so . . . that it's hard to commit a violent act (result)
When their team wins (when)
when their team loses (when)
because they give some students, especially poor ones, an opportunity to get out of a difficult situation and improve their chances for a successful life (why)
If a young basketball player from a poor village in Nigeria can get a scholarship to play for, say, UCLA (under what condition)
than it ever was (comparison)
If a young woman coming from a ghetto is accepted on the University of Missouri swim team (under what condition)
wherever she goes (where)
In spite of the fact that school sporting programs have some deficiencies that need to be ironed out (contrast)
because I'm one of those students (why)

3.

2. Many citizens support gun control because they believe that the easy availability of guns is a key ingredient in violent crime. *or* Because they believe that the easy availability of guns is a key ingredient in violent crime, many citizens support gun control.
3. Many citizens do not support gun control, although they recognize that guns are part of the crime problem. *or* Although they recognize that guns are part of the crime problem, many citizens do not support gun control.
4. Unless teenagers have meaningful activities, they are likely to get involved in crime.
5. There is potential danger wherever we go. *or* Wherever we go, there is potential danger.
6. If criminals commit three serious crimes, they will be sentenced to life in prison without possibility of parole.
7. The Brady Law to control handguns was finally passed after its supporters had lobbied for years for its passage. *or* After its supporters had lobbied for years for its passage, the Brady Law to control handguns was finally passed.
8. While politicians argue about the war on drugs, the drug problem continues to grow. *or* The drug problem continues to grow while politicians argue about the war on drugs.

4.

2. on account of the fact that   3. such . . . that
4. more . . . than   5. as much . . . as
6. In spite of the fact that   7. If

5.

2. The prison escapee was driving so rapidly that he lost control of the car and was apprehended.
3. If they get enough attention from their parents, children probably won't turn to crime.
4. Some children watch so much television *or* such a lot of television that they have trouble telling reality from fantasy.
5. The sheriff's office has put more agents on the streets in case there is additional trouble.
6. Provided their governments appropriate enough money, nations everywhere can gain headway against crime.
7. Today there is more awareness about the underlying causes of violence than there was in the past.
8. Many juvenile criminals today receive light sentences although they commit serious crimes.
9. Today there isn't as much abuse of certain drugs as there used to be. That's a positive sign.
10. In spite of the fact that he had exhibited good behavior, the prisoner was denied parole.

6.

2. a 3. b 4. b 5. a 6. b 7. b 8. a 9. a 10. b

UNIT 13 Adverbials: Viewpoint, Focus, and Negative

1.

Part 1:

2. almost missed
3. Even . . . Nancy
4. only ten
5. Only Eric
6. even lent
7. only wanted
8. only one
9. just wanted
10. just three

Part 2:

2. just 3. simply
4. even, just 5. sadly
6. seldom 7. rarely
8. unfortunately
9. certainly 10. not only
11. only 12. clearly
13. only then

2.

(In some cases, more than three placements are possible.)

2. Unfortunately, violence has increased in public schools. Violence unfortunately has increased in public schools. Violence has increased in public schools, unfortunately.
3. Luckily, some parents are able to spend a great deal of time with their children. Some parents are luckily able to spend a great deal of time with their children. Some parents are able to spend a great deal of time with their children, luckily.
4. Surely, we must be willing to make some sacrifices. We must surely be willing to make some sacrifices. We must be willing to make some sacrifices, surely.
5. Fortunately, some young people manage to survive unhappy childhoods. Some young people fortunately manage to survive unhappy childhoods. Some young people manage to survive unhappy childhoods, fortunately.
6. Evidently, some schools have no policies on bringing guns to campus. Some schools evidently have no policies on bringing guns to campus. Some schools have no policies on bringing guns to campus, evidently.
7. Frankly, it is important to place limits on your children's behavior. It is, frankly, important to place limits on your children's behavior. It is important to place limits on your children's behavior, frankly.

3.

2. I almost got up and called
3. We were only talking
4. guess we just lost
5. simply call and tell
6. Even your little brother
7. called almost
8. just hope you
9. only you can
10. you should even

4.

2. All too seldom do families eat meals together.
3. On no account can domestic violence be ignored.
4. Young people should start paying their own bills. Only then will they begin to truly appreciate their parents.
5. Little does a teenager know about how difficult it is to be a parent.
6. Hardly ever do they understand the need for discipline.

UNIT 14 Other Discourse Connectors

1.

however: contrast   so: result   Therefore: result
First: relation in time   Also: addition   so: result
though: contrast   In fact: addition   then: relation in time
Meanwhile: relation in time   so: result   however: contrast
for: cause   and the sandwich tasted: addition   but: contrast
First: relation in time   Second: relation in time
Third: relation in time   Fourth: relation in time
So: result   However: contrast   Nonetheless: contrast

2.

2. First   3. second   4. however   5. therefore   6. Also
7. Meanwhile   8. otherwise   9. And   10. In fact

3.

2. However   3. Meanwhile   4. otherwise   5. In fact
6. for example   7. Because of this   8. Nonetheless

5.

Almost we → We almost
we have → have we
Jonathan got even → even Jonathan got
she takes → does she take
Only we were → We were only
Even they don't → They don't even
I approve → I don't approve
those school officials realize → do those school officials realize
the train comes → comes the train

6.

2. F   3. T   4. T   5. F   6. F   7. F   8. F   9. T

8.

2. b   3. a   4. a   5. b   6. a   7. b   8. a   9. b   10. a

4.

in spite of → even though or though or although or in spite of the fact that
however → but
on account of → on account of the fact that
Although → However
besides → and
also → and
Because → Therefore or So
Or → Otherwise
also → and
although → however or though
otherwise → or

5.

2. b   3. a   4. a   5. b   6. a   7. a   8. b

UNIT 15 Adverbial Modifying Phrases

1.

. . .saying that the success of the conference depends on the good faith actions of Mr. Tintor, the country's president.

. . .by agreeing to free and unconditional talks.

Interviewed about Mr. Amalde's comments, . . .

. . .speaking on condition of anonymity, . . .

Acknowledging that the current vaccine is ineffective, . . .

Having conducted successful repairs and identified flaws on Magna Maria, Wasa's existing instrument, . . .

To be known as Illyria, . . .

. . .to be a viable state.

2.

Subjects	Combine?
2. standard, problems	no
3. population, supply	no
4. Governments, They	yes
5. parents, people	yes
6. leaders, citizens	no

3.

2. When giving money to beggars on the street, some tourists mistakenly think they are doing their part to help the poor.
3. Unless provided with firsthand knowledge of poverty, tourists cannot truly understand the plight of the poor.
4. If sponsored by people in wealthier nations, orphans in poor countries can escape the cycle of poverty.
5. Poor people will not be able to escape poverty until given job opportunities.

4.

Incorrect sentences:

By arguing that I don't have enough money anyway, the request is ignored.

Having landed in the capital, a taxi took me to my hotel in the center of town, and that's where I met her.

Sitting on a dirty blanket on the sidewalk in front of the hotel, my eye was caught by her.

While talking later with a nun at a nearby convent that administers gift money from other countries, much worthwhile information was given to me.

Selling her matches, her spirit shone through, simply trying to scratch out a semblance of a living.

5.

2. Given the choice between disaster and some kind of restriction on our right to have as many children as we want, we may have to choose the latter.
3. Having grown slowly between the years 500 and 1700, the world's population then began to accelerate.
4. Clearing more and more land for farms every year, farmers all over the world unfortunately destroy animal habitats.
5. To ensure that their citizens are healthy, many governments provide immunizations to all children.
6. By providing contraceptive devices to their citizens, health officials in some countries are trying to deal with the problem of overpopulation.
7. We must stabilize the world's population growth to prevent ecological disaster.
8. Having witnessed two devastating conflicts in this century, we must do everything in our power to prevent future world wars.

6.

2. Observing that population and food supply grow at different rates, Malthus warned us of a problem.
3. To prevent unrest, governments everywhere must ensure full employment.
4. Having recognized that overpopulation was a problem, the Chinese government took action.
5. Having established a policy of limiting births, Chinese government officials now have to enforce it.
6. Leaders of governments throughout the world must do something comprehensive to prevent a major disaster.
7. If carried out right, the adoption of ZPG would cause the population to decrease.
8. By sponsoring a needy child in the Third World, we make the world a little better.

7.

2. b 3. b 4. b 5. a 6. a 7. a 8. b 9. b 10. b

PART V Review or SelfTest

I.

1. B: as soon as you back the car out of the garage
2. A: than he used to be
   B: unless I threatened him
3. A: when the plane gets in
   B: in case I'm not home
4. A: that I can hardly move
   B: that I end up gaining a few pounds / whenever I come home to visit
5. A: as there used to be
   B: provided that you have cable
6. A: since you didn't turn in your term paper / even though you did well on the tests
   B: because I couldn't think of anything to write about

II.

2. However 3. thus 4. otherwise 5. in fact 6. Moreover

III.

2. Though they had been leaving the children with Sarah's mother, this wasn't a satisfactory situation.
3. One of them was going to have to quit working unless they could find a solution to the problem.
4. When one of their neighbors proposed the creation of a day care co-op involving seven families, their problem was solved.
5. Each day, one of the parents in the co-op cares for all of the children while the other parents are working.

IV.

The even kids → Even the kids
Only I hope → I only hope
almost we didn't → we almost didn't
Little we knew → Little did we know
Never I have been → Never have I been
just we could spend → we could just spend
Never again I will → Never again will I

V.

2. . . . rewards; however, . . .
3. . . . 5:30 P.M., and . . .
4. . . . good, they . . .
5. . . . exercise; also, . . .
6. . . . children, someone . . .
7. . . . until 6:30, and . . .
8. . . . success; none . . .

VI.

2. A 3. C 4. B 5. B 6. C 7. D 8. A

PART V From Grammar to Writing: Sentences and Fragments

A.

F 2. <u>As soon as you learn the hand signals</u>.
S 3. <u>Although China is overpopulated</u>, <u>it is trying to correct the problem</u>.
S 4. <u>We won't solve the problem of violence</u> <u>until we control guns</u>.
F 5. <u>If a young basketball player from Nigeria can get a scholarship</u>.
F 6. <u>Because I was one of those students</u>.
S 7. <u>The economy is perhaps too dependent on the automobile</u>.
S 8. Carried out right, <u>this procedure would cause the population to stabilize</u>.
F 9. <u>By the time the train finally arrived in Santa Maria</u>.
S 10. <u>We need to make some personal sacrifices</u> <u>if we want to help</u>.

B.

company that is
new positions, Dorothy and Patrick
stressful because
on time, they had
a week, they are
work when it is
happier because

C.

2. CX . . . living room, it . . .
3. CPD . . . increase, but natural resources . . .
4. CX no comma
5. S no comma
6. CPD . . . taxes, nor does she . . .
7. CPD . . . at once, for we . . .
8. CX . . . colors, though . . .
9. CX . . . dining car, a violent . . .

D.

Suggested Answers:
2. Although I tried to board the train and find a seat, there wasn't one available.
3. Because heavy rail tracks are already there, heavy rail has gotten the best press.
4. Heavy rail tracks are already there; therefore, heavy rail has gotten the best press.
5. You ran a red light, and you don't seem to know the hand signals.
6. You ran a red light; also, you don't seem to know the hand signals.

PART VI Adjective Clauses

 U N I T 16 Review and Expansion

1.

whom others regard as a take-charge leader
who gets things done
who regard the world as their oyster
who is president of her high school class
that benefit everyone
whose behavior is similiar to that of the active-positive in the sense of acting on the world
who is a good example of an active-negative
which is surprising
others regard as a "nice person"
who allows the world to act on him
when he didn't have a lot of friends
one can easily take advantage of
which is what people like about him
where unfortunate things are likely to happen
who is always worried that disaster is just around the corner
that deals with infractions by students

2.

2. which I find somewhat amazing 3. which bothers me
4. which is what everyone likes about him
5. which is mystifying

3.

2. which is why 3. the other prisoners looked up to
4. he's been working for 5. the psychiatrists considered
6. which is why 8. a fact which makes me
9. whom the other prisoners respected
10. for which he has been working
11. whom the psychiatrists considered
12. evidence which makes me

4.

something who we could ➔	something we could *or* something that we could *or* something which we could
tests show ➔	tests that show *or* tests which show
that they tell ➔	that tell
a person whom is ➔	a person who is
things involve ➔	things that involve *or* things which involve
in some way, who doesn't ➔	in some way, which doesn't
guys which live ➔	guys who live

5.

2. b 3. b 4. a 5. b

6.

2. b 3. a 4. b 5. b 6. a

UNIT 17 Adjective Clauses with Quantifiers; Adjectival Modifying Phrases

1.

seen on TV

most of whom answered yes to the question

including the United States, Canada, Mexico, and Japan

regarded as an expert in the field of mass media

most responsible for redirecting our thinking about mediums of communication, especially television

seen on a screen in a movie theater and on a TV set

each of which contains a separate photograph.

projected on the screen

composed of millions of dots

requiring more mental energy

convinced that it leads to mental laziness

many of whom report an almost irresistible tendency to fall asleep while watching television

2.

2. all of whom have played the role of James Bond
3. all of which have earned over $100 million
4. both of which were directed by Akira Kurosawa
5. most of which are loved by children
6. neither of whom is well known to American mass audiences

3.

2. based on Michael Crichton's novel
3. starring John Travolta and Olivia Newton-John
4. directed and produced by Kevin Costner
5. featuring Harrison Ford, Carrie Fisher, and Mark Hamill

4.

2. Westerns, examples of which include *Dances with Wolves*, *Unforgiven*, and *Wyatt Earp,* have been making a comeback in recent years.
3. Musical animated films, including *Aladdin, The Lion King,* and *Beauty and the Beast*, have also become very popular.
4. It looks as though sequels to big movie hits may lose their appeal, in which case moviemakers will be forced to become more creative.

5.

most of them ➔ most of which
illusion is presented ➔ illusion presented
some of them ➔ some of whom
everyone is famous ➔ everyone famous
friends, many of them ➔ friends, many of whom
with a fellow works ➔ with a fellow working
movies are made these days ➔ movies made these days
twists and turns are calculated ➔ twists and turns calculated
in that case ➔ in which case

6.

2. F 3. T 4. F 5. F 6. F 7. T 8. F 9. F 10. T

PART VI Review or SelfTest

I.

I work with in my secretarial job
whom I'll call "Jennifer"
who always greet you in a friendly manner and never have
    an unkind word to say
whom I'll call "Myrtle"
who rarely gives compliments and can sometimes be
    critical
who was my friend
which is why I didn't seek out her friendship
when all three of us, Jennifer, Myrtle, and I, were working
    together
who tends to jump to conclusions
whose name he wouldn't reveal
whom I expected to stand up for me
which was a lie
who had stolen the money
who took the money
that tells us not to judge a book by its cover

II.

2. in which   3. that   4. which   5. most of whom   6. who
7. who   8. whose   9. who   10. whose

III.

2. no change
3. no change
4. (that)
5. no change
6. (that)
7. no change
8. no change

IV.

2. which is why he can be termed an extrovert
3. which is why they often have many friends
4. which is why they tend to value accomplishment
5. which is why they don't always feel satisfied with their
   accomplishments

V.

2. B   3. C   4. C   5. A   6. D   7. B   8. A   9. D   10. D

PART VI From Grammar to Writing: Punctuation of Adjective Clauses

A.

2. Tom, who is clearly an extrovert, loves meeting new
   people.
3. Sandra, who is very quick to make friends, loves to
   have friends over for dinner.
4. Tom and Sandra have two married sons, both of whom
   live abroad.
5. no change
6. no change
7. no change
8. no change

B.

1. no change
2. no change
3. *The Passenger*, directed by Michelangelo Antonioni and
   starring Jack Nicholson, is not well known in North
   America.
4. Many Canadians, including Donald Sutherland and
   Michael J. Fox, are major international film stars.
5. no change
6. no change

C.

The zoology class, which meets at 8:00 every morning, is . . .
Calculus, which I have at noon every day, looks . . .
There are four of us in our suite, including . . .
Sally, who is from San Antonio, is great; . . .
I also really like Anne, who is . . .
Heather, the other girl from Texas, is . . .

PART VII Noun Clauses and Complementation

UNIT 18 Noun Clauses: Subjects and Objects

1.

it doesn't go nearly far enough
whoever gets something from the nation
what we receive
that it is time to reinvoke John F. Kennedy's famous call to
    action
what your country can do for you
what you can do for your country
that Congress pass new legislation creating a job corps and
    requiring all youths to serve in it
whatever they are most skilled at or interested in
Whoever worked in the job corps
What this country needs

2.

2. I'll get a job   3. whatever I'm told   4. whoever hires me
5. I'm going into the army   6. what I want as a career
7. the army will help me decide   8. what I have to do
9. whatever your boss tells you
10. if you might have a point

3.

2. whatever I want   3. whichever one interests me
4. whoever needs help   5. whatever I can
6. however much time you want   7. whoever is
8. whatever needs to be done

4.

Whomever says ➜ Whoever says
That I like ➜ What I like
is what I ➜ is that I
The other thing what ➜ The other thing that
I just wonder that ➜ I just wonder what
I hope what ➜ I hope that

5.

2. a   3. b   4. a   5. b   6. b   7. a   8. a   9. b   10. b   11. a

UNIT 19 Complementation

1.

that the Board of Education isn't taking our concerns
    seriously
that the board do something positive
that the board sincerely negotiate with us on our request
    for higher salaries, smaller classes, better discipline, and
    a real commitment to education
that the board has refused even to talk with us

2.

2. that a lot of the teachers don't want to teach
3. that we are *or* we're there to learn
4. that he or she is there to teach
5. that she would not *or* wouldn't tolerate any nonsense
6. that she was there to help us as much as she could
7. that the whole system needs to be changed

3.

2. It is essential that salaries be raised at least 5 percent
    per year.
3. It is desirable that teachers be given release time to
    complete special projects.
4. It is important that no instructor be asked to teach more
    than five classes per day.
5. It is essential that strict discipline be maintained in the
    classroom.

4.

players going ➜ players were going
that you were there ➜ that you be there
that you turned in ➜ that you turn in
that we be there ➜ that we were there
that he or she learns ➜ that he or she learn
that fact what ➜ the fact that
People say what ➜ People say that
that teachers like Mrs. Ochoa be ➜ that teachers like
                                            Mrs. Ochoa are

5.

2. F   3. T   4. T   5. F   6. F   7. T   8. T   9. F   10. T

PART VII — Review or SelfTest

I.

1. B: Whatever you want to do
2. A: where we want to go on vacation
   B: that Hawaii would be nice
3. A: who wins the prize
   B: whoever gets the most points
4. A: she is quilty
   B: the fact that she waited so long to contact the police
5. A: what I'm seeing
   B: that they've been able to do this well
6. A: that I need more time to complete the assignment
   B: Take however long you need to do the job well
7. B: that we need to ban weapons of all kinds
8. B: that she's very unhappy

II.

I report to that's called → I report to what's called
tutor whatever comes in → tutor whoever comes in
I'm amazed what they're → I'm amazed that they're
impressed by who she's learned → impressed by what she's
learned
we work on whoever → we work on whatever
that's that we do → that's what we do
for whatever long → for however long

III.

2. where she is
3. that Bill is an asset to our firm, the fact that he's ill a great deal
4. that we need to do, whatever is necessary
5. whoever it is, that it isn't Ron *or* that it's not Ron

IV.

2. C 3. B 4. C 5. A 6. B 7. A 8. D 9. D

PART VII — From Grammar to Writing: Writing Direct and Indirect Speech

A.

2. "Sally, how would you evaluate your education?" the reporter queried.
3. "I absolutely despise going to school!" Sally responded.
4. "Jim," Frank said, "you're crazy if you think it's going to be easy to get a job."
5. "Frank," said Jim, "don't be a fool!"
6. The Teachers' Union spokesperson asked the superintendent, "When are you going to start taking our concerns seriously?"

B.

1. Spokesperson Frances Baldwin said that the Board of Education had even refused to talk to them.
2. Board President Bates responded that there was simply no money for salary raises.
3. TV reporter Joan Matthews asked Fumiko if she agreed with Sally that most teachers don't want to teach.
4. Frank asked Jim what he would do if he couldn't find a job after he quit school.
5. Reporter Jim Bresler asked Zeya if she intended to go to college when her term was over.

C.

1. responded
2. commented
3. claimed
4. maintained
5. added

PART VIII Unreal Conditions

 UNIT 20 Unreal Conditionals and Other Ways to Express Unreality

1.

if we all paid more attention to our intuitive feelings, we
  would do better

if a new situation presents itself, you don't have to weigh
  the evidence on both sides of the question

if you accept the job, you'll soon be bored and will hate it

if you just approach the job with the right attitude, things
  will turn out well

you end up liking it

as if you liked the work

you hadn't been so hasty

"If only I'd waited a little longer,"

If you'd listened to your intuition, you wouldn't be in this
  situation

By now you probably would have found a job more to your
liking

2.

2. had 3. hadn't been cleaned 4. were *or* was
5. hadn't been changed 6. 'd given up
7. does *or* will do 8. 'd known

3.

2. If the doctor had arrived sooner, he might have been
  able to save the boy.
3. If the boy had not *or* hadn't been doing a man's job, he
  probably wouldn't have been killed.
4. If the saw had cut the boy's finger instead of his hand,
  the boy could probably have survived.
5. The boy might not have been cut by the saw if the
  sister hadn't said "supper" at a crucial moment.
6. If the work boss had said "Call it a day," the boy would
  have escaped his fate.
8. The doctor probably wishes (that) he had *or* he'd
  arrived sooner.
9. The boy's parents probably wish (that) they had not *or*
  hadn't allowed the boy to work at a man's job.
10. Other parents probably hope (that) this kind of
  accident does not (doesn't) *or* will not (won't) happen
  to their children.

4.

world owe her ➜ world owed her
wish she won't ➜ wish she wouldn't
If I would have ➜ If I had
I might had ➜ I might have
probably would get ➜ probably would have gotten
if I would have ➜ if I had
If only I wouldn't have ➜ If only I hadn't
hope she never asked ➜ hope she never asks
hope I didn't agree ➜ hope I don't agree

5.

2. b 3. b 4. a 5. b 6. a 7. a 8. b 9. a 10. a

 UNIT 21 Inverted and Implied Conditionals; Subjunctive in Noun Clauses

1.

Subjunctive verb forms:
(that she) come, get
(that Mary) look into

Implied conditionals:
If so . . .
With a little bit of practice . . .

2.

2. let 3. got 4. started 5. were

3.

2. her way be considered   3. an argument be won
4. an argument be fair   5. you adopt
6. you give   7. something be done
8. a course of action be followed

4.

2. had she stayed   3. otherwise   4. with   5. If so   6. If not
8. if she had stayed   9. if she didn't find work   10. if she had
11. if they were hiring   12. if they weren't hiring

5.

essential that I found ➔ essential that I find
(essential that I) just came ➔ (essential that I) just come
Had I know ➔ Had I known
as if I have ➔ as if I had
as if I be ➔ as if I were *or* am
it's time I'm telling ➔ it's time I told
What if I had come ➔ What if I came

PART VIII Review or SelfTest

I.

2. If he had changed the oil, the engine wouldn't have
   seized.
3. If the engine hadn't seized, the other car wouldn't have
   rear-ended him.
4. He wouldn't have had to pay a towing bill.
5. He wouldn't have had to replace the engine.
6. He could have made it to the job interview if all this
   hadn't happened.
7. If he had made it to the job interview, he might have
   gotten the job.
8. Brandon hopes that he has learned his lesson.

II.

2. as though it were going to   3. as if he were
4. as though he had been   5. as if she were
6. as though you thought

6.

Comprehension
2. F   3. F   4. T   5. F   6. T   7. T   8. F   9. T   10. F   11. F
Optional Dictation
2. that you keep   3. demands that he take   4. that he have
5. as if she owned   6. were   7. 'd rather she didn't
8. important that we not excite   9. It's time you took
10. I were you I'd sit down   11. 'd insist that he find
12. What if he were to   13. suggest that you give

III.

2. not lose her temper   3. bring the dog in at night
4. get rid of the animal
5. call the animal control bureau

IV.

2. we'd realized   3. he keeps *or* he'll keep
4. there's *or* there will be   5. we could contact
6. weren't   7. we had
8. this won't be *or* this isn't
9. we knew   10. it is *or* it will be

V.

2. B   3. A   4. C   5. A   6. C   7. A   8. D   9. B   10. D

PART VIII From Grammar to Writing: Avoiding Run-on Sentences and Comma Splices

A.

2. Thain asked Aurora to pull over; his intuition told him the old man needed their help.
3. Kate knew she had to change her relationship with her boss, but she didn't know how to do it.
4. Although *or* Though *or* Even though Aurora wished they had gotten to the yard sale on time, she was glad they had stopped to help the old man.

B.

2. Thain and Aurora drove to a pharmacy. They got the old man his insulin.
3. Aurora wanted to get to the yard sale; there was a chest of drawers for sale.
4. Aurora didn't want to stop for the old man, but Thain persuaded her it was necessary.
5. Although *or* Though *or* Even though Harold says he will seek professional help to overcome his anger, there is no assurance that he will carry out his promise.
6. Feeling dominated by her mother-in-law, Nancy needed to take assertive action.

C.

2. Nancy says she wants to do something worthwhile. If so, she should join the Peace Corps.
3. I need to get a bank loan; otherwise, I'll have to file for bankruptcy.
4. Jack and Margo would like to send James to a private school. However, the school is expensive, and James doesn't want to go.
5. Becky and David love their new neighborhood; in fact, they're going to buy a house there.

D.

Note: The periods and semicolons below can be interchanged so long as the capitalization is correct.

. . . it works. Last summer . . .
. . . I work. We interviewed . . .
. . . Sarah. On paper, Bob . . .
. . . better qualified; he had . . .
. . . job. However, Sarah . . .
. . . impressed us. She . . .
. . . simply. Bob . . .
. . . everything. All of us . . .
. . . Sarah better. In fact . . .
. . . wasn't wrong; she's turned . . .

Index